Bombs in the Backyard

Nevada Studies in History and Political Science

Bombs in the Backyard:

Atomic Testing and American Politics

A. Costandina Titus

Second Edition

University of Nevada Press : Reno & Las Vegas

Nevada Studies in History and Political Science

University of Nevada Press, Reno, Nevada 89557 USA
Copyright © 1986 by A. Costandina Titus
New material copyright © 2001 by A. Costandina Titus
All rights reserved
Manufactured in the United States of America
Book design by Steve Renick
Library of Congress Cataloging-in-Publication Data
Titus, A. Costandina, 1950–
    Bombs in the backyard : atomic testing and American politics /
    A. Costandina Titus. — 2nd ed.
        p. cm. — (Nevada studies in history and political science ; no. 25)
    Includes bibliographical references and index.
    ISBN 0-87417-370-1 (alk. paper)
        1. Nuclear weapons—Testing—Environmental aspects—United States.
    2. United States—Politics and government—1945–1989.   3. United
    States—Politics and government—1989–.   I. Title.   II. Series.
    U264.T58   2000
    361.1'79—dc21   00-051245
The paper used in this book meets the requirements
of American National Standard for Information
Sciences—Permanence of Paper for Printed
Library Materials, ANSI Z39.48–1984.
Binding materials are chosen for strength and durability.

University of Nevada Paperback Edition, 2001
10 09 08 07 06 05 04 03 02 01   5 4 3 2 1

To my parents, Joe and Betty Titus

Contents

List of Illustrations		xi
Preface		xiii
1.	From *Atomos* to A–Bomb	1
2.	An Awesome Dawn	11
3.	Politics of Control	22
4.	Victims of Proliferation	36
5.	Bombs in the Backyard	55
6.	Selling the Bomb	70
7.	Living Under the Mushroom Cloud	86
8.	Political Fallout from Above-Ground Tests	101
9.	More Likely Than Not	114
10.	Time to Build a Monument	131
11.	Transitions of the 1990s	145
	Conclusion	167
	Notes	170
	Bibliography	213
	Index	231

Illustrations

Following page 114

Map of the Nevada Test Site
Marines' atomic-maneuvers map, mid-1950s
Soldiers at the Nevada Test Site removing fallout, 1955
The press corps observing detonation from News Nob, 1957
Typical mushroom cloud, mid-1950s
Atomic cloud seen from downtown Las Vegas, 1951
Atomic cloud seen from Last Frontier Hotel
Preparing mannequins for Doom Town maneuvers, 1958
Miss Atomic Bomb, 1957
Cartoon from U.S. Atomic Energy Commission book, 1957
Cartoon from U.S. Atomic Energy Commission book, 1957
"Our Little A-Bomb" contest winner, 1953
Official seal of Clark County, Nevada, 1950s

Preface

During the last decade, the issue of "official negligence" has appeared on the American political scene as certain groups have begun to demand that the government first accept responsibility for allegedly harmful actions and then provide appropriate compensation. Government programs involving hazardous waste disposal, Agent Orange deployment, and nuclear weapons testing have come under attack. The self-proclaimed victims who are leading this charge share a common goal: They want the government to compensate them for misfortunes they have suffered through no fault of their own.

These challenges to authority have attracted considerable attention for several reasons. First, they arose at a time when the American public, still haunted by memories of Vietnam and Watergate, was less trusting of their government than at any other point in its history. Second, the groups involved are placing unprecedented demands on the system along two fronts: They are pushing environmental law beyond disease prevention into the realm of compensation, a legal and political quagmire that the government has previously sought to avoid; and, even more important, they are asking the government to openly admit error, an extremely difficult if not impossible step for any system to take, especially in matters of national security. Third, the evidence presented in these charges against the government is rife with the elements which make a good story: mystery, conspiracy, and personal tragedy.

Those who have enjoyed the greatest coverage lately are the so-called victims of atomic testing. Several recent books have made an excellent case against the government for deliberately misleading the public about the dangers of nuclear weapons testing. Based primarily on firsthand accounts by witnesses and participants in the program, and on selected, recently declassified archival material, these works effectively portray the Atomic Energy Commission (AEC) as a villainous organization with no regard for human life.

While there is little doubt that public safety was a low priority for government in its pursuit of bigger and better bombs, we must recognize that these books present only part of the story. They address the politics of atomic testing solely from the standpoint of the victims and tend to ignore the context in which the crucial decisions were made; as a result, they overlook the important questions of how and why. By focusing on the AEC's policy in relation to fallout, these works also fail to recognize that minimizing the dangers of the testing program was merely one component in an overall plan to generate public support for nuclear weapons proliferation; indeed, the government's primary objective was to convince the public not that there was no risk but that the risk was worth taking. These books offer no analytical framework within which to consider the atomic testing program as it has evolved since 1942; they disregard such keys to policy analysis as statutory provisions, appropriations patterns, and bureaucratic organization schemes. Consequently, they draw no comparisons between what the government did thirty years ago and what it is doing today, nor do they make sound predictions about what to expect in the future.

This study attempts to fill the gaps in the literature on this important topic. It is addressed to two audiences. For the generalist, including those interested in contemporary American history, public policy issues, or the sad drama of the alleged victims of fallout, the book contains ample background as well as detailed analysis of the current state of the compensation fight. For those already familiar with the history, politics, and health issues of atmospheric nuclear testing, this book offers an interpretive framework that links the first atomic dawn with the latest court decision and presents the record as a coherent, even a predictable story.

As events are chronicled from the days of the "Manhattan Project" to the recent attempts by Congress to enact compensatory legislation, two major themes emerge. The first is one of continuity. Precedents set during Roosevelt's administration are still the policy of today. For example, secrecy has been the watchword of the atomic weapons program since its inception. The Manhattan Project started by FDR in June 1942 was so top secret that Vice President Truman denied knowing of its existence when he moved into the Oval Office following Roosevelt's death. And in 1950 the decision to build a continental test site was made under conditions of absolute secrecy, because President Truman did not want to scare people about "blowing up bombs in their backyards." Later, research on the "Star Wars" defense at the Nevada Test Site was so secretive that local ranchers and miners were denied access to their lands bordering the testing zone.

Another illustration of this continuity can be found in the acts passed by Congress in 1946 and 1977 establishing the Atomic Energy Commission and the Department of Energy, respectively; in both cases Congress ignored an obvious conflict of interest and left it up to the agency to establish radiation safety standards. Likewise, Congress reduced the civilian nature of both agencies substantially by allowing the military to maintain control over all decisions involving weapons.

The refusal to accept responsibility for soldiers also has persisted. During the fifties when troops were involved in atomic maneuvers at ground zero, the AEC allowed the military to set personnel exposure limitations. In 1977, when marines were sent to the South Pacific to clean up Eniwetok, their safety was monitored not by the Department of Energy but by the Defense Nuclear Agency. Consistency also can be found in the AEC's policy of repeated denial that radiation from testing has caused any serious damage to either people or animals; this was the official line during the period of atmospheric testing, and it was steadfastly maintained through the eighties.

The second theme to emerge is that the federal government has not been alone in understating the real dangers of atomic weapons testing. During the fifties and early sixties the national press, and especially the southern Nevada papers, strongly endorsed the testing program, presenting the public with positive headlines and patriotic editorials. Eyewitness coverage of particular shots focused on the spectacular visual effects of the explosions and failed to address more serious questions about the possible harmful effects of fallout. The state of Nevada also avoided the issue of potential long-term consequences and welcomed the test site because of the immediate economic boom it brought to the area; state officials at every level were eager to accommodate the needs of the new facility, which brought in federal dollars.

Finally, the American people, by and large, have acceded to the government's position on safety in weapons testing. During the Cold War years, they were easy prey for Joseph McCarthy and feared the threat of spreading Communism. They ignored warnings from such renowned scientists as Linus Pauling and Herman Muller and voted against a presidential candidate who called for a halt to nuclear weapons testing. Even recently, with increasing evidence about the potential dangers of radiation, there was widespread support among the residents of southern Nevada for continuing the atomic weapons testing program in their own backyard.

These two themes do not encompass the entire story of the politics of atomic testing and compensation for its alleged victims. But together, they help to explain how the odds have been stacked against those currently seeking redress of test-related grievances. Viewing weapons-testing policy as the result of a consistent pattern of government denial and public acquiescence allows the reader to better understand the complexities of this difficult episode in recent American history. Indeed, it forces one to analyze the plight of today's "atomic victims" within the context of a nation undergoing unprecedented perceived threats to its existence.

Acknowledgments

My heartfelt thanks go to several people who have offered their assistance throughout the course of this project on atomic testing: Senator Howard Cannon, who provided the initial opportunity for me to explore this subject; Joseph A. Fry, who critiqued the manuscript and made valuable suggestions for revision; Andrew C. Tuttle, who lent both moral and material support to my efforts; Christine Chairsell, who spent many hours tracking down details; Shari Brown, who patiently typed and retyped; and, of course, Thomas C. Wright, who helped in ways too numerous to mention.

Others who deserve acknowledgment include Judge Roger Foley, James W. O'Neil, Ray Goldsworthy, Margaret Purdue, Mary Manning, Paul Duckworth, Alan and Larry Johns, David Millman, Vera Thompson, and the late Anna Dean Kepper.

I am also indebted to the students of my summer school classes of 1983 and 1984 for indexing the local newspapers of the 1950s, the Las Vegas News Bureau for affording me access to their picture files, and the University of Nevada, Las Vegas for granting me a sabbatical leave during which I was able to complete this manuscript and a CFAR grant in 1999 when I wrote the epilogue chapter.

After being away from the subject of atomic testing for some fifteen years, I was able to chronicle developments in the post–Cold War era by relying on the kindness of several people: Carlos Blumberg and Christina Frye helped me gain access to legislative records, while David Newton assisted in tracing and citing atomic court cases. Tim Carlson shared valuable information on the workings of the NTSDC; and both Darwin Morgan and Kevin Rohrer of the DOE provided helpful materials from within the agency. The Johns brothers remain an inspiration to me, while Troy Wade epitomizes a Cold Warrior at his best. Finally, I am eternally grateful to Shirley Davis for her help with this manuscript; her patience and support made it possible to finish on schedule.

From Atomos to A-Bomb *I*

A Brief History
of Nuclear Development

Although it is common knowledge today that the world is composed of tiny particles known as atoms, scientific acceptance of the existence of atoms is of relatively recent origin.[1] First suggested around 450 B.C. by the Greek philosopher Leucippus, the atomic hypothesis was rejected for some two thousand years on the authority of Aristotle, who taught that matter consisted of continuous elements rather than separate atoms. It was not until the Renaissance, when experimentation began to replace metaphysics, that the atomic theory again attracted interest. Once reconsidered, however, it was pursued with vigor, and over the next three hundred years most of the scientific inquiry conducted throughout the world contributed in some degree to its development. The prevailing view during this period can be summed up in this statement by Isaac Newton from his work *Opticks:* "It seems probable to me that God in the Beginning form'd matter in solid, massy, hard, impenetrable, moveable particles."[2]

Newton's theory of impenetrability was to be proven wrong as several major breakthroughs occurred during the nineteenth century that added significantly to the understanding of atomic phenomena. In 1803 the British chemist John Dalton determined that every chemical element is composed of atoms which are identical and which can be distinguished from the atoms of other elements by their weight. He further theorized that the smallest unit of a chemical compound is an entity composed of a specific combination of atoms of various elements; this entity is known today as a molecule. Thirty years later Michael Faraday, while studying the effects of electricity passed through chemical compound solutions, concluded that atoms yield definite amounts of electricity. This finding in turn led to the discovery of the electron, one of the components of the atom itself.[3]

By the end of the nineteenth century it had become evident that atoms have a structure of their own that can be penetrated. Research emphasis then shifted as a result of several major findings which showed atoms of certain heavy metals to be radioactive. This shift

began in 1895 when the German scientist Wilhelm Röntgen discovered that, as cathode rods strike the walls of a glass tube in which a
gaseous discharge is occurring, a radiation is emitted which is capable
of penetrating opaque objects. Röntgen called this radiation *X-rays, X*
meaning unknown. Because the equipment for producing X-rays was
readily accessible and the technique fairly simple, researchers rushed
to experiment with the new phenomenon.[4]

Interest in X-rays was not limited to the scientific community. The
public's response to this amazing new discovery was also enthusi-
astic.[5] Thomas Edison arranged for the first demonstration of X-rays
in the United States to be held at the National Electric Light Association exhibition in New York City in May 1896. Immediately thereafter, X-ray exhibits became popular events at county fairs across the
nation as people lined up for a chance to "see their bones." Personal
X-rays were soon considered a status symbol, and the titillating
possibility of using the rays for naughty purposes permeated even
polite conversation, as illustrated by the following poem, which appeared in a popular photography magazine:

X-actly So!

The Roentgen Rays, the Roentgen Rays,
What is this craze?
The town's ablaze
With the new phase
of Xray's ways.
I'm full of daze
Shock and amaze;
For nowadays,
I hear they'll gaze
Thru cloak and gown—and even stays
These naughty, naughty Roentgen rays.[6]

The real significance of X-rays in the development of atomic energy is that their production resulted in another crucial discovery made
later that same year. The observation that production of X-rays is
accompanied by fluorescence of the glass walls of the discharge tube
led scientists to examine other materials known to be capable of
fluorescing, to see if they also would emit penetrating radiation. A
French investigator, Henri Becquerel, was particularly interested in
the element uranium. He soon found that uranium emits radiation
which, like X-rays, will penetrate cardboard and blacken a photo-

graphic plate. At first he assumed the radiation was a consequence of fluorescing, but he later determined it to be an intrinsic property of the uranium itself.[7]

Becquerel's discovery attracted the attention of Marie Curie, who began experiments of her own in radioactivity, as she named the phenomenon. She made a systematic examination of all known elements to determine which ones were radioactive. She found only one, thorium. However, her continued research on uranium-bearing materials led to the identification in 1898 of two new elements, polonium and radium, both of which were radioactive.[8]

The luminous quality of radium soon produced a popular craze even greater than that caused by X-rays. "Radium roulette" was played in New York casinos on a spinning wheel which glowed in the dark, luminescent clothing was the rage in women's fashions, and an elixir containing radium was successfully peddled by Dr. W. J. Morton as "liquid sunshine," the cure for diseased organs. Radium was also considered a beneficial additive for fertilizer and a therapeutic way to induce menopause artificially. Indeed, the potential uses of the new element seemed boundless.[9]

Meanwhile, Ernest Rutherford, a young physicist from New Zealand working at the Cavendish Laboratory in Cambridge, found that the rays emitted by the various radioactive elements were of two kinds, which he called *alpha* and *beta*. A third kind, the *gamma* ray, was discovered a year later by Paul Villard in France.[10] And so, by the dawn of the twentieth century, scientists had established the existence of radiation and had determined that atoms were not indestructible, but experimentation thus far had been intermittent and inconclusive about the implications of these discoveries.

Many of the mysteries were soon to be unraveled, however, as an international network of the world's greatest physicists, all involved in atomic research, evolved during the first few decades of the new century. As one famous scientist wrote later:

> Our understanding of atomic physics . . . had its origins at the turn of the century and its great synthesis and resolutions in the nineteen-twenties. It was a heroic time. It was not the doing of any one man. It involved the collaboration of scores of scientists from many different lands . . . It was a period of patient work in the laboratory, of crucial experiments and daring action, of many false starts and many untenable conjectures. It was a time of earnest correspondence and hurried conferences, of debates, criticism and brilliant mathematical improvisation. For those who participated, it was a time of creation.[11]

Personnel, notes, and equipment were exchanged freely across international boundaries. Even during World War I the physicists remained much closer to one another than did their intellectual counterparts in other disciplines. In one instance when James Chadwick, who later discovered the neutron, was interned at Ruhleben, near Berlin, at the outbreak of the hostilities, his German teachers, Walter Nernot and Heinrich Rubens, helped him set up a small laboratory in the prison camp. In May 1918 he wrote to Rutherford: "They were extremely willing to help and offered to lend us anything they could. In fact, all kinds of people lent us apparatus."[12]

As soon as the fighting ended, these physicists resumed full-scale international collaboration. At that time there were three recognized centers of atomic research: Cambridge, where Rutherford ruled "like a sharp-tongued and easily irritated monarch"; Copenhagen, where Niels Bohr "guided, restrained, deepened and finally transmitted the enterprise"; and Göttingen, where the triumvirate of Max Born, James Franck, and David Hilbert "instantly asked questions about each new discovery made in England and supposed to have been correctly explained in Denmark."[13] It was not long before Robert Oppenheimer of the United States, who was to become known as the "father of the atomic bomb," Enrico Fermi of Italy, who would design the first uranium reactor, and several others joined the ranks of these distinguished participants in the race to unchain the atom.

Internationalism continued to rule in science up until the very eve of the Second World War. Discoveries were shared by Germans in Nazi-controlled Germany; by German, Austrian, and Italian émigrés; and by Frenchmen, Danes, Americans, and Soviets. Even as late as February of 1939, when a small group of American scientists attempted to restrict the publication of information of potential military significance, there was considerable opposition worldwide. Then, in September of that same year, two events occurred that made continued international cooperation among the scientists impossible: Germany invaded Poland, bringing England and France into war, and Niels Bohr and J. A. Wheeler published a paper that described nuclear fission, the process that was to become the key to building an atomic bomb.[14] These events changed the character of atomic research. From being open and international, work on the atom suddenly became secret and linked to national defense. This shift would profoundly affect the nature of the atomic weapons testing program in the United States.

The extremely significant discovery of nuclear fission resulted from experiments begun by Fermi in which he bombarded uranium atoms with neutrons. It was found that when fission, or splitting, of the uranium atom occurs, some free neutrons are released in addition to the two newly created massive fission fragments. These free neutrons are then capable of bombarding other atoms, causing more fission to occur and thereby creating the possibility of a self-sustaining chain reaction.[15] When scientists announced that this process could produce enormous amounts of energy, three million times greater than that released by burning coal and twenty million times more powerful than TNT, the inevitable question arose: Could this energy be harnessed for making a super bomb?[16]

In the United States, the first attempt by scientists to bring the possibility of building an atomic bomb to the attention of the military was met with little enthusiasm. In March of 1939 Enrico Fermi, then a professor at Columbia University, advised Admiral S. C. Hooper, director of the Navy's Technical Division, of the latest developments in atomic science and their potential effects on the techniques of battle. At that time, although the European situation was tense, the war had not yet broken out, and the United States seemed far removed from the threat of involvement in the emerging conflict. Consequently, the government's response to Fermi's information was a polite Thanks, but don't call us, we'll call you.[17]

Ironically, on the same day that Fermi met with Admiral Hooper, Hitler's troops marched into Czechoslovakia and within one week had halted all further sales of uranium from the Joachimsthal mines, Europe's richest source of the mineral. This occurrence, reinforced by news of a full-scale uranium project being conducted under the auspices of the German Army Weapons Department, caused increasing concern among many British and American scientists, especially those who had recently fled Europe after having experienced life under Hitler. Led by Leo Szilard, Eugene Wigner, and Edward Teller, these refugees were determined to bring their fears to the attention of President Roosevelt. Albert Einstein agreed to lend his support to the effort and on August 2, 1939, signed a letter to the president that emphasized that studies of uranium fission foreshadowed the development of atomic power for both driving ships and making bombs. The letter went on to point out that the Germans were aware of and actively working toward the development of these possibilities.[18]

Einstein's message did not reach the president until some ten weeks later, after the war in Europe had begun. The letter was finally delivered on October 11 by international financier Alexander Sachs who was a longtime friend and advisor to FDR. After listening to Sachs, the president called in his military aide, Brigadier General

Edwin M. "Pa" Watson, and said to him, in words which have since become famous, "Pa, this requires action."[19] Despite these words, however, little was accomplished during the year following the exchange.

President Roosevelt's first act was to appoint the Advisory Committee on Uranium chaired by Lyman J. Briggs, director of the National Bureau of Standards. It was further composed of one member from the army and another from the navy. In addition, the paltry sum of six thousand dollars was appropriated to support the study of uranium fission in the upcoming year. Nonetheless, research continued in a piecemeal, scattered fashion and no coordinated affort was made to develop an atomic weapon. Five months later, in March of 1940, Einstein wrote a second letter to FDR, again urging his support of atomic fission research. The following June, the National Defense Research Committee (NDRC) was created to mobilize scientific endeavors for military purposes. Under the direction of Vannevar Bush the agency pursued two objectives: increasing the uranium stockpile and stepping up experimentation with the chain reaction. Again, however, efforts were intermittent and underfinanced.

Two events in the summer of 1941 finally spurred the American government into action: Britain's prestigious MAUD (Military Application of Uranium Detonation) Committee issued its report concluding that an atomic bomb was possible, and Emilio Segre and Glenn Seaborg made a crucial discovery at Berkeley which solved several problems Fermi was having in his attempts to create a chain reaction. They isolated an artificial element, later to be known as plutonium, that would fission better than uranium. Finally, on December 6, 1941, just a day before the Japanese attack on Pearl Harbor, President Roosevelt made the decision to apply substantial financial and technical resources to the construction of an atomic bomb. He convened a special committee, dubbed the S-1 Section, and charged it with determining whether, and at what cost, the United States could make the bomb.[20]

Reporting back to the president six months later on June 17, 1942, the S-1 Section recommended an "all-out" effort of unprecedented magnitude. The report went on to state that the project would initially cost upwards of $100 million; would involve the construction of production plants for preparing fissionable material, as well as for building the bomb itself; and would likely, granted adequate funds and priorities, produce something soon enough to be of military significance in the current war. President Roosevelt approved the report and America's national atomic research project was launched.[21]

The U.S. Army Corps of Engineers created a new district, the Manhattan Engineering District (MED), on August 13, 1942, to carry out the special task of building an atomic bomb. For security reasons, this work was officially named "DSM Project" for Development of Substitute Materials, but soon became known as the "Manhattan Project." A month later, on September 17, 1942, Brigadier General Leslie R. Groves, the construction engineer who had been responsible for building the Pentagon, was placed in command of all army activities of the project. The Military Policy Committee, comprised of two scientists, Vannevar Bush and James B. Conant, and two military men, General W. D. Styer and Admiral W. R. Purnell, was also appointed to determine the general policies of the whole project. This program of joint administration continued through April 1943 with the army playing an increasingly important role as the industrial effort got under way. By May of 1943 all research contracts had been transferred to the Corps of Engineers and the army maintained complete control throughout the remainder of the operation.[22]

The ultimate goal of the Manhattan Project was to beat the Germans in the race to build a powerful new weapon, but before that could be accomplished several plants had to be designed and constructed to provide fissionable material needed for the making of a Super-bomb. After careful consideration, two sites were chosen for the location of these facilities: Oak Ridge, Tennessee, and Hanford, Washington. The plant at Oak Ridge was designed to separate uranium 235 from uranium 238, while the one at Hanford housed a number of reactors used for the production of plutonium. Both areas soon grew into sizable self-contained communities as various support services were developed for the scientists and their families. A third secret city was built at Los Alamos on the grounds of an expropriated boy's school in the hills near Santa Fe, New Mexico. Called "The Hill," this remote and beautiful spot was to become the birthplace of the world's first atomic bomb.[23]

Scientists were recruited from universities and research centers located around the country and abroad to participate in the Manhattan Project. They left behind homes, jobs, even families, without explanation, to go into seclusion and work on a top secret military project which they felt would make history. As described by journalist Robert Jungk, "It was probably the first time in history that so brilliant a group of minds had voluntarily undertaken to adopt a mode of work and existence so unlike their normal way of life."[24]

The scientists recognized the importance of the need for secrecy, but the everyday application of many security measures was often difficult to accept for people accustomed to collaborating and sharing information. Letters were read and censored, homes were bugged, bartenders turned out to be FBI agents, and members of different divisions were prohibited from discussing their work with one another. In one case, Henry D. Smyth, who later authored the official report on the entire project, found himself facing a dilemma when, as director of two departments simultaneously, he had to get his own permission to talk to himself. In fact, the project was so top secret that Vice President Harry Truman had to be informed of its existence by Secretary of War Henry Stimson upon assuming the presidency following FDR's death.[25]

Yet, despite these elaborate precautions, atomic secrets were leaked. It was later discovered that Klaus Fuchs, a German scientist who had immigrated to England and joined the Manhattan Project as part of the British delegation, had been slipping information to the Russians throughout his stay at Los Alamos. David Greenglass, brother of Ethel Rosenberg, was also found guilty of supplying top secret information to the Communists during his stint as an army machinist at Los Alamos.[26]

The scientist chosen by General Groves to be the director of the Los Alamos laboratory was forty-year-old Robert Oppenheimer, a slight, soft-spoken, well-read physics professor from the University of California. The choice was a controversial one because "Oppie," while recognized by many as a brilliant scientist, had no administrative experience of any kind and had never won the Nobel Prize, thereby lacking the prestige enjoyed by some of his colleagues. There was also a question about his security clearance based on evidence that he had associated with members of the Communist party during his youth.[27] Nevertheless, he had a special capacity for inspiring those around him and imparting to them the excitement he felt for participation in this pioneering work. He was no "dry as dust" specialist but rather a Renaissance man who quoted Dante and Proust and spoke a number of languages. He possessed what one of his associates called "intellectual sex appeal."[28]

Although General Groves had occasional problems dealing with this distinguished but undisciplined group of "crackpots," he never regretted the appointment of Oppenheimer as their director. In his own account of the Manhattan Project, he wrote in 1962:

> I have never felt that it was a mistake to have selected and cleared Oppenheimer for his wartime post. He accomplished his assigned mission and he did it well. We will never know whether anyone else could

have done it better or even as well. I do not think so, and this opinion is almost universal among those who were familiar with the wartime operations at Los Alamos.[29]

For two and a half years the scientists of the Manhattan Project worked day and night to finish building their "gadget," as they euphemistically referred to the bomb. Hundreds of new inventions and patents were developed in the course of the work, 150,000 people were employed in various capacities, and over $2 billion were expended. On several occasions, projects costing millions of dollars had to be scrapped when they proved to be dead ends. But the scientists, driven by General Groves and inspired by Oppie, persevered in their efforts.

As the war continued and the bomb neared completion, the question of its fate became a matter of primary importance. The scientists were concerned about the bomb's immediate use and about the longer-term development and control of atomic power. Some began to fear the tremendous ramifications of what they had accomplished and expressed remorse for having participated. Many argued against releasing the bomb on Japan and called for a purely technical demonstration instead.[30] Others, however, accepted the military's position that using the bomb would prevent the necessity of an invasion of Japan, which could prolong the fighting for another year and result in thousands of additional deaths before the war was over.[31]

In the end, of course, it seemed a foregone conclusion that the bomb would be dropped. In fact, the story is told that, following the U.S. capture of Carl Friedrich von Weizsäcker's papers in Strasbourg on November 15, 1944, which revealed that the Germans were two years behind the Americans in their atomic research, Samuel Goudsmit, a physicist-turned-intelligence officer, commented, "Isn't it wonderful that the Germans have no atom bomb? Now we won't have to use ours." A major attached to the unit responded with surprise, "Of course you understand, Sam, that if we have such a weapon, we're going to use it."[32] And so it was that during the spring of 1945, while some scientists put the finishing touches on the "gadget" and others circulated petitions against its use, arrangements were already being made for its military deployment: Airplanes were equipped, pilots selected, and targets identified.[33]

There was no guarantee, however, that the bomb would work. The majority of the scientists believed that the theoretical hypotheses would be proved valid, but the possibility of failure had to be acknowledged. No one was willing to risk the first trial of the device over enemy territory, where failure would wipe out the crucial psychological impact of the weapon. Furthermore, it was essential to obtain technical data on the various effects of the bomb, such as explosive force, heat, blast, shock, and radiation. If the bomb were used first under military conditions, the measurement and retrieval of this valuable information would be greatly hindered. Thus, it became clear that a test of the device was needed before it could be deployed against Japan.[34]

An Awesome Dawn 2

As the government prepared for and conducted its initial test of an atomic weapon, the precedents were set for many of the standards and practices which would be followed throughout the entire eighteen-year period of atmospheric testing. A close look at the details of the first test, from the selection of the site to the monitoring of fallout, reveals that the questions of government negligence and liability arose with the very first mushroom cloud. In fact, some of the problems later revealed by spokespersons for alleged victims of government action at the South Pacific and Nevada proving grounds were recognized and "handled" as early as 1945.[1]

Kenneth Q. Bainbridge, a Harvard physics professor who had worked three years at the MIT Radiation Laboratory, was named project director for the first atomic test. He was charged with making "preparations for a field test in which blast, earth shock, neutron and gamma radiation would be studied and complete photographic records made of the explosion and any atmospheric phenomena connected with the explosion."[2]

Bainbridge's first task was to choose a suitable location for conducting the test. Los Alamos was ruled out immediately for both space and security reasons. Convenience and facility of transportation were major considerations, however, so they looked first at places with easy access to the New Mexico lab. Other criteria for the needed site related to minimizing the effects of the blast: the land had to be flat; the weather had to be good with little rainfall and low, predictable winds; and the area had to be sparsely populated, not only for the safety of the residents but for the guaranteed secrecy of the project. Several areas were considered, including the Tularosa Basin in New Mexico; the desert near Rice, California; San Nicholas Island off the coast of Southern California; the lava region near Grants, New Mexico; an area southwest of Cuba, New Mexico; sand bars off the coast of Texas; and the San Luis Valley in Colorado near the Great Sand Dunes National Monument.[3] Interestingly, the southern Nevada site, which was to become the home of the only permanent nuclear testing ground within the continental United States, was not even suggested as a possibility.

After rejecting these potential sites, the project officials finally decided to conduct the test on a part of the Alamogordo Bombing Range in the bleak Jornada del Muerto (Journey of Death) desert near White Sands, New Mexico. The land was already in the possession of the government, an advantage that was to weigh heavily in the future selection of additional testing sites. The area was flat, dry, barren, and fairly isolated, the nearest inhabitant lived twelve miles away, and the closest town, Carrizozo, was twenty-seven miles away.[4]

Despite its obvious suitability, the locale suffered from one condition that proved endemic to all such sites eventually selected as testing grounds: It was almost constantly windswept. This was considered a minor problem, however, and was overlooked in light of the positive features of the location. Such disregard for the importance of the wind was to have serious consequences in the years to come. Wind direction and speed were too often discounted in decisions to conduct or delay given tests, and as a result, many people and animals were exposed to radioactive fallout which was carried outside the testing area by the prevailing air currents.

The scheduled test was referred to by the code name "Trinity," an unusual, perhaps even heretical, choice about which there has been considerable speculation. Some claim it was taken from the name of the nearby turquoise mine which had been cursed by the Indians and abandoned many years earlier. Others said it simply referred to the fact that three bombs were currently under construction and nearing completion.[5] Still another account credits Oppenheimer with having derived the name from a Holy Sonnet by one of his favorite poets, John Donne:

> Batter my heart, three-person'd God; for, you
> As yet but knock, breathe, shine, and seek to mend;
> That I may rise, and stand, o'er throw me, and bend
> Your force to break, blow, burn, and make me new.[6]

Excitement mounted during the final days leading up to the Trinity test. There was great speculation among the residents of Los Alamos about the success of their invention. The major topic of conversation was whether the bomb would go off or not, or, as the scientists referred to it in their discussions, whether it would be a "boy" or a "girl." Some of the less optimistic penned a satirical verse which became known as the "Los Alamos Blues":

From this crude lab that spawned the dud,
Their necks to Truman's axe uncurled,
Lo, the embattled servant stood
And fired the flop heard round the world.[7]

Oppenheimer himself had doubts about the success of the project; in fact, he bet his friend George Kistiakowsky, who was in charge of the explosives division, ten dollars against a month's salary that the bomb would not detonate. There was a betting pool on the yield of the explosive force that would result and the trend was definitely toward the lower numbers. Edward Teller, one of the few confident scientists, predicted that the explosion would equal 45,000 tons of TNT. Project consultant I. I. Rabi later won the pool with the guess of 18,000 tons, a number he picked only because all the low numbers were taken by the time he entered the contest. The actual yield was nineteen kilotons.[8]

The scientists also discussed what might happen if their calculations proved wrong and the bomb turned out to be infinitely more powerful than anyone had imagined. In an attempt to mask their fears, they joked about the possibility of throwing the earth off its axis or igniting the atmosphere.[9] Ironically, such scenarios provided the plots for several of the "sci-fi" movies which were to become so popular during the fifties.[10]

On July 15, 1945, after secretly transporting themselves and their gadget some two hundred miles south from Los Alamos to the Trinity test site, the Manhattan Project personnel began the final countdown on an event that would change the course of history. The bomb itself, nicknamed "Fat Man" after Winston Churchill, was an implosion-type plutonium device, 60 inches in diameter and 128 inches in length. It weighed ten thousand pounds. The bomb was mounted on a steel-supported oakwood platform inside a sheet-metal shack and then hoisted to the top of a 103-foot tower.[11] As it was raised slowly to the top, at about a foot a minute, scores of mattresses were piled beneath it in hopes of softening the impact should a cable snap and the five-ton weapon plunge to the ground.[12]

The site operations were organized around the tower (or "ground zero," as the detonation point was called), with three stations, each situated ten thousand yards away to the south, west, and north. Teams of scientists were assigned to these centers to observe and measure the sequence of events—Station South 10,000 served as the main control point. The observation shelters were built of wood with walls reinforced with concrete and buried under several layers of earth.[13] Five miles further away from ground zero was Base Camp, the nearest point to the explosion where anyone was allowed to be out in the open. Two other important spots at the testing site were the old McDonald Ranch which served as assembly headquarters for the bomb, and Compania Hill, a barren knoll twenty miles northwest of the tower, from which visiting VIPs, scientists not directly involved in the activities of the detonation, and authorized journalist William L. Laurence of the *New York Times* would be allowed to witness the event.[14] The hill was not unlike "News Nob" established later at the Nevada Test Site (NTS) from which the press witnessed and reported on test blasts.

Little planning was done to measure the bomb's lethal effects on humans or their environment. The purpose of the test was to see whether the bomb worked, and few of the scientists or military men were interested in what it would actually do to living things and their habitat. The suggestion was made to erect fake buildings with dummies inside on the test site, but General Groves vetoed the idea because it would stretch security and require too much time and manpower.[15] Such operations, however, would become the order of the day for later weapons testing; elaborate "Doom Towns" were constructed in the southern Nevada desert and stocked with household goods to determine how an ordinary American family would fare under nuclear attack.

Medical personnel were also involved in the final stages of preparation, but in light of current understanding of the effects of radiation, their precautions seem highly inadequate. Worried about the glare from the explosion, they issued sunburn lotion and welder's dark glasses to everyone present for use during the test.[16] They also distributed protective clothing to all Trinity personnel: coveralls, caps, gas masks, cotton gloves, and special booties to be worn over regular shoes.[17] All those present at the blast were further advised to lie face down on the ground, with their arms over their heads and their feet toward the explosion.[18] The radiation-exposure limit was set at five roentgens for all personnel, a dangerously high level compared to safety standards today, but, as has often been the case, other considerations were deemed more important than personal safety. In this situation, medical experts succumbed to pressure from the scientists who wanted liberal dosage standards so they could roam the test site freely after the shot to check their recording instruments.[19]

Elaborate monitoring procedures were also established under the direction of Stafford Warren, chief radiologist, who was later to become the head of the Atomic Energy Commission's Division of Biological and Medical Research. Teams of fallout monitors were posted along the highways bordering Trinity with one roving monitor in charge; they were to report the progress of the fallout cloud and check the level of fallout with Geiger counters. They would relay this information back to Warren at Base Camp, using code names from the story "The Wizard of Oz" to identify themselves. Arrangements also were made for Major Hymes Friedel, stationed in Santa Fe, to assume command should Base Camp be wiped out by the blast; this contingency plan clearly demonstrates the uncertainty of the scientists about the results of their creation.[20]

Finally, plans were devised to evacuate the area if this became necessary. Designated escape routes from the three stations were established with vehicles standing by to leave on a moment's notice; these were manned by drivers familiar with the desert roads at night. A force of 160 enlisted men under the command of Major Q. O. Palmer was stationed north of the test area with enough vehicles to evacuate nearby ranches and towns in case of an emergency. In addition, some twenty military intelligence officers were located in towns up to one hundred miles away where they served a dual function: They would be available to direct an evacuation if needed, and they carried barographs to record the blast and earth shock at remote points "for legal purposes."[21] This direct quotation from an AEC publication indicates that, from the beginning, the government was concerned with questions of liability.

As the final hour drew near, the weather refused to cooperate and thunderstorms deluged the Trinity site. General Groves, Oppenheimer, and Bainbridge were faced with the dilemma of postponing the test or going ahead on schedule. Of all the factors weighed in the decision, the political implications of a delay were paramount. President Truman, meeting in Potsdam with Churchill and Stalin, anxiously awaited the results of the test; its success or failure would make a significant difference in any negotiations he made for issuing an ultimatum to Japan and/or bringing the Soviet Union into the Japanese campaign.[22] General Groves felt that delays would increase the risk of security leaks and possible sabotage attempts. Postponing the test also meant increased psychological strain for the scientists whose nerves were already frayed from the exertion of the previous months. Finally, delay would result in prolonged exposure of delicate instruments which were in place at the test site and were essential for firing and then measuring the impact of the bomb itself.[23] On the other hand, the dangers of exposure to radioactivity would be greatly increased if the active cloud from the explosion were caught up in a thunderhead. "Rain would bring down excessive fallout over a small area instead of permitting it to be widely distributed and, therefore, of little or no consequence."[24]

The test was originally scheduled for 4:00 A.M., a time when the explosion would attract the least amount of attention because most people would be asleep. By 2:30, however, the weather had worsened and the test had to be delayed, first for an hour and then for another thirty minutes. At 4:00 the rain stopped and at 4:45 the crucial weather report came: "Winds aloft very light, variable to 40,000 surface calm. Inversion about 17,000 feet. Humidity 12,000 to 18,000 above 80 percent. Conditions holding for next two hours." Although the weather was far from ideal, it had improved. The decision was made to go ahead with the blast and the zero hour was set for 5:30.[25]

At precisely 5:29:45 A.M. Mountain War Time on July 16, 1945, the first atomic bomb was detonated with results beyond anything imagined. The light in the bell-shaped fire ball was greater than any ever produced on earth and so intense that it could have been seen from another planet. The temperature at its center was more than ten thousand times that at the surface of the sun, and the pressure, caving in the ground beneath, was over 100 billion atmospheres. The radioactivity emitted was equal to one million times that of the world's total radium supply, and the yield of the explosion was equal to nineteen thousand tons of TNT.[26] Almost immediately after the explosion, the fire ball transformed itself into "a swirling column of orange and red, darkening as it rose until it looked like flames of burning oil. Suddenly, a narrower column rose and mushroomed into a parasol of billowy, white smoke surrounded by a spectral glow of blue. Seconds after the first flash . . . came the blast and thunder. This was much less impressive than the extraordinary pyrotechnic display, but five minutes later, the hills still echoed with a faint, continuous rumble."[27] The steel tower that held the bomb had vanished after being completely vaporized in the explosion.

None of those present reacted to the phenomenon with professional detachment. Personal accounts by witnesses are invariably filled with theological references. General Thomas Farrell wrote: "Seconds after the explosion came, first, the air blast pressing hard against the people, to be followed almost immediately by the strong, sustained awesome roar which warned of doomsday and made us feel we puny things were blasphemous to dare tamper with the forces heretofore reserved for the Almighty."[28] Oppenheimer recalls being reminded of an ancient Hindu verse from the *Bhagavad-Gita:*

If the radiance of a thousand suns
Were to burst at once into the sky,
That would be like the splendor
        of the Mighty One . . .
I am become Death,
The shatterer of worlds.[29]

And Laurence, whose assignment it was to record the event for
history, wrote: "In that moment hung eternity. Time stood still.
Space contracted to a pinpoint. It was as though the earth had opened
and the skies split. One felt as though he had been privileged to
witness the Birth of the World—to be present at the moment of
Creation when the Lord said: Let there be light."[30]

After the blast, the radiological monitoring teams went to work.
At first there were no signs of danger and before long the scientists
with instruments in the forward area moved in to pick them up.[31]
Official pictures of these groups reveal that no special provisions were
made beyond the wearing of protective clothing. There was extensive
traffic along the highways of the site between the various stations and
Base Camp. Around daybreak, less than two hours after the explosion, in a lead-lined tank driven by Sgt. Bill Smith, Herbert Anderson
and Enrico Fermi drove to ground zero, where they recovered instruments and took soil samples from the bomb's crater.[32] This practice of allowing people to move about the test site a short time after a
blast and without special protection was repeated when military units
were sent to "clean up" Japan after the war, and participated later in
mock nuclear conflict maneuvers during atomic test blasts in Nevada.

Radiation monitoring outside the Trinity area posed a greater problem for Warren and General Groves, both of whom knew that the
army was not eager to pursue too diligently the problems of widespread fallout. The possibility of endless lawsuits haunted the military, who wanted to put the test and its aftereffects to bed as soon as
possible. Given these restraints, however, they sought to do a con-
scientious monitoring job.

The active cloud drifted northeast at approximately ten miles per
hour, dropping fallout across a region one hundred miles long and
thirty miles wide. By noon, heavy fallout had been identified in an
oval extending ten miles north of the Trinity crater with readings in
some places as high as thirty-five roentgens per hour. At 4:20 P.M., the
Geiger counter at Carrizozo shot off the scale and the question of
evacuation was raised, but within an hour the cloud had passed and

the readings had dropped. The cloud drifted beyond Carrizozo to several towns outside the jurisdiction of the monitors; fallout was detected in Coyote, Ancho, and Tecolote. Vaughn, 112 miles to the north, was thought to be especially "hot." But by dusk the situation had improved and the tension over excessive radioactivity had diminished; most of the officials were convinced that the majority of the fallout had been confined to the test site and the area ten miles to the north of it. That evening, General Farrell notified the Pentagon that the danger had passed.[33]

Unknown to the scientists at that time, however, a part of the cloud had left its predicted path and passed over several cattle ranches along the Chupadera Mesa west of Carrizozo. Although the cows were not as severely damaged as the sheep of Iron County, Utah, which were exposed to fallout in 1953, they did lose the hair along their backs and suffered from serious blistering of the exposed skin. When the affected ranchers filed complaints, Lt. Colonel Stanley L. Steward from the Alamogordo Air Base, and Dr. Louis H. Hempelmann from Los Alamos inspected the cattle. Four Herefords were purchased immediately from rancher Louis Halda and sent directly to Los Alamos where it was confirmed that radiation had caused their ailments. In December, Stewart and Hempelmann returned to the area, "(1) to survey the extent of the damage and number of cattle involved, and (2) to buy up all those cattle which the Alamogordo ranchers felt could not be sold at premium prices on the open market." The cattle purchased and shipped to Oak Ridge for intensive, long-term evaluation included thirty-one cows, fifteen steers, one bull, and four calves that had been *in utero* at the time of the test.[34] Subsequent reports on their condition indicated that the radiation damage was superficial with changes confined to the animals' skin. No change was noted in the blood nor were any genetic abnormalities detected.[35] Descendants of this herd are in existence and can be viewed at the Oak Ridge facility.

It is not surprising that the ranchers were placated by the government's purchase of their damaged cattle. It meant an immediate payoff and, furthermore, people were not likely to challenge the government in the fall of 1945 for conducting tests that had helped to end the war.[36] The government took no chances; however, just as officials were concerned about measuring the earth shock effects "for legal purposes," so were they aware of possible suits over livestock damage. In a letter written on June 7, 1948, Hempelmann commented, "It was decided at [that] time that all cattle should be observed for the duration of their natural lives so that evidence as to their well being would be available in case of future legal proceedings."[37]

In addition to buying off aggrieved parties, the government set another precedent on the morning of the Trinity shot—the practice of maintaining absolute secrecy in the matters of nuclear weapons development. Despite the early hour of the blast, its effects did not go unnoticed. The flash of light was seen in Albuquerque, Santa Fe, Silver City, Gallup, and El Paso. Windows rattled and the earth shook, and the people wanted to know what had happened. In response, the commanding officer of the Alamogordo Army Air Base issued the following press release: "A remotely located ammunition magazine containing a considerable amount of high explosives and pyrotechnics exploded. There was no loss of life or injury to anyone, and the property damage outside of the explosive magazine itself was negligible. Weather conditions affecting the content of gas shells exploded by the blast may make it desirable for the Army to evacuate temporarily a few civilians from their homes."[38]

This concern for secrecy perhaps was understandable during wartime, but it did not end with the war. Instead, secrecy consistently has dominated atomic policy over the years. Under the cloak of national security, questions concerning atomic weapons testing and development have been resolved without the benefit of public discussion. Even Congress has been denied access to information. Many times when members of the Joint Committee on Atomic Energy (JCAE) requested information from the AEC, they were informed that such data was classified and, therefore, unavailable. This was especially true during the mid-fifties when Lewis Strauss was chairman of the AEC and Clinton Anderson, Democrat from New Mexico, chaired the JCAE. Anderson resented Strauss's insistence on keeping the commission's plans secret from the congressional watchdog committee and a serious feud developed between the two men. As Drew Pearson wrote in his national column, they "are so incensed at each other, the atmosphere fairly crackles when they meet."[39]

Immediately following the Trinity test, President Truman was notified of its success. A cablegram from the War Department reached Secretary of War Stimson at 7:30 P.M. Berlin time. It read: "Operated on this morning. Diagnosis not yet complete but results seem satisfactory and already exceed expectations." Elated, Stimson wired back: "I send my warmest congratulations to the Doctor and his consultant."[40]

On the evening of July 26, the United States, Great Britain, and China issued an ultimatum to Japan to surrender or suffer annihilation. Truman, Churchill, and Chiang Kai-shek called upon the government of Japan "to proclaim now the unconditional surrender of all Japanese armed forces, and to provide proper and adequate assurances of their good faith in such action." The alternative was "prompt and utter destruction."[41] Although there was no mention of the bomb per se, the force of the Allies' intent was clear. Two days later, Premier Suzuki of Japan said in a press conference that the government did not consider the ultimatum "a thing of any great value" and planned to "just ignore it" and "press forward resolutely to carry the war to a successful conclusion."[42]

During the following week, arrangements for deploying the weapon were finalized. Then, at 8:16 A.M. on the morning of August 6, 1945, "Little Boy," a gun-type uranium bomb with a yield of thirteen kilotons, was dropped from 31,600 feet on the city of Hiroshima. The B-29 carrying the bomb was flown by Col. Paul Tibbets, Jr., and was named *Enola Gay,* after his mother.[43]

The Japanese were warned, in no uncertain terms, to give up immediately or be subjected to the ravages of a second bomb. They failed to surrender, and seventy-five hours later, at 12:01 P.M. on August 9, a duplicate of the Trinity device was dropped from the B-29 *Bock's Car.* It fell from 29,000 feet, down onto the port of Nagasaki with a yield of twenty-three kilotons; it killed nearly 100,000 people and carved out a crater one mile square in the center of the city.[44] Two days later, Japan surrendered and the war was over.[45]

Dropping the bomb on Japan brought an end not only to the war but to the five-year period of silence that had shrouded the operations of the Manhattan Project. Once the world learned of the atomic bomb's existence, it was decided that Henry Smyth's official account of the project should be made public. The government realized that news of the bomb would generate tremendous excitement that might result in reckless statements by individual scientists who had been involved. Although hesitant to release any information which could aid other nations in duplicating the bomb, top officials decided that the report was the lesser of two evils. Carefully written and revised so as not to reveal anything vital, the report allowed the government "to seize the center of the stage from irresponsible speakers."[46] Furthermore, as James Conant advised Secretary of War Stimson, "its publication will help us defend against the inevitable cry for more information about the project."[47]

This approach to public relations presaged the government's policies during the years to come. Carefully worded official statements on atomic matters were released regularly to the press; they invariably carried more clout with the general public than comments made by individual scientists who were often portrayed as disgruntled or disloyal. Selected educational materials were also widely distributed for presentation to public schools and organizations.[48] From the beginning, the American people learned only what the AEC wanted them to know. But they were satisfied with these bits of information; they felt they were being informed and therefore failed to ask important questions about the burgeoning atomic weapons program. This is ironic in light of Smyth's own comments in his official report on the Manhattan Project: "In a free country like ours, such questions should be debated by the people and decisions must be made by the people through their representatives. . . . The people of the country must be informed if they are to discharge their responsibilities wisely."[49]

Less than a month after the atomic bomb was dropped on Japan, a U.S. military inspection team landed on the island of Kyushu. It reached Hiroshima on September 8 and Nagasaki a few days later. In all the areas examined, the scientists found ground contamination of radioactive materials to be below the hazardous limit.[50] Consequently, despite the general lack of knowledge about the effects of nuclear fission particles, the government declared the area safe for occupation. On September 23, just forty-five days after the bombing, a force of one thousand U.S. Marines and a smaller detachment of Navy Seabees moved into the devastated area where they remained until late autumn. No unusual precautionary measures were taken: the men drank the water from the reservoir, worked for long hours cleaning up the heavily damaged areas, and wore no protective clothing or special gear. They were not issued radiation dosage badges or any other equipment for measuring radioactivity.[51] During this time a joint committee of American and Japanese scientists was formed to study the medical effects of the bomb on the residents of the target areas,[52] but no consideration was given to the possible harmful effects of lingering radiation on those entering and occupying the zones after the blasts.[53]

Following the war, the participants in the Manhattan Project were honored and hailed as heroes; President Truman praised them for having contributed to "the greatest achievement of organized science in history." Most of the scientists, however, sought to put the gadget behind them. Following Oppenheimer's lead, they drifted back to their teaching and research positions at universities across the country.[54] They soon learned, however, that they could no longer afford the luxury of living and working in an ivory tower. Their contribution to science had opened the lid to a Pandora's box and out had flown social, political, and moral problems that would have to be addressed.

3 Politics of Control

*The Atomic Energy Act
of 1946 and Its Successors*

At the end of World War II, the United States government faced the difficult challenge of regulating atomic energy. During the previous five years, an enormous industrial complex of research, development, and production facilities had been created and allowed to operate under conditions of utmost secrecy. Once the bomb was dropped on Japan, however, this mode of operation became both impossible and unacceptable. Suddenly, the closely guarded secrets of the Manhattan Project found themselves at the center of the political arena where new, uncontrollable forces began to shape the nation's atomic future.

Once the American people learned about the power of the atom, a power possessed solely by the United States, they became obsessed with the subject. Their fervor was fanned by a press that, indulging in unrestrained sensationalism, speculated daily about the design, capability, and future use of atomic devices. Various proposals for creating a suitable regulatory agency were introduced in Congress, interest groups were formed to lobby legislators and educate the public on the implications of the bomb, and several ambitious politicians sought to advance their own careers by becoming involved in atomic energy matters. Demands for controlling the awesome new power were also voiced by the international community. Such was the nature of the political climate which spawned the Atomic Energy Commission, an agency created with inherent biases which made future problems of government negligence and liability predictable, if not inevitable.

In announcing U.S. possession of the atomic bomb following its deployment against Japan, President Truman emphasized three major points that would set the tone for United States atomic policy during the next decade. First, while recognizing the need for international control, Truman asserted that the United States should continue its own development of both military and civilian uses of atomic power. Toward this end, he made it clear that the secret of the bomb would be closely guarded until means could be found to effectively "protect us and the rest of the world from the danger of sudden destruction." Second, he declared that atomic energy had tremendous potential for human welfare and should become a "forceful influence for world peace." And third, he told the American people he would ask Congress to immediately establish a commission to control the production and use of atomic power in all its forms.[1]

Two months later, on October 3, 1945, President Truman submitted to Congress a proposal for atomic legislation that addressed his three points. This draft resulted in part from work conducted earlier by the Interim Committee, a presidential advisory group created the previous April to make recommendations on use of the bomb and, in anticipation of future problems, to advise the president on policies that would be appropriate in the aftermath of the war.[2] At first, the committee was preoccupied with the issue of whether to use the bomb against Japan. By the time it convened on July 19, however, this was no longer a question. The Trinity test shot had been successfully conducted and combat use of the weapon was imminent; the members suddenly realized that postwar planning would have to be conducted hurriedly.

Aided by two lawyers from the War Department, Kenneth C. Royal and William L. Marbury, the Interim Committee drafted a bill which would establish a nine-man commission, consisting of five civilians, two representatives from the army, and two from the navy. The term of office for the members was to be indefinite so the commissioners could be insulated from political pressure, and the appointment was to be only part-time, so the members could retain other positions. The powers granted to the commission by this proposal were sweeping: The commission would hold custody of all raw materials and deposits, all plants, facilities and equipment, all technical information, and all contracts related to the production of fissionable materials. It would also establish and administer its own security, personnel, and audit regulations. In effect, the bill would prohibit almost any activities related to atomic power outside the commission's control; no one could conduct atomic research without the commission's consent and even then it held the authority to "direct, supervise, regulate, and inspect" such activities.

The Interim Committee submitted this proposal to the White House in mid-August where, as was customary, it then circulated for comment among the members of Truman's cabinet. The greatest concern came from the State Department, which found several changes necessary before it would agree to sponsor the bill. The preamble had to be rewritten to state that atomic energy would be used for promoting world peace as well as for national defense. The State Department also required that one member of the commission have experience in foreign relations. By September 2, the War Department had accepted these revisions and the bill was ready to be sent to Congress.[3]

Despite the urgency of the matter, however, the administration hesitated.[4] In a special address to the Congress on September 6, President Truman listed twenty-one recommendations for conversion to a peacetime economy, but made no mention of atomic energy.[5] The primary cause for this delay was the fear that once domestic legislation was introduced, President Truman's freedom of action on international policy would be severely limited. At this point the issue of international control had not been resolved. Some members of the administration, led by Secretary of War Stimson, advocated a partnership with the Soviet Union to prevent an all-out arms race; others, including Secretary of the Navy James Forrestal, opposed sharing any information about the bomb. In the end, President Truman followed Stimson's lead; when he finally submitted his atomic energy plan to Congress on October 3, he further proposed to discuss with other nations an agreement under which cooperation might replace rivalry in the field of atomic power.[6] In the months to come, this international proposal would meet with even greater opposition and difficulty than the president's plan for domestic control of atomic energy.[7]

The administration's bill was introduced in Congress simultaneously by Senator Edwin C. Johnson of Colorado and Congressman Andrew Jackson May of Kentucky, both ranking Democratic members of the Military Affairs Committee in their respective houses. Differing little from the original legislation drafted by the Interim Committee, the May-Johnson bill (H.R. 4280) took the general position that weapons development was the most important aspect of atomic energy and placed control largely in the hands of the military.[8]

Quick and easy passage of the measure, as had been anticipated by the administration, was not forthcoming. The greatest opposition came from the scientific community, whose members saw the strict security provisions of the proposed legislation as a threat to physics itself because these restrictions could be applied even to what one was allowed to say in the classroom. Despite reassurances from their own leaders, including Oppenheimer and Bush, that the bill was a needed interim measure, many scientists feared that too much power was being placed in the hands of the military from whence it could never be retrieved.[9]

Furthermore, the War Department misread public sentiment on the matter. The fighting was over and the people were tired of military discipline; political leaders trusted unquestioningly during the war were now seen as ordinary politicians pursuing their own interests. The attempt to rush the bill through the military committees of Congress made many suspicious of the War Department's motives, while others feared the indefinite nature of the broad powers which would be granted to the new commission. Representative May's political ineptness and untoward harassment of witnesses testifying before his committee drew severe criticism and hampered the bill's passage.[10] Finally, a maneuver by Michigan's Republican Senator Arthur H. Vandenberg also delayed the bill by preventing it from being sent to the Military Affairs Committee of the Senate whose members, like their counterparts in the House, were prone to rush it through. This was accomplished through the creation of a special eleven-member committee in the Senate to consider "the entire question of the atomic bomb and atomic energy."[11]

The final straw came when President Truman withdrew his support from the measure in mid-November 1945. He offered no substitute but later endorsed a bill introduced on December 20 by Senator Brien McMahon, the young Democrat from Connecticut who chaired the Special Senate Committee on Atomic Affairs.[12] The McMahon bill (S. 1717) also mandated the creation of an atomic regulatory agency, but its priorities differed from those of its predecessor in two significant ways: First, it stressed the importance of peacetime applications of atomic power in addition to weapons development; and second, it called for civilian rather than military control of the industry.[13] Conspicuous by its absence, however, was any concern for or mention of public health and safety which might be affected by the future development of atomic power.[14]

Hearings on the McMahon bill began on January 22, 1946. Throughout the following spring extensive debate ensued among the members of the Special Senate Committee on how best to structure a commission to deal with atomic power. Faced with an unprecedented situation, the senators carefully considered taking seemingly drastic action such as restricting information despite First Amendment guarantees, and creating a federal monopoly over the atomic energy industry in direct contradiction to one of the most sacred American economic traditions. The committee also looked closely at the patent and royalty problems that would result from state ownership, and at the merits of a full-time commission vis-à-vis a part-time one with members whose loyalties could be divided. Perhaps the most important, and certainly the most publicized issue, however, was civilian versus military control. While some sought absolute exclusion of the military, the more conservative members of the committee, including Vandenberg, who had previously opposed the May-Johnson bill, considered such a suggestion patently absurd.[15]

The final bill was a hybrid, but probably represented the best compromise possible, given the differences in individual levels of understanding, depths of emotional commitment, and ideological orientations among the policymakers involved. It was passed unanimously by the Senate on June 1, 1946,[16] and emerged substantively intact from the House just three weeks later by a vote of 265 to 79.[17] A conference version was passed on Friday, July 26,[18] and President Truman signed the bill into law the following Thursday morning, August 2, exactly seven years after Einstein had written his letter urging Franklin Roosevelt to develop an atomic bomb.[19] The new law, P.L. 585, officially known as the Atomic Energy Act of 1946, "put the citizens of the United States through their government in complete charge and ownership of one of the most complex, diverse, exciting, and difficult enterprises which the world has ever seen."[20]

The Atomic Energy Act did not take effect until midnight on December 31, 1946, over a year and a half after the end of the war. Until that time, the Manhattan Project remained under the direction of General Leslie Groves who, with little or no direction from above, made extremely important policy decisions that laid much of the foundation on which the AEC was later to operate.[21] He demobilized the Manhattan Engineering District and carefully replaced the wartime officers with "men who were young enough to break into the atomic field, but who were senior enough in rank to have demonstrated their ability to accept heavy responsibilities, and whose age would be an asset in their dealings with our scientific personnel."[22] Along with Vice Admiral W. H. P. Blandy of the United States Navy, Groves was instrumental in setting up and conducting two atomic weapons tests at the South Pacific island of Bikini during the spring of 1946. He also appointed Dr. Norris Bradbury, a navy reserve officer, to replace Oppenheimer as director of the Los Alamos laboratory, and he made arrangements to convert Los Alamos into a permanent facility rather than risk security leaks that might result from moving the operation to a less secluded locale.[23] Although General Groves denied allegations that these decisions were made to insure the military's continued influence over atomic power,[24] there is little question that they were, in effect, instrumental in doing just that.

Despite the optimism of many, when the AEC assumed control on January 1, 1947, there was little change in the policy direction which General Groves had established. Although the 1946 law placed nuclear development in the hands of civilians, this soon proved to be window dressing. Certain characteristics of the newly established agency allowed the military to continue to exert disproportionate influence over the decision-making process and to keep weapons development the top priority of the AEC for the next thirty years.

Both the purpose and the structure of the new commission, as outlined in the statute, illustrate this point. In the opening paragraph of the Atomic Energy Act, Congress stated unabashedly that the "paramount objective" of the AEC "at all times" will be "assuring the common defense and security." There could be no doubt about the priorities of the agency. This was made even more explicit when Congress directed the AEC to develop and use atomic energy only "so far as practical" for "improving the public welfare, increasing the standard of living, strengthening free competition in private enterprise, and [last of all] promoting world peace."[25]

Toward this end, the AEC was statutorily divided into four departments: Research, which was later split into one section for physical research and another for biological and medical studies; Production, which was responsible for creating fissionable material; Engineering, which was concerned with building reactors; and Military Application, which dealt with "that ace in the hole—the atomic bomb."[26] Despite the fact that the commission was to be a civilian body, P.L. 585 required that the Military Application Division be headed by a member of the armed forces.[27] And, in keeping with Congress's directive, the functions of this division clearly dominated the commission's activities from the beginning. During the first fifteen years of the AEC's existence, 70 percent of its expenditures went to the weapons-development programs carried out by this department.[28]

The commission itself was composed of five full-time civilian members named by the president and approved by the Senate for staggered five-year terms of office. One of the five commissioners was further designated as chairman. In addition, the president appointed the chief executive officer—the general manager—who was also subject to Senate confirmation.[29] Although AEC members technically were required to be civilians during the extent of their service on the commission, this did not preclude the appointment of military officers who could simply resign from active duty and then accept the new position. In fact, three of the first five general managers named to direct the AEC were military men when tapped for the job: Major General K. D. Nichols, Brigadier General K. E. Fields, and Major General A. R. Luedecke.[30] Lewis L. Strauss, an original com-

missioner and later an extremely powerful chairman of the AEC
during the midfifties, was a reserve admiral in the U.S. Navy.[31] This
informal connection between the military and the commission further
entrenched the former's influence over atomic policy-making.

In addition to the commission itself, three important support committees were mandated by the Atomic Energy Act of 1946. The
General Advisory Committee, composed of nine outstanding atomic
scientists chosen by the president for six-year terms, advised the
commission on scientific and technical matters relating to materials,
production, research, and development. Its first chairman was Robert
Oppenheimer.[32] Second, the Joint Committee on Atomic Energy in
Congress consisted of nine members from the Senate and nine from
the House, with not more than five from either house representing the
same party. The JCAE was vested with full jurisdiction over "all bills,
resolutions, and other matters . . . relating primarily to the Commission or to the development, use or control of atomic energy."[33] It was
a watchdog mechanism designed to provide Congress with the means
for keeping abreast of the commission's activities.[34]

The third committee was the Military Liaison Committee that,
according to Commissioner Sumner T. Pike, one of the original
members of the AEC, "was a happy thought of Senator Vandenberg."[35] The Military Liaison Committee consisted of representatives
of the Departments of War and Navy, selected by the respective
Secretaries.[36] The committee was to rule on any matters related to the
"military application" of atomic energy, and, as Pike went on to say,
"in these infant days of nuclear energy development, there are few
things which may not possibly have some military significance."[37]
The committee could also appeal, through the service secretaries to
the president, to overturn any commission decision which it felt
inappropriate. Furthermore, the burden of responsibility for keeping
informed about military activities was placed on the commission.
Created as a counterpart within the military was the Armed Forces
Special Weapons Project (AFSWP) which was responsible for all
military participation in developing atomic weapons.[38]

The security provisions established by the 1946 legislation provided
additional opportunities for the military to dominate atomic policy-
making. Influenced by testimony from General Groves and the shocking discovery of a Canadian spy ring that had fed U.S. atomic secrets
to the Soviets during the war, the members of the Special Senate
Committee revised and renamed Section 10 of the McMahon bill.
"Dissemination of Information" became "Control of Information,"

and the distinction between "basic scientific" and "related technical" information was deleted, along with the declaration establishing free dissemination as the cardinal principle in the information field. The new emphasis was on restrictions, including the right of service secretaries to prescribe additional regulations on information concerning military applications.[39]

The law also provided for security investigation of anyone who was to work for the commission or its contractors, and established a new special category of information called "restricted data." Defined in Section 10 of the statute, restricted data was "all data concerning the manufacture or utilization of atomic weapons, the production of fissionable materials, or the use of fissionable materials in the production of power." The death penalty was set as punishment for anyone disclosing restricted data "with intent to injure the United States or secure an advantage to a foreign power."[40] Because the great majority of the AEC's work related in some capacity to weapons development, the military was party to the classification of almost all of the information generated by the various divisions of the commission. As a result, it was always in a position to determine what information was suitable for public release.

Although handicapped by these provisions for military control, David Lilienthal, first chairman of the AEC, took the mandate of civilian authority very seriously. The only political independent appointed by Truman to the commission, Lilienthal came to Washington from his post as chairman of the Tennessee Valley Authority where he had learned that man can work in harmony with nature. As chairman of the AEC, he followed the same principles he had used at TVA and attempted to establish an agency which was independent, even aloof, from both the JCAE and the military. His success was limited, however; he won for the AEC the custody battle over the bombs in 1948, but he soon fell prey to the growing demands for increased production of weapons.

Lilienthal's opposition came from sources other than just the military. On Capitol Hill, Senator McMahon, now chairman of the JCAE, and William Borden, a former wartime bomber pilot who was director of the committee, argued that the United States could never have enough bombs, and Henry ("Scoop") Jackson, then Democratic Representative from Washington, took the position that anything short of doubling the authorized output of fissionable material would undermine the security of the country. The scientific community had its hawks as well, among them Edward Teller, Ernest Lawrence, and

Luis Alvarez, about whom Lilienthal wrote: "[There] is a group of scientists who can only be described as drooling with the prospect [of a positive H-bomb decision] and bloodthirsty."[41]

Lilienthal also faced a serious opponent within the commission—Lewis Strauss. Not only did Strauss vote against Lilienthal on the question of building a hydrogen bomb and oppose him internally, but he was active in seeking support for his position from outside. He lobbied both Senator McMahon and General Kenneth Nichols, who had been General Groves's number two man in the Manhattan Project and was currently commander of the Armed Forces Special Weapons Project. Nor did Strauss hesitate to carry this proweapons message to the general public. Speaking before the New York Chamber of Commerce, he once commented that only "when sword and spear have been beaten into ploughshare and pruning hook," can the principles of the bomb be used for peaceful purposes.[42]

Lilienthal lost the battle over the H-bomb or "Super" as it was called during the early years of its development.[43] The final blow came in the fall of 1949 when the Soviets detonated their own atomic device, dubbed "Joe One" after Stalin. President Truman responded to the news by calmly assuring the public that this action had not taken the government by surprise. Internally, however, his administration was in an uproar. Among the members of the "Z Committee," the president's top advisors on atomic weapons development, Lilienthal opposed responding to the Soviet threat by producing an H-bomb; Dean Acheson, secretary of state, was ambivalent; and Louis Johnson, secretary of defense, was wholeheartedly in favor of building the Super. On the Policy Planning Staff (PPS), George Kennan opposed the Super while Paul Nitze campaigned for its development. Within the AEC, pro–Super commissioner Lewis Strauss faced steadfast opposition not only from Lilienthal but also from Robert Oppenheimer, chairman of the General Advisory Committee. On another front, the Joint Chiefs of Staff, chaired by General Omar Bradley, were strongly in favor of building the H-bomb and argued that it would help restore to the United States some of the advantage lost by the Soviet test. In the end, President Truman found this position persuasive and announced on January 31, 1950, his decision in favor of the new weapon.[44]

Lilienthal left office the following month. With Kennan having retired as head of the PPS at the beginning of the year, there was little opposition left within the administration to an all-out weapons development program. By the end of March, the Joint Chiefs and the PPS, now under the directorship of Nitze, had outlined four new alternative approaches for American policy toward the Soviets. Interestingly enough, Kennan's previously touted policy of "containment" was not even considered one of the viable options; it was seen as not only likely to result in failure but also containing too much political risk. From these recommendations, the National Security Council drew up a policy statement, NSC-68, which became a blueprint for United States mobilization in the cold war. Approved by President Truman in mid-April 1950, the document not only provided the rationale and funds for building the Super, but also became the seminal expression of the contemporary American belief "that the Cold War is in fact a real war."[45]

Gordon Dean succeeded Lilienthal as chairman of the AEC. As a result of NSC-68, Dean faced even heavier demands for weapons production expansion. Like Lilienthal, Dean sought to fulfill the mandate of civilian control, but it soon became clear that the military was going to win. In the two and a half years following the Soviet detonation of an atomic bomb, the United States government approved three plans to increase its capacity to produce fissionable material. The stockpile increased from zero in January 1947, when the AEC took over the Manhattan Project, to such a large number in 1953 that President Eisenhower was able to offer the equivalent of five-thousand-bombs-worth of fissionable material in support of his "Atoms for Peace" plan.[46] The age of overkill had begun and there was no turning back.

Eight years after its passage, the Atomic Energy Act of 1946 was revised and many of its original restrictions were loosened.[47] Drafted and guided through the Congress by Republican Representative Sterling Cole of New York, current chairman of the JCAE, the revised bill kept the structure of the AEC relatively intact but put forth two new objectives. First and foremost, the bill was designed to facilitate commercial development of atomic energy. By 1953 many felt that government monopoly over atomic energy was no longer appropriate. Industrialists wanted to operate on their own, and there was general agreement that the profit motive would serve as a great incentive for private industry to develop nuclear power. Consequently, licensing provisions were made to allow the private ownership of nuclear facilities, the private use of fissionable material, more liberalized patenting rights, and industrial access to needed technical information.[48]

Second, the revised statute sought to foster increased international cooperation in the field of nuclear energy development. In keeping with the proposals for international cooperation set forth in President Eisenhower's "Atoms for Peace" speech before the United Nations on

December 8, 1953, the new law restated the purpose of the AEC to reflect this shift in emphasis. Although Chapter I, Section 1(a) of the act made it clear that developing atomic energy for military purposes was still the top priority of the commission, a reordering of secondary objectives in Section 1(b) reflected the new concern for world peace:

> Atomic energy is capable of application for peaceful as well as military purposes. It is therefore declared to be the policy of the United States that—
> a. the development, use, and control of atomic energy shall be directed so as to make the maximum contribution to the general welfare, subject at all times to the paramount objective of making the maximum contribution to the common defense and security; and
> b. the development, use, and control of atomic energy shall be directed so as to promote world peace, improve the general welfare, increase the standard of living, and strengthen free competition in private enterprise.[49]

An "international atomic pool" was also recognized and the president was authorized to enter into cooperative agreements with other nations.[50]

At the same time, however, the power of the military was increased. As delineated in Section 3, any international cooperative efforts or uses of atomic energy for peaceful purposes had to be "to the maximum extent consistent with the common defense and security."[51] Furthermore, as stated in Section 144, international cooperation was authorized "*Provided, however,* That no such cooperation shall involve the communication of Restricted Data relating to the design or fabrication of atomic weapons: *And provided further,* That the cooperation is undertaken pursuant to an agreement for cooperation entered into in accord with section 123."[52] Section 123, in turn, required the Department of Defense to submit to the president a full report and recommendation on any proposed cooperation agreement before it could go into effect.[53]

In addition to its role in international affairs, the military was again given special powers over domestic policy-making. The Division of Military Affairs was the only department actually named in the statute; other divisions, not to exceed ten, were to be created as needed by the AEC. The director of the division was required to be an active member of the armed forces,[54] and the Department of Defense was given the authority to prohibit access to restricted data if the secretary felt that such access could "endanger the common defense and security."[55] Furthermore, the powers of the Military Advisory Committee were transferred directly to the Department of Defense. Whereas under the 1946 statute, the commission was required "to advise and consult with the committee,"[56] under the new law, the commission was mandated to do the same "with the Department of Defense, through the Committee."[57] This subtle but significant rewording continued throughout Section 27, suggesting that no longer would decisions be made by a temporary advisory group but rather by the permanent military establishment.

The revised statute also strengthened the power of the military indirectly by irrevocably separating the functions of the commission into two distinct categories: those dealing with atomic energy and those with atomic weapons. In the years to come, the commission increasingly would be called upon to act as a regulatory body over the private atomic energy industry in this country. Throughout the same period, the commission would simultaneously be involved in a program of international cooperation in the production of atomic energy; numerous countries would be aided with dollars, information, equipment, and expertise in their efforts to develop nuclear power as a source of energy. As a result of these activities, decisions concerning weapons development would be left more and more in the hands of the Military Applications Division, with little pretense of civilian control. So again in 1954, as in 1946, despite claims to the contrary, the military was given carte blanche over the development of atomic weapons, first by Congress and subsequently by the AEC itself.

The 1954 statute also resembled its predecessor in its lack of concern for protecting public health and safety. The only relevant restriction referred to atomic power plants but not to atomic weapons testing. According to Chapter 10 of the act, the commission was simply prohibited from issuing an atomic energy license to anyone who might be a threat "to the common defense and security or to the health and safety of the public."[58] This phrase appeared frequently throughout the text of the statute with reference to activities of the industry. Congress washed its hands of the potential problem when it deliberately authorized the commission to set "safety standards to protect health and to minimize danger to life or property."[59] With little direction from the JCAE, the commission was able to define this vague mandate as it saw fit and set standards that did not inhibit its own pursuits.

One striking difference between the two statutes, however, was the inclusion in 1954 of Section 167, "Claim Settlements." This provision allowed the AEC to "consider, ascertain, adjust, determine, settle, and pay, any claim for money damage of $5,000 or less against the United States for bodily injury, death, or damage to or loss of real or personal property resulting from any detonation, explosion, or radiation produced in the conduct of the Commission's program for testing atomic weapons."[60] A one-year statute of limitations was imposed on the filing of claims, and damages that could be determined as having resulted from negligence on the part of the claimant were disallowed. Any settlement reached was final, thereby eliminating the possibility of further appeal through the judicial process.[61]

No such provision was included in the original Atomic Energy Act. Under the Federal Tort Claims Act of 1946, however, the AEC could settle claims only up to one thousand dollars.[62] The five-thousand-dollar provision was included in 1954 in response to the growing number of claims being filed by neighbors of the Nevada test site. Congress saw this as a way to avoid lengthy and expensive court cases; it also provided a means by which to quickly compensate dissatisfied citizens living in an area where it was crucial to maintain public support for the testing program. The main problem with the provision, however, was that it created a conflict of interest by allowing the AEC to determine whether its own actions were responsible for causing harm. Consequently, the provision offered little protection for people with claims for damages more serious than broken windows or cracked foundations.

For some twenty years the AEC continued to operate under the provisions of the Atomic Energy Act of 1954 as amended, with the military controlling weapons development, and the civilian divisions of the commission involved primarily in atomic energy programs. Then, on October 11, 1974, Congress passed the Energy Reorganization Act.[63] The names were changed but the *modus operandi* continued as before. The 1974 law abolished the AEC and established two new agencies to take its place: the Energy Research and Development Administration (ERDA) "to bring together and direct Federal activities relating to research and development on the various sources of energy"[64] and the Nuclear Regulatory Commission (NRC) to license and regulate the private atomic power industry.[65] This formalized the division of policy-making which had occurred *de facto* in 1954.

After three decades of military domination of atomic policy, the Senate attempted to write into the 1974 statute some checks on the power of the defense establishment. First, the Senate included a provision in its version of the bill that at least 7 percent of ERDA's annual appropriations be assigned to each of the nondefense divisions. Such an allocation still would have meant 75 percent for defense expenditures. Nonetheless, the provision was seen as too restrictive and was struck from the bill by the conference committee. Second, the Senate included a provision requiring that the administrator of ERDA, appointed by the president and approved by the Senate, had to have been a civilian for at least five years prior to assuming the position. The conference committee recognized the conflict of interest, but shortened the requirement to only two years.[66]

This interim arrangement lasted for three years, until August 4, 1977, when Congress, as promised, passed the Department of Energy Organization Act and consolidated the various energy-related agencies into one cabinet department.[67] The name of the Military Applications Division was changed to Department of Defense Programs and placed under the direction of an assistant secretary named by the president with Senate approval; the old Military Liaison Committee was transferred intact to this same division.[68] Decisions concerning nuclear weapons are still controlled by the military, and current expenditure figures indicate that defense programs have continued to be supported above all others.[69]

Congress's original intention was to place control of atomic power in the hands of civilians, but over the years the agency it created and perpetuated was to prove to be a wolf in sheep's clothing. Stated in the legislation itself, the primary objective of the AEC was to use atomic power to protect this country's national security and its policies consistently reflected that priority. Much of its membership came from the established ranks of the military, and its operations allowed for special military considerations in decision making and imposing restrictions. It is little wonder then, that from the beginning finding alternate uses of atomic energy has taken a back seat to the development of its military applications.

4 *Victims of Proliferation*

Testing in the South Pacific

Although the United States was the first country to develop and employ an atomic bomb, American scientists at the time had little real knowledge about the force and effects of such a device. The military realized that acquiring this information was crucial if the country were to maintain its preeminence in the field of atomic weapons. Consequently, shortly after the end of World War II, the Joint Chiefs of Staff began to argue for establishing a full-scale testing program. Within a few months President Truman had approved the program and permanent testing grounds had been established in the Marshall Islands, southwest of Hawaii. By 1963, when the Partial Test Ban Treaty went into effect, 106 nuclear weapons, including the hydrogen bomb, had been detonated in the South Pacific. During this period a major accident occurred that forced the AEC to establish policies for compensating victims. These policies, as well as others related to use of military personnel and maintenance of safety standards, were to persist throughout the era of atmospheric testing.

The original call for atomic weapons testing came specifically from the navy, whose leaders wondered what a bomb like those dropped on Japan would do to a warship or battle fleet. Senator Brien McMahon addressed this question in a speech on August 25, 1945, and further suggested testing the bomb on captured Japanese naval vessels. The Joint Chiefs of Staff took McMahon's hint and began immediately to make the necessary arrangements. On January 10, 1946, President Truman approved the plan for "Operation Crossroads" and authorized the creation of Task Force One, under the command of Vice Admiral Blandy, for the sole purpose of carrying out the tests.[1]

The task force's initial assignment was locating an acceptable site for the testing ground. Not only did the site have to meet conditions similar to those considered in the selection of the Trinity site in New Mexico, it also had to have a large sheltered area for anchoring target vessels. Accordingly, Bikini Atoll, a semicircular chain of some thirty small land dots located in the Marshall Islands region of Micronesia, twenty-four hundred miles southwest of Hawaii, was chosen as the test site. Bikini seemed ideal: It had a lagoon twenty miles long and ten miles wide, the average depth of the water was two hundred feet, the weather was excellent with eighty-degree temperatures year round and an annual rainfall of eighty inches, it was remote from fishing areas and steamer lines, and it was close to the island of Kwajalein (250 miles north), which could be used as a base for the bomber plane.[2]

The only problem with Bikini was that it was inhabited. The United States government resolved this simply by relocating the 167 people who lived on the atoll. Commodore Ben Wyatt, American military governor of the Marshall Islands, went to Bikini on Sunday, February 10, 1946, and informed the people, speaking through a translator, that they would have to leave their homes so the United States could test nuclear weapons on the island. Addressing the islanders at the end of their church services, Wyatt compared them to the children of Israel whom God had saved from their enemy and would now lead to the Promised Land. He then asked, "Would you be willing to sacrifice your island for the welfare of all men?" Telling the United States government to look somewhere else was simply not a realistic option. Left with no choice, Bikini Chief Juda Kessibuki responded, "If the United States government and the scientists of the world want to use our island and atoll for furthering development, which with God's blessing will result in kindness and benefit to all mankind, my people will be pleased to go elsewhere."[3]

The Bikinians were offered three sites for their relocation: Ujae, Lae, or Rongerik. They chose the latter, an uninhabited island 140 miles east of Bikini. Their relocation became a major media event as photographers swarmed to capture the friendly islanders on film. Less than a month later, on March 7, they left their ancestral homeland aboard navy landing vessels with the promise that they could return to Bikini once the testing was over.

Once the Bikinians were moved to Rongerik, preparations began posthaste for the first test, scheduled for May 15. Admiral Blandy's choice of the date was largely influenced by the need to act before the scientists of the Manhattan Project returned to their university positions for the fall term. Forty-two thousand military personnel and several hundred civilians were sent to the South Pacific to assess the naval effects of an atomic blast. In addition, one hundred fifty aircraft and two hundred ships, including legendary battleships like the *Pennsylvania*, the *Arkansas*, and, ironically, the *Nevada*, and such well-known aircraft carriers as the *Independence* and the *Saratoga*, were dispatched to the scene. Captured ships from the defeated enemy, the *Nagato* and *Sakawa* from Japan, and the *Prinz Eugen* from Germany, were also hauled in as part of the seventy-three-ship target fleet.[4]

Also present was the U.S.S. *Appalachian* which sailed from San

Francisco into the testing zone as the official press ship. Carrying 170 reporters from around the world, the ship offered the latest in communications technology; it could transmit 258,000 words a day with simultaneous translations into five languages, and it housed labs with extensive film processing capabilities.[5] This public coverage of the Bikini tests was quite different from the secrecy of the Trinity shot eleven months earlier, when only one journalist, William Laurence, had been allowed to witness and later record the details of the test blast.

Prior to the testing, Operation Crossroads had been the subject of several months of intensive media buildup which consistently depicted the upcoming tests as "benign, circumscribed, and well-meaning."[6] Relaying the military's line, the media presented the tests as matters of self-defense and even humanitarianism. *U.S. News & World Report* informed readers that "only the coming tests can give the final answer to the main question of how today's modern warship can stand up in combat in an age of atomic warfare."[7] *Newsweek* entitled its coverage, "Significance; The Good That May Come From the Tests at Bikini."[8] And *Science News Letter* reported, "One of the answers being sought in the tests will be to see whether more sensitive or exact devices may be needed to indicate quickly enough the need for special medical treatment of atom bomb victims."[9] By the time of detonation, the world was anxiously awaiting the results of these important experiments.

Despite the elaborate arrangements which were in place by mid-May, President Truman ordered a postponement of the first test. He felt that it was essential for key congressmen to be in Washington on May 15 because they were heavily involved in considering legislation to create an atomic energy commission. The president could not spare them on the Hill, but neither did he want to conduct the tests without inviting them to attend. Furthermore, a postponement would enable the president, through his United Nations emissary Bernard Baruch, to proclaim U.S. support for worldwide nuclear controls before proceeding with weapons tests.[10] Consequently, he delayed the test for six weeks.

Then, at thirty-four seconds past 9:00 A.M., Bikini time, on July 1, 1946, the fourth atomic bomb ever exploded was dropped from a B-29 called *Davis Dream* over the lagoon of Bikini Atoll. The "Able" shot involved a twenty-three-kiloton bomb called "Gilda" (named after a Rita Hayworth movie), which was detonated a thousand feet above the target vessels. As a result of the explosion, five ships were sunk immediately and nine others were heavily damaged.[11] Nonetheless, the blast was a disappointment to some observers who had heard so many stories about the bomb's capabilities. As Dr. David Bradley, a radiation monitor whose diary is a primary source of information on Operation Crossroads, wrote: "Expecting much more dire and dramatic events our crew was disappointed. There was much pooh-poohing of the bomb over the interphone, and at last the co-pilot growled: 'Well, it looks to me like the atom bomb is just about like the Army Air Force—highly overrated.' "[12]

The general public's attitude toward the bomb was also changed. Whereas the people had once been completely intimidated by a weapon which could destroy a city and force a nation to surrender, after July 1 they viewed the bomb as a terrible but finite force against which there were defenses. As William Laurence noted: "Before Bikini the world stood in awe of this new cosmic force. . . . Since Bikini this feeling of awe has largely evaporated and has been supplanted by a sense of relief unrelated to the grim reality of the situation. Having lived with a nightmare for nearly a year, the average citizen is now only too glad to grasp at the flimsiest means that would enable him to regain his peace of mind."[13]

Along these same lines, *Time* magazine reported: "Awful as it was, it was less than the expectations of many onlookers."[14] And *Newsweek* wrote: "Man . . . set off his fourth atom bomb this week. . . . Yet . . . he could sigh with relief. Alive he was; given time and the sanity of nations, he might yet harness for peace the greatest force that living creatures had ever released on this earth."[15] Richard G. Hewlett and Oscar E. Anderson, Jr., addressed this change in the public's attitude in their official history of the AEC: "To the extent the test dulled men's minds to the dangers that faced the world, the effect was bad. To the extent it supplanted emotionalism with realism, the effect was good."[16]

Within hours after the Able blast, radiation monitors flying over the target area declared it safe for human occupation. By early afternoon the first of the small boats, originally situated twenty miles from ground zero, began to enter the lagoon with boarding parties. Typifying the attitude at the time, Dr. Bradley optimistically wrote, "It would appear that at least for the time being we have escaped from the real threat of atomic weapons, namely the lingering poison of radioactivity. The great bulk of highly dangerous fission products was carried aloft into the stratosphere where it can be diluted to the point of insignificance in its slow fall-out."[17]

The second shot in the Crossroads series, code-named "Baker," occurred three weeks later, on July 25. Unlike Able, which was dropped from a plane, Baker was detonated beneath the surface of the lagoon to test the effects of an underwater nuclear blast on the hulls of eighty-seven battleships and submerged submarines. The scientists realized that an underwater blast would be different from those previously conducted in the air; they predicted that a chimney of water half a mile in diameter would rise up thousands of feet in the air and tons of water would be vaporized to steam by the intense heat, condensing eventually into a cloud around the top of the chimney. There was also concern over the creation of a tidal wave that could engulf the target fleet and then sweep over the islands.

But of greatest importance to the Radiological Safety Section was the rain of radioactive fission particles that would follow the blast. Quoting Dr. Bradley, "Whereas the cloud in the Able test climbed rapidly to 30,000 feet, the cloud this time is not expected to go half as high. Instead, it will at once begin to rain down upon the target area, and the rain will certainly be deadly from the entrapped fission products." He went on to say that "we are inclined to take our cue from Dr. Hirschfelder, our task force oracle, who says that the ships will not be safe to go aboard for months."[18]

Nonetheless, by Monday, July 29, only four days after the blast, full-scale cleanup operations were being conducted aboard some of the target ships. Following the navy principle "a clean sweep-down, fore and aft," the ships were scrubbed down with soap and water in an effort to decontaminate them. When washing proved ineffective, the paint was sandblasted off the ships. Valuable scientific equipment and laboratory animals also had to be retrieved from the ships, both above and below the water. According to Dr. Bradley: "The main objective, of course, [was] to get the target ships underway once more as soon as possible. The Navy seem[ed] confident that this [would] not be long."[19] As a result, the people in command, following the precedent set at Trinity, placed a low priority on safety precautions that were seen as cumbersome, psychologically debilitating, and time consuming.

This attitude inadvertently was summed up by Dr. Bradley on September 8, six weeks after the blast, when he explained why some of the cautionary measures being taken at that time were not employed earlier when the situation was even more dangerous:

> In the first place, it is a good policy in public or industrial health to be as cautious and conservative as is consistent with the job to be done. In the first hectic week or two following the last shot when ships had to be pumped or left to sink, when there were important instruments and

experimental animals to recover, and when the problem of decontamination was less well understood—in those days, if such extreme
precaution had been required, nothing at all could have been done and
the experiment would have been a total failure.[20]

Additional evidence of this situation can be found in recent testimony by military men involved in the exercise. Typical is the statement by Jack Leavitt who enlisted in the navy in 1941. Describing his
duty on Bikini, he reports having been assigned to board the U.S.S.
Pensacola and "scrub down the decks to wash off any radioactive
fallout." He goes on to say that "at no time did I or anyone working
with me—that is, naval personnel—have a Geiger counter, nor any
other testing device to measure danger of radiation." Similarly, Frank
Karasti, who boarded the destroyer *Hughes* a day after Baker, tells:
"Out of the four hours we spent on her, two were spent vomiting and
retching as we all became violently ill." George McNish of Tampa,
Florida, tells basically the same story: "We had scientists dressed
like for outer space, with instruments like I had never seen. But
when it came to diving or bringing up samples, all we had were
skin and tanks."[21]

The government's own publications from the time corroborate
these eyewitness accounts. Photographs from the official pictorial
record of the Crossroads test series reveal that people were allowed to
wander about dangerous areas without protective gear. One snapshot,
labeled "Davy Jones's locker," is an underwater picture of silt on the
bottom of the lagoon which was formed from pulverized coral. The
caption reads: "Divers sank into this silt up to their shoulders." In
another, crew members of the submarine *Skate,* one of the target
vessels, are standing on her wrecked bridge beneath a sign that reads,
"Keep Clear—Danger! Very Radioactive." A third shows sailors and
reporters aboard a badly damaged ship; written in chalk on the wall
behind them is the warning, "No Souvenirs." Others feature sailors in
shorts and tee shirts swabbing the decks of contaminated ships.[22] The
following passage from Dr. Bradley's account confirms that military
personnel wore no special gear and were allowed in areas where
radiation checks were still being conducted:

I've often wondered what the Navy men thought when they came upon
some mysterious figure, decked out in galoshes, gloves, coveralls, and
mask, creeping along the passages of an able-bodied ship, waving a
magic black box over the water pipes and listening intently through
earphones as though tuned in on the supernatural. They must feel that
the good old Navy is being taken over by screwballs.[23]

Dr. Bradley noted a number of specific safety-related problems: Soap and water offered no relief from the "damned Geigers";[24] the presence of radioactive material on the ships of the line fleet would present complications when the ships had to be drydocked for repairs;[25] there was a "real hazard from elements present which cannot be detected by the ordinary field methods";[26] the accuracy of the urinalysis conducted for the crews "who have since Baker plus one been off and on aboard the hottest target ships" was extremely doubtful;[27] and sandblasting could present a danger from inhaled radioactive dust.[28]

His diary also reveals the cynical attitude toward safety procedures and equipment by some of the scientists and medical personnel. He recorded the following conversation about the effectiveness of gas masks in filtering out contaminated air:

Radiation monitor :	"So you think that the gas masks are superfluous?"
Dr. Hirschfelder :	"Yes, I do."
Radiation monitor :	"And if you ran into a cloud of hot stuff, you would not bother to wear one?"
Dr. Hirschfelder :	"I, well . . . Yes. Yes, I probably would, though I couldn't tell you why."[29]

The papers of Stafford L. Warren, who served as medical adviser to the radiological section at Bikini, reveal his concerns regarding inadequate safety precautions. Discovered recently at the UCLA library, this collection of memos and reports filed during Operation Crossroads charge that fleet commanders pursued "a blind, hairy-chested approach to the matter of radiological safety."[30]

To counter charges of negligence the government has persistently maintained that the crews at Bikini received less than the minimum-allowed dosage of radiation, as proven by the film badges they wore. That defense has been a weak one, however. Many former military men claim never to have been issued film badges, and indeed the government itself was forced to admit that badge information could be found for only 11,500 of the 42,000 present during the Crossroads operation.[31] Furthermore, even if all the men had been issued film badges, such devices reflected dosage levels only up to a certain saturation point. They offered no protection against the dangers of exposure to radiation; they simply allowed a person to tell, after the fact, how much radiation he had been exposed to. As one of the crewmen decontaminating the *New York* commented after receiving his film badge: "Sure, but that only tells you afterwards. A lot of good that is when you've been fried all day in Xrays."[32]

A third shot in the Crossroad series, named "Charlie," was scheduled for March 1947. However, President Truman cancelled the planned deep-water test in September 1946 without explanation. It has been suggested that this was done because of the radiation hazards created by the first two blasts, but, in light of continued testing in the South Pacific over the next decade, this is not a satisfactory explanation. It is more likely that the president cancelled Charlie because the Atomic Energy Act had been passed in August and the AEC was scheduled to take over operations on January 1, 1947. The president felt that the new civilian commission should set up its own testing program rather than assume responsibility for one already in progress. Furthermore, cancellation of the test was intended as a sign of good faith by the United States in the negotiations for international control of atomic energy.[33]

After Crossroads, almost two years passed before the next series of tests was conducted in the South Pacific. During the interim the AEC assumed control over atomic power and soon found that due to the international situation, "the dawn of a new day in which atomic energy would serve the cause of peace rather than the demands of national defense" had to be postponed.[34] The commissioners had to give much more attention to the military aspects of atomic energy than they had expected, and had to spend much more of their time in consultation with officials from the defense establishment. There was a constant debate over whether the government would build a stockpile of nuclear weapons and, if so, who would have custody over it.[35]

Despite superficial tension between some of the civilian and military members of the AEC, actions taken by the commission during this period generally supported the policies of the Department of Defense. At the first meeting of the General Advisory Committee, held on February 2, 1947, the scientists made thermonuclear weapons their top research priority,[36] and in the spring, the commission began to make arrangements for a series of weapons tests in the South Pacific to be conducted the following year.[37] This commitment to military needs was further strengthened when, in its January 1948 report to Congress, the AEC declared that "its goal . . . was the scientific and engineering perfection of improved designs and that thorough testing of weapons and components [was] necessary to improved design."[38]

President Truman, despite his vocal advocacy of civilian control over atomic power, also took actions oriented toward military development. On September 20, 1946, he fired Secretary of Commerce Henry Wallace for criticizing the weapons-development program. Wallace not only publicly attacked the president's step-by-step plan for atomic disarmament as being unrealistic, but he also argued that an armaments race would lead to war, not peace.[39] The president's call for Wallace's resignation made one thing very clear: Any criticism of the government's new hard-line policy against the Soviet Union and, by association, any limitations on America's nuclear strength, would not be tolerated. And, in June 1947, Truman approved the AEC's plans for the second test series.[40]

With such support, arrangements proceeded quickly for the second test series. Los Alamos was made responsible for the technical leadership, the military provided the logistics and supplies, and the commission supplied the funds and the test weapons. By mid-September a ten-thousand-member joint AEC-Pentagon unit, Task Force Seven, had been created under the command of General John E. Hull. Later that month Hull led a group of scientists and military personnel on a scouting expedition in the South Pacific to choose an appropriate test site. The primary consideration was size—the island had to be large enough for towers and instrumentation for the three shots which would constitute "Operation Sandstone."[41]

On October 11, the task force announced that Eniwetok Atoll was their choice for the test site.[42] Located three hundred miles from the naval base at Kwajalein, Eniwetok was also part of the Trust Territory of the Pacific Islands. A tranquil, lovely spot, the area was described in *Scholastic* magazine as "a sort of coral necklace of forty tiny island beads far out in the vast Pacific . . . about halfway between Hawaii and the Phillipines."[43]

Once again a small native population was uprooted and relocated. Proceeding forthwith, by December 20 the government had moved the 142 inhabitants of Bijire and Aomon islands to Ujelang, a smaller, less desirable atoll 124 miles to the southwest.[44] On March 16, 1948, three months after the natives had been moved from the atoll, General Hull arrived in Eniwetok aboard the U.S.S. *Mt. McKinley* to begin the final preparations for Operation Sandstone. This test series differed from its predecessor in several important ways. First, the Bikini tests had been conducted specifically to measure the impact of atomic weapons on naval vessels, whereas the primary purpose of the Eniwetok tests was to study the weapons themselves and the improvements that had been made in their designs.[45] The question being asked was, could we "get a bigger bang than ever before"?[46] Second, in response to the changing international situation, Operation Sandstone, unlike Operation Crossroads, which was conducted in the spotlight, was shrouded in secrecy. For security reasons, the dates of the tests were not announced and the only outsiders allowed to witness the event were members of the JCAE.[47] Furthermore, the ships carrying personnel to the assignment were plastered with posters depicting a fish with an open mouth. "Don't be a sucker" they warned, "Keep your mouth shut."[48] Third, the tests were justified not just in terms of their contribution to national security but also because "the scientific and technical operations of the proving ground will provide new fundamental data and a broader understanding of the phenomena of nuclear fission, for peaceful as well as military application of atomic energy."[49]

The Sandstone tests consisted of three detonations from 200-foot towers: "X-Ray," a thirty-seven-kiloton bomb, was fired on Enjebi Island on April 15; "Yoki," a larger bomb with a yield of forty-nine kilotons, was fired May 1 on Aomon Island; and "Zebra," an eighteen-kiloton bomb, was fired on May 15 on Runit Island.[50] Although there were no ships to scrub down, stories and pictures of the retrieval and cleanup maneuvers after the blasts were reminiscent of those from Bikini. The evidence strongly suggests that radiation-safety practices were again casual at best.[51] In fact, the problems may have been even greater at Eniwetok, where speed was considered crucial. Because many of the significant fission products created by the bomb were short-lived radioisotopes, postblast samples had to be flown back to Los Alamos as quickly as possible. As a result, within four minutes of the blast, helicopters delivered technicians to the target island where they reeled in a cable of samples from near the ground-zero tower. These samples were then loaded on planes and delivered to radiochemists in Los Alamos less than thirty hours later. Furthermore, for security reasons, Task Force Seven wanted to conduct these tests and be gone before the Soviet Union could monitor their results.[52]

From the scientists' perspective, the tests were a smashing success resulting in "substantial improvements in the efficiency of use of fissile material."[53] The new design principles were verified and the way was now paved for producing bombs with bigger and better yields. Sandstone also established a new standard for coordination between the military and the civilian scientists which was thereafter frequently cited as "a model of harmonious cooperation."[54] More important, the test series gave a lift to those politicians, industrialists, generals, and scientists who were pushing Congress for greater nuclear weapons outlays; it thereby firmly established the mushroom cloud as a predominant fixture on the contemporary American political, social, and economic scene.

The AEC did not use the South Pacific testing ground again for three years. During that time, several events occurred that had sweeping ramifications for the atomic weapons development program: On August 29, 1949, the United States lost its monopoly over nuclear weapons when the Soviets detonated Joe One.[55] A year later, in June 1950, American troops were sent to fight against Communist forces in Korea.[56] Furthermore, the arrest of Klaus Fuchs in England on February 2, 1950, as an atomic spy who had fed secrets to the Russians during the days of the Manhattan Project caused increased public alarm and speculation about the weapons capacity of the Soviet Union.[57]

Pressured by the military and certain members of the AEC, President Truman made two crucial decisions in response to these events: He announced that he was ordering full-speed-ahead development of the H-bomb,[58] and he approved the establishment of continental testing grounds that could be more easily maintained and defended than the remote site in the South Pacific.[59] The media applauded the president's actions, and Congress and the public followed suit.

Despite the existence of the new continental test site, the AEC returned to Eniwetok in the spring of 1951 for "Operation Greenhouse," a four-shot series conducted by Joint Task Force Three under the command of Air Force General Elwood R. Quesada. The primary objective of the exercise was to test some of the mechanisms being devised for the thermonuclear H-bomb.[60] From that point until October of 1958 when President Eisenhower ended the South Pacific testing program as part of a voluntary moratorium on testing, fifty-seven additional tests of a similar nature were conducted in the Marshall Islands, thirty-six on Eniwetok, and twenty-one on Bikini.[61] After President Kennedy renewed testing in 1961 following the Soviet violation of the voluntary moratorium, the AEC returned to the South Pacific where thirty-five atmospheric tests were conducted on Christmas Island and Johnston Island between April and November of 1962.[62]

With a single exception, the South Pacific tests were conducted without incident, but that one exception was to pose serious problems for the AEC. The accident in question occurred on March 1, 1954, when the AEC detonated "Bravo," the first in a series of six hydrogen bombs being tested as part of "Operation Castle."[63] The detonation took place on Bikini and produced a much higher yield (fifteen megatons) than had been anticipated. Following the blast, which gouged a five-hundred-meter chasm in the island, the wind suddenly shifted direction and carried the 20-mile-high mushroom cloud of radioactive particles of pulverized coral 240 miles eastward. As a result of this shift, the cloud heavily contaminated more than seven thousand miles of the surrounding Pacific Ocean and passed over several small islands, including Rongerik, Rongelap, and Utirik, showering twenty-eight Americans and some two hundred fifty natives with radioactive fallout.[64]

When the AEC radiation safety monitors stationed at Rongerik detected that radiation levels were exceeding their instruments' maximum scale of one hundred millirads per hour, they donned special clothing and stayed inside their tightly closed building until they were evacuated thirty-four hours later. The local residents of the other two islands were not so fortunate and suffered much higher rates of exposure as they awaited evacuation. The people of Rongelap were not evacuated for more than twenty-four hours after the Americans left Rongerik, which was only twenty-five miles away, and the Utirik population was not removed until more than three days after the blast had occurred. The islanders were taken to the base at Kwajalein. Those from Utirik returned home two months later in May 1954 "in spite of slight lingering radiation," but those from Rongelap were forced to remain for three years.[65]

In an AEC news release issued on March 31, Chairman Lewis Strauss commented on the accident and denied that any serious harm had been done:

> None of the 28 weather personnel have burns. The 236 natives also appeared to me to be well and happy. The exceptions were two sick cases among them, one an aged man in advanced states of diabetes, the other a very old woman with crippling arthritis. Neither of these cases have any connection with the tests. Today, a full month after the event, the medical staff on Kwajalein have advised us that they anticipate no illness, barring of course disease which might be hereafter contracted.

Strauss went on to refute the charge that the AEC had allowed this to occur intentionally so the islanders could be used as guinea pigs, calling the accusations "utterly false, irresponsible, and gravely unjust to the men engaged in this patriotic service." He concluded with the AEC's standard line: "One important result of these hydrogen bomb developments has been the enhancement of our military capability to the point where we should soon be more free to increase our emphasis on the peaceful use of atomic power—at home and abroad. It will be a tremendous satisfaction to those who have participated in this program that it has hastened that day."[66]

Despite Chairman Strauss's original claim to the contrary, the islanders exposed to the Bravo cloud did suffer from serious radiation-related maladies. Although the medical records for the radiation safety monitors are not available, it is known that the people of Rongelap received 175 rems and the people of Utirik received 14 rems.[67] After their evacuation to Kwajalein, many experienced itching and burning of the skin, eyes, and mouth, nausea, vomiting, and diarrhea. Later, in the second stage of acute radiation poisoning, some began to wholly or partially lose their hair, and skin burns appeared on the necks, shoulders, arms and feet of the most heavily exposed. It was not until 1964, ten years after the Bravo shot, that the first thyroid tumors and cancers appeared. Since then, nineteen of twenty-one Rongelapese who were under twelve at the time of the blast have developed thyroid tumors. In Utirik, prior to 1977, the AEC treated eleven cases of thyroid tumors out of a population of only 157; suddenly then, this already-high incidence of the condition rose sharply to the point that it equalled the rate experienced by the more heavily exposed Rongelapese.[68]

Under the United Nations Trusteeship Agreement, signed in July 1947, the United States government agreed to "protect the health of the inhabitants" of Micronesia.[69] Having admitted to being responsible for exposing the islanders to radiation, Congress was forced to respond to the health problems that arose in later years as a result of this exposure. Accordingly, on August 22, 1964, Congress passed P.L. 88-485, which appropriated $750,000 to be paid in equal amounts to each of the affected inhabitants of Rongelap or their heirs.[70]

Thirteen years later, on October 15, 1977, in response to the increasing number of cancer cases among the islanders, Congress passed P.L. 95-134, which increased compensation for the victims of Bravo in three ways: First, a sum of $25,000 was to be paid to anyone who had the thyroid gland removed or who developed hypothyroidism; second, $1000 was to be paid to any individual who had been a resident of Utirik at the time of the blast; and third, the Secretary of the Interior was mandated to provide adequate ongoing medical care and treatment for any person suffering from radiation illness as a result of being exposed to fallout from the Bravo blast.[71] In both statutes, however, Congress included the statement that such payment "shall be in full settlement and discharge of all claims against the United States government" arising out of the 1954 incident.[72] The government attempted to stave off the possibility of suit by offering a modest settlement to the injured parties.

The islanders were not the only victims of radioactive fallout from the Bravo cloud. A small Japanese tuna trawler, *Fukuryu Maru* ("Lucky Dragon"), with its twenty-three crew members was drifting approximately ninety miles northeast of Bikini at the time of the blast. Around 3:50 A.M. the men noticed a brilliant flash in the west, and at 7:25, white ashes began to descend on their ship. Shortly thereafter, the crew members experienced eye pain, headaches, and nausea, their faces turned black and their hair fell out. Upon returning to its home port of Yaizu two weeks later, the *Lucky Dragon* was quarantined and its crew hospitalized. The radioactive fish it carried were confiscated and buried but, unfortunately, not until some had been cut up and sold.[73]

The AEC's position with regard to the plight of the Japanese fishermen was summed up by Chairman Strauss in a statement of March 31. He first blamed the Japanese for being "well within the danger zone," and then went on to say: "The reports which have recently come through to us indicate that the blood count of these men is comparable to that of our weather station personnel."[74] A similar "thumbs-up" statement was issued by Democratic Rhode Island Senator John Pastore, who passed through Japan after witnessing the second test in the Castle series on March 26. Upon visiting with the fishermen, he reported extreme optimism about their recovery.[75] Nonetheless, one of the crew members, radio operator Aikichi Kuboyama, age forty, fell into a coma on August 29 and died on September 23. The AEC never issued a formal statement on his death, but an internal memorandum clearly spells out the commission's position:

> At a time when he was convalescing satisfactorily from his radiation injury, he developed hepatitis which was presumably of infectious type caused by a filterable virus. From this he grew steadily worse with severe liver pathology and generalized jaundice. After a prolonged illness, he died from the effects of hepatitis. Such hepatitis is not in itself a direct consequence of radiation injury and does not constitute a part of such injury.[76]

Perhaps even more significant than the ailments of the exposed crew members was the impact of the incident on the Japanese fishing industry. Not only were the fish from the *Lucky Dragon* radioactive, but the catches of other boats fishing in the waters near the designated danger zone were also found to be contaminated. Overall, 457 tons of tuna had to be discarded.[77] As was typical by this time, the AEC again followed a strategy of denial. Strauss commented: "With respect to the stories concerning widespread contamination of tuna and other fish as a result of the tests, the facts do not confirm them. The only contaminated fish discovered were those in the open hold of the Japanese trawler."[78] In a similar statement, the AEC reported: "The opinion of the Atomic Energy Commission scientific staff, based on long-term studies of fish in the presence of radioactivity, is that there is negligible hazard, if any, in the consumption of fish caught in the Pacific Ocean outside the immediate test area subsequent to tests."[79]

These reassurances did little to restore confidence among buyers in Japan's fish markets; consequently, prices sagged. Furthermore, the United States Food and Drug Administration laid down rigid restrictions on tuna imported into this country. On one hand, the Americans were asserting that there was no danger and that the Japanese were being unrealistic about the levels of radioactivity in fish; on the other, they rejected even potentially contaminated tuna bound for consumption in the United States.[80] The controversy escalated as Japanese newspapers decried the double standard and demanded that the United States pay for damage incurred. Leftist politicians raised a great outcry and labor unions claimed that testing would "doom the Japanese nation to ruin." Japanese scientists also contested the findings of the AEC. One professor, Mitsu Taketani, suggested in a radio broadcast that the contaminated fish be sent to United States Ambassador John M. Allison for his dinner.[81] The incident prompted India's Jawaharlal Nehru to call for an end to the tests in the Pacific, saying: "This only reminds me of the genies that came out of the bottle, ultimately swallowing the man."[82]

In the end, the United States yielded to pressure and made two concessions: The AEC enlarged the danger area surrounding the test site by eight times, and "increased the scope and intensity of its survey of the area to make sure all craft approaching or inadvertently entering the area [were] warned."[83] The United States also agreed to pay, *ex gratia*, to the government of Japan, without reference to the question of legal liability, two million dollars for purposes of compensation for injuries or damages sustained from the Bravo shot. The term *ex gratia* made it clear that the United States assumed no responsibility for the accident and that compensation was made out of sympathy. The Japanese government allocated about three-fourths of the total to the tuna industry. Of the rest, $37,000 went to the city of Yaizu where the *Lucky Dragon* had docked, $71,000 to crew members for medical expenses, and an average of $5,000 apiece to the crew members for compensation.[84]

This action absolved the United States of any further responsibility and the incident was soon forgotten. Such was not the case in Japan, however. As British historian Richard Story wrote: "This affair caused resentment in Japan at least equal to that occasioned by the atomic attacks on Hiroshima and Nagasaki."[85] The Japanese people strongly identified with the ill-fated vessel and its crew members. More than 400,000 attended the funeral of Kuboyama, and within a year some 30 million had signed a petition against nuclear weapons. This in turn led to the convening of the first World Conference Against A- and H-bombs in Hiroshima on August 5, 1955. The *Lucky Dragon* itself was renovated and placed in Tokyo's downtown Peace Park as a permanent reminder of the incident.[86] The United States government was able to put the incident aside with a small contribution to the victims, but those who suffered could not so soon forget.

The problem of the displaced islanders was not resolved as easily. The plight of the Bikinians since that first move in 1946 has been a traumatic one. Their initial choice of Rongerik as a new home was a mistake because the atoll was smaller than Bikini and its potential for agriculture even lower. Many of the fish in its lagoon proved to be poisonous. By March of 1948, the islanders were literally starving and had to be moved to a temporary camp on Kwajalein where their leaders were again allowed to choose a spot for relocation. This time they chose Kili, a fertile island four hundred miles south of Bikini which had been used as a coconut plantation by the Germans and Japanese. Unfortunately, however, the Bikinians were fishermen, not planters, so their existence continued to be bleak.[87]

In the spring of 1967, approximately ten years after the testing had stopped, the AEC reviewed the results of a radiological survey of Bikini and declared the island once again safe for human habitation. Two years later the first Bikinians returned to their now-devastated atoll to participate in the resettlement program. Homes were built, the topsoil was turned, and fifty thousand new trees were planted. The future looked bright when the government announced in 1973 that the project would soon be completed and the remaining Bikinians could return home by Christmas.

Shortly thereafter, however, Secretary of the Interior Rogers C. B. Morton became alarmed by the findings of several new radiological surveys of the area and ordered the resettlement halted. Morton wrote to Secretary of Defense James Schlesinger in March 1975 requesting that a thorough survey of the area be undertaken. The Defense

Department declined to take action because of the high costs of the proposed study. The Bikinians, frustrated and confused by contradictory information they were receiving, filed suit in federal court in October 1975 to force the government to stop the resettlement program until such a survey was taken. The U.S. agreed to do so, but it was not until early 1978, after much bureaucratic squabbling, that the study was conducted. By August of that year, the atoll had been declared off limits and those inhabitants who had returned were once again moved to nearby islands. This time they were told that they would not be able to return to Bikini for approximately one hundred years.[88]

In the interim, Congress, "in recognition of the hardship suffered by the people of Bikini due to displacement from their atoll since 1946," set aside a trust fund for the islanders. In June 1975, with the passage of P.L. 94-34, Congress appropriated $3 million *ex gratia* to the Bikinians. This was increased twofold in 1978 when Congress passed P.L. 95-348, which provided an additional $12 million for the relocation and resettlement of the Bikinians who had mistakenly been allowed to return.[89]

But this trust fund has not been enough to satisfy the displaced islanders. Represented by Senator Henschi Balos in the legislature of the Marshall Islands and by attorney Jonathan Weisgall, their lobbyist in Washington, they filed suit in federal district court in Honolulu seeking an injunction forcing the government to renovate the atoll. A tentative agreement was reached in March 1985, however, and the suit was dropped. The Bikinians agreed to endorse the Compact of Free Association which, if approved by Congress, will end the Marshall Island Trusteeship and constitute "full settlement of all claims, past, present, and future . . . in any way related to the Nuclear Testing Program." In return, the administration pledged support for $75 million to be paid to the Bikinians over the next fifteen years in compensation for damages to property and health. The Reagan administration also promised that funds would be made available for resettlement "at a time which cannot now be determined."[90]

Like the Bikinians, the people of Eniwetok were promised they could return to their homes as soon as the testing was over. In 1956, however, nine years after they had been relocated to Ujelang Atoll, these natives were still unable to return. At that time they were paid $25,000 in cash and $150,000 in trust for use of their atoll. In 1969 they received another $1,020,000 in trust for the hardships they suffered as a result of being displaced, their continued displacement in the foreseeable future, and the decline in productivity of their subsistence agriculture. To the islanders of Eniwetok, however, money could not and never would be a substitute for their islands. Still displaced in the late 1970s, they saw the Bikinians going home and they wanted to do the same, "because it is the only place which God has set aside for them and for no other people."[91]

In response to their plea and advised by the Departments of Energy, Defense, and Interior that the atoll could be made safe for inhabitants, Congress authorized funding for a massive Eniwetok cleanup and resettlement campaign that was mobilized in May 1977. The government felt that the conditions which had doomed the Bikini revitalization project several years earlier would not be major problems in Eniwetok for two reasons: First, in Bikini, all the islands had been contaminated by fallout, whereas in Eniwetok all but two of the tests had been conducted on the northern islands leaving those to the south relatively free from contamination; and second, most of the debris from the Bikini tests lay in the lagoon, but in Eniwetok, where the majority of the tests were conducted on or over the land, the debris could be more easily retrieved.[92]

Once approved, the cleanup tasks soon got underway. Military units removed radioactive scrap, scraped away the top layer of soil in many areas, and filled bomb craters with radioactive debris and then covered them over with cement. This massive operation was carried out by the Nuclear Defense Agency which claimed that "the most important consideration . . . was the radiological safety of the individuals involved in the operations." Reports by soldiers who participated in the project and by members of the press who visited the atoll indicate, however, that this claim was not supported in practice. According to them, enforcement of safety standards was haphazard.[93]

At this time, the Department of Energy published a colorful brochure for distribution to the approximately 450 people expected to resettle the atoll. The document explained, in layman's terms, how the government was trying to get rid of the "tiny things that came from the bomb," meaning radiation. It further spelled out certain living pattern restrictions which the natives would have to follow upon their return to Eniwetok.[94] Similar guidelines had been established previously for the returning Bikinians, but when checked for radiation dosage levels in May 1978, it became evident that they were not adhering to the restrictions against eating locally grown food. Indeed such regulations seemed impossible to enforce.[95]

The cleanup project was completed in 1980 and several hundred natives have since returned to resettle the southern islands which have been declared "relatively uncontaminated." The question of resettling the northern islands where most of the testing occurred remains unresolved. This has caused a problem for the Eniwetok people who have traditionally been divided into two distinct groups: the Dri-Enjebi of the north and the Dri-Eniwetok of the south. The Dri-Enjebi are now reluctant to live on the lands of their ancient rivals.[96] Other problems have arisen as a result of this partial resettlement. For example, Runit Island will be quarantined forever, but other islands less then three miles away have been designated "safe for picnics and food gatherings." As a local resident commented, "What will happen if birds, crabs, turtles, and other animals that land on the off limits island are eaten by the people?"[97]

Some scientists argue that, like Bikini, none of the islands in the Eniwetok atoll is safe for human habitation. Edward Martell of the National Center for Atmospheric Research has stated that "the resettlement of such sites is extremely likely to have tragic consequences, particularly for the younger members of the inhabitants. Progressively worse consequences are to be expected for each successive generation in the affected population group."[98] Nonetheless, despite the Bikini experience, the resettlement of Eniwetok continues in the south as demands increase for Congress to provide assistance for the renovation of the northern islands as well.

Bombs in the Backyard 5

The Nevada Test Site Operations

Although the South Pacific testing program was considered a success by both the military and the AEC, it soon became evident that operations there created considerable logistical problems for the government. Not only was it inconvenient for political officials to visit the remote site, but it was also extremely difficult to coordinate such a long-distance effort; transporting thousands of men and tons of equipment halfway around the world was costly in terms of time and money. The problem of maintaining top security for these endeavors presented an additional cause for concern. Consequently, in 1947, shortly after the first Bikini series, the military's special weapons program initiated a top secret project, code-named "Nutmeg," to identify potential locations for a future continental test site. The advantages of a continental facility were obvious; nonetheless, the report concluded that the decision to hold future tests within the continent would depend not on "the physical feasibility of conducting the tests without harm, but upon the elements of public relations, public opinion, logistics, and security."[1] As Commissioner Sumner Pike commented in March 1949, it would take a national emergency to justify testing within the United States.[2]

That emergency arose during the summer of 1950 when the United States became involved in the Korean Conflict. Coming on the heels of the Soviets' detonation of Joe One, this conflict posed a serious threat to American superiority in the international arena. By mid-December, the deteriorating situation prompted President Truman to exhort "our farmers, our workers in industry, and our businessmen to make a mighty production effort to meet the defense requirements of the nation."[3] Both the AEC and the JCAE abetted the president in his drive to step up weapons development. Facilities were expanded for the increased production of fissionable material and work on the super H-bomb was accelerated. The proposal for a continental test site, where lead times would be reduced and less costs incurred, was revived as a means of building up the nuclear stockpile, especially of low-yield weapons. Despite warnings from the scientific community about safety hazards, President Truman, on December 18, 1950, approved the establishment of such a facility in southern Nevada and six weeks later, on January 27, 1951, the first atomic weapon was tested over a section of the desert known as Frenchman Flat.[4]

The site selected for the home of the new continental testing program was part of the Las Vegas-Tonopah Bombing and Gunnery Range situated in the desert of Nye County some sixty-five miles northwest of Las Vegas. It was chosen from a list of five possibilities, which included Alamogordo/White Sands, New Mexico; Dugway Proving Ground, Utah; Pamlico Sound/Camp Lejeune, North Carolina; and a fifty-mile-wide strip between Fallon and Eureka, Nevada.[5] Following the selection, the AEC and the air force signed an agreement on December 21, 1950, by which a 350-square-mile area of the bombing and gunnery range was surrendered to the AEC as a permanent test site. The AEC was also allowed to use Indian Springs Air Force Base facilities to support the test site. The establishment, referred to as the Nevada Proving Ground (NPG) until 1955, was officially a branch of the AEC's Albuquerque operation.[6] The site was expanded for the first test series to 415,000 acres, approximately 640 square miles. The lease arrangement with the air force became permanent on February 19, 1952, when 435,200 acres were withdrawn under Public Land Order 805 and set aside for "nuclear testing purposes." Subsequent expansions in 1958, 1961, 1964, and 1967 have brought the site to its present size of approximately 850,000 acres or 1,350 square miles, which includes a rectangular section 28 miles wide by 40 miles long, and two protruding additions at the northwest and southeast corners to take in the Pahute Mesa and Mercury areas[7] (see map).

The southern Nevada location was chosen over the others for several reasons. It was the largest of the areas suggested. It was already under complete federal control that precluded any jurisdictional problems with state and local governments. The site was near needed operational facilities, but was not vulnerable to outside attack. Camp Mercury, a temporary air base located at the tip of the site, could easily be converted to a permanent testing operation center. The selection of southern Nevada had the support of Nevada Democratic Senator Pat McCarran, a powerful member of the Appropriations Committee, and it was anticipated that many state residents would welcome the testing program because of its potential contribution to the economy.[8]

Two other features of the location which figured prominently in its selection were isolation and meteorology. The area surrounding the site was sparsely populated: The people closest to ground zero lived at Indian Springs and Cactus Springs, some twenty-five miles to the southeast. Directly south were tiny settlements at Mt. Charleston. Further in that direction, no one was closer than the residents of Las Vegas, approximately seventy miles away. To the east, several families lived along U.S. Highway 93 but none was closer than sixty miles, and thirty-eight miles to the north a small community of sixteen people was located at Groom Mine. Other distances, calculated from Yucca Flat, the site of most of the atmospheric tests, include Death Valley Junction, fifty-seven miles; Beatty and Lathrop Wells, forty miles; Alamo, fifty miles; Tonopah, eighty-five miles; Caliente, eighty-seven miles; Overton, ninety-five miles; and Pioche, one hundred miles. In Utah, St. George stood 135 miles away.[9] This remoteness was especially appealing to the government for several reasons: Maintaining security in an unpopulated area surrounded by desert would be relatively simple; should an accident occur, it would affect only a few people; and monitoring the radiation exposure of a small population meant less time, less trouble, and less expense for the AEC.

The weather at the Nevada site, with its low rainfall and predictable winds, was also considered appropriate for atmospheric testing. Unfortunately, as in New Mexico during the Trinity test, these weather conditions were to prove less predictable than originally supposed. This was noted by Los Alamos biologist Frederick Worman who wrote in 1965: "The data . . . indicate that the unexpected may be expected at the test site."[10] Often in the years between 1951 and 1958 the unexpected did occur and shifting winds carried the radioactive cloud created by a blast outside the boundaries of the test site, scattering fallout on the inhabited areas in its path.

The geology of the area, which was to become so important in later years when testing moved underground, was given little consideration during the original selection of the site. In the first place, it seemed irrelevant to atmospheric testing and in the second, little was known about what lay beneath the desert floor. Detailed base maps were nonexistent; in fact, the best available picture of the regional geology was a reconnaissance map drawn by S. H. Ball in 1907.[11] Since 1956, however, when the first underground test was conducted, the AEC has sponsored extensive geological research on the site. Scientists have produced ground-water hydrology reports, geophysical measurements, and stratigraphic studies, as well as detailed base maps, for the entire region.[12] But, like the weather, these geological formations have not always behaved as expected. Consequently, several major accidents have resulted from underground testing at the site since 1956; most of these have involved "venting" of radiation, but cave-ins have also occurred.[13] As the government now looks toward this area as a possible high-level nuclear waste disposal site, these questions concerning the geology of the area will become increasingly important.

The 1950 decision to begin atomic testing within the continental United States was made in great secrecy and with extreme caution.[14] Secretary of Defense George Marshall and his deputy, Robert Lovett, cautioned Truman against announcing the tests, thinking it unwise in the current international situation to reveal the extent of the United States' nuclear arsenal.[15] In the end, however, the president decided he had to notify the American public of the new test operations, and on January 11, 1951, the AEC released an official announcement.

The announcement was short and to the point, explaining simply that test activities at the new site would include "experimental nuclear detonation for the development of atomic bombs—so-called 'A-bombs'—carried out under controlled conditions." The AEC went on to reassure the public that radiological safety and security conditions had been reviewed and it had been found "that the tests may be conducted with adequate assurance of safety under the conditions prevailing at the bombing reservation. All necessary precautions, including radiation surveys and patrolling of the surrounding territory, will be undertaken to insure that safety conditions are maintained."[16] The AEC also circulated handbills throughout southern Nevada which reiterated this message and assured the neighbors of the new facility that "no danger from or as a result of AEC test activities may be expected outside the limits of the Las Vegas Bombing and Gunnery Range."[17] Such statements were to become commonplace over the next decade; even today, similar reassurances are given to the public when underground blasts are conducted.

The first series of tests at the NPG was code-named "Operation Ranger." Conducted almost immediately, Ranger consisted of five nuclear detonations between January 27 and February 6, 1951. The primary objective of the operation was "to provide sufficient data to determine satisfactory design criteria for nuclear devices" scheduled to be detonated in the South Pacific later that spring. Toward that end, five devices, ranging from one kiloton to twenty-two kilotons, were airdropped over Frenchman Flat, a dry lake bed located in the southwestern corner of the proving grounds. Four were detonated at a height of 19,700 feet above the ground, and one at 29,700 feet.[18]

The Ranger shots were relatively uneventful with the exception of the fourth, an eight-kiloton device detonated on February 2 that shattered windows in Las Vegas and prompted one scientist to report that "the factors controlling this are poorly understood." He also recommended that tests in the future not be conducted on consecutive days, that facilities for hot showers be installed, and that a larger pool of experienced radiation monitors be used.[19] For the time being, however, there seemed to be little cause for alarm. Safety monitors had detected no "significant levels" of radioactivity outside the testing area, and no one had received any detectable injuries during the series. Consequently, the operation was declared a success and praised for its efficiency, safety, and speed.[20] Testing seemed to have found a permanent home in Nevada.

Arrangements were quickly approved for the expansion of facilities at the proving ground. Eight million dollars were appropriated and construction was begun on utility and operational buildings. The original test center, a hastily built facility that included a control room, administrative office, first-aid station, and shower for personnel decontamination, was replaced. A new communications system was installed, as were several detonating towers and additional personnel accommodations. As a safety measure, ground zero was moved twenty miles north from Frenchman Flat to Yucca Flat, a desert valley located in the north-central part of the proving grounds and completely surrounded by mountains. Personnel was also increased; not only were additional AEC scientists assigned to the program, but special arrangements were made with the Department of Defense for soldiers to participate in atomic warfare maneuvers during the next test series, "Buster-Jangle," already scheduled for the following October.[21]

In July, Army Colonel H. McK. Roper, Executive Secretary of the AEC's Military Liaison Committee, sent Chairman Gordon Dean a memo requesting the participation of soldiers in the atomic weapons tests being conducted in Nevada. According to Roper, this would allow the military to accomplish two things: troops could be indoctrinated in methods and strategies of atomic warfare, and the psychological effects of an atomic explosion on soldiers could be observed. The original plan for military participation called for an army regimental force of five thousand soldiers to establish an actual combat position close to ground zero. As soon as it was safe, the troops would "engage in a coordinated ground force advance over the area neutralized by the explosion." Dean replied two weeks later that the AEC had approved Roper's plan, provided that the military accept full responsibility for its own accommodations. While the AEC was willing to help, Dean made it clear that the Commission "was not able to assume the burden of furnishing facilities for their [the troops'] administrative movement, security control, or support."[22]

On September 12, a convoy of trucks from the army's Third Corps Artillery arrived at the NPG; construction soon began on Camp Desert Rock, which was to be the home of some ninety thousand soldiers during the next decade. When soldiers arrived at Camp Desert Rock, they were presented with an "Information and Guide" booklet that explained the importance of strict security measures. Each page was stamped "RESTRICTED" and contained numerous warnings against talking too much: "To assist in maintaining the security of Exercise Desert Rock it is desired that you maintain secrecy discipline regarding classified information observed here. Everyone will want to know what you have seen—officials, friends, and the enemy." The booklet also included warnings about health hazards, not from radiation, but from indigenous reptiles and poisonous insects.[23]

To train the soldiers in maneuvers appropriate for atomic warfare, elaborate plans were drawn up for mock battles against an "aggressor enemy." The scenario for the Buster-Jangle series, written by Lieutenant General Joseph Swing's staff, assumed that two enemy armies had landed on the northwest coast of the United States two months earlier. Their assault had driven U.S. forces to the southwest. By the end of October, the U.S. Sixth Army had withdrawn to a line stretching from Los Angeles through southern Nevada. Unable to break through the line, the U.S. troops were forced to use an atomic bomb to clear a path into enemy-held territory. This would precipitate a northward retreat by the enemy, followed by a U.S. counteroffensive. Such maneuvers allowed the military to experiment with the tactical use of atomic weapons against conventional ground forces. Basing its battle plans on the "typical formations and current tactical doctrines of Communist armies," the military left no doubt as to who the aggressor enemy would be. Similar plans were subsequently contrived for each of the later tests at which troops were present.[24]

The military's second objective—observing the psychological impact of the bomb—was achieved with the help of civilian researchers. In the summer of 1951, the Department of Defense contracted with George Washington University to establish the Human Resources Research Office (HumRRO), which was charged with the job of conducting research into training methods, motivation, and morale of "atomic soldiers." In July, Dr. Meredith Crawford, dean of the College of Arts and Sciences at Vanderbilt University, was named director of the program. HumRRO's first assignment was to study the attitudes and knowledge about atomic effects of soldiers involved in the Buster-Jangle series, also known as Exercise Desert Rock I. The behavioral scientists gathered their data by issuing questionnaires to the men at different intervals before and after their participation in the test. For additional information, human behavior specialists from Johns Hopkins University Operations Research Office (ORO) were also hired by the Pentagon. Their methods of investigation involved not only questionnaires but personal observations of and conversations with the soldiers before, during, and after the testing exercise. They also measured heart rate and blood pressure of the participants.[25]

Operation Buster-Jangle began on schedule with the detonation of a small 0.1-kiloton device on October 22, 1951. The series consisted of seven shots, including one tower detonation, four airdrops, a surface blast, and a crater shot, with yields ranging from a tenth of a kiloton to thirty-one kilotons. The troop exercises during several of these shots included observer programs and tactical maneuvers. Observer programs, conducted at shots "Dog," "Sugar," and "Uncle," generally involved lectures and briefings on the effects of nuclear weapons, observation of a nuclear detonation, and a subsequent tour of a display of military equipment exposed to the blast. Tactical maneuvers were conducted after shot Dog, an airdropped nuclear device detonated with a yield of twenty-one kilotons on November 1. The army units involved in the tactical maneuvers included: a) 1st Battalion, 188th Airborne Infantry Regiment, 11th Airborne Division from Camp Campbell, Kentucky; b) 3rd Medical Platoon, 188th Airborne Medical Company from Camp Campbell; and c) Platoon, Company A, 127th Engineer Battalion from Fort Lewis, Washington. In sum, 2,796 soldiers participated in the troop-observer program and 883 in the tactical-troop maneuvers.[26]

After the exercise, the two research teams submitted their findings on the psychological impact of the bomb. These top-secret reports, later declassified, painted very different pictures of the situation. The HumRRO scientists presented an upbeat, positive report which concluded that a "reasonable attitude" toward the bomb could be obtained through widespread and thorough indoctrination, careful planning, strong leadership, and test-site experience. Eighty-three percent of the men said they would volunteer to participate in another similar exercise, 78 percent expressed confidence in the experts not to allow any troops to be harmed, and 62 percent boasted that they would have no problem being sent into actual atomic combat.[27]

The ORO scientists, however, found that physiological evidence belied the soldiers' verbal responses; changes in heartbeat and blood pressure indicated that the men were more concerned about the bomb than their "brave talk" would have suggested. The psychologists also noted that, whereas the paratroopers assigned to this exercise performed adequately, this may not be the case with typical troops who would be less motivated and less skilled. Nonetheless, the report went on to criticize the exercise for its "artificiality" and strongly recommended repeating the maneuver "under more realistic conditions."[28]

The Pentagon took this suggestion to heart and soon appealed to the AEC to allow troops to be stationed closer to ground zero during the next exercise. Brigadier General A. R. Luedecke, deputy chief of the AFSWP, further advised the AEC that the military services desired and were prepared to "accept full responsibility for the safety of all participating troop units and troop observers." This set off quite a debate within the commission. Colonel K. E. Field of the Military Application Division naturally supported the Pentagon's request; Carroll Tyler, manager of the Santa Fe Operations Office who was in charge of the proving ground, reminded the commission that policy prohibited anyone from being within six miles of a blast and advised disclaiming any responsibility should the military choose to ignore this regulation; and Shields Warren, director of the Division of Biology and Medicine, strongly opposed the action.[29] In the end, the AEC yielded to pressure from the military and abdicated all its safety and health responsibilities to the Pentagon. The commissioners rationalized their decision by noting that realistic training in any field is subject to risk and possible injury. This proved to be an unfortunate decision because troop safety at the Nevada site, as in the South Pacific, was a low priority for military leaders.

Once the Pentagon gained complete control over the use of troops, several significant changes were instituted. First, as anticipated, combat units began to be placed routinely in trenches as close as two miles from ground zero. In addition, during three tests, volunteer officers were allowed to remain as close as two thousand yards from the blast, a fact that was originally kept secret from the public, but later appeared in the *Guinness Book of World Records*. Second, the amount of radiation to which soldiers could be exposed was doubled from 3 to 6 rems, while AEC standards for civilian test-site workers remained 3.9 rems for an entire series. Third, army-trained radiation monitors soon replaced AEC specialists and assumed responsibility for film badging and laboratory analysis, tasks for which they were not adequately trained or equipped to handle.[30] Finally, soldiers no longer waited several hours after a shot before entering the blast zone; as Brigadier

General H. P. Storke, commander of Camp Desert Rock during the "Upshot-Knothole" series in spring 1953, proudly told his men: "In this exercise, for the first time in known history, troops successfully attacked directly toward ground zero immediately following the atomic explosion." These changes were all intended to make the maneuvers more realistic and the results of the experiments more accurate. The military made no pretense about the use of soldiers as guinea pigs: "You can remember, with a sense of pleasure and accomplishment, that you were a real pioneer in experimentation of the most vital importance to the security of the United States."[31]

Atmospheric testing in Nevada continued along these lines throughout most of the fifties. Many of the tests were defense oriented and involved troop maneuvers as well as experiments to determine the effects of a nuclear blast on various kinds of military equipment. In addition to soldiers, hundreds of jeeps, tanks, bunkers, and other forms of hardware were scattered across the desert floor at different distances from ground zero. One particularly bizarre experiment became known as the "Charge of the Swine Brigade." To determine which fabrics afforded the best protection from burns, the army fitted 111 White Chester pigs in specially tailored uniforms with seams, zippers, and drawstrings matched exactly to the specifications of the army's own standard GI-issue field jackets. The pigs were then exposed to the blasts of two successive shots. Seventy-two of the pigs were killed outright, but the army was still able to gain what it considered valuable information about the thermal protection properties of its uniforms.[32]

Other tests conducted during this period were designed to aid in civil defense preparations. Approved by Congress on January 11, 1951, just days prior to the opening of the NPG, the Federal Civil Defense Administration (CD) was mandated to establish community bomb shelters and instruct the public on how to protect itself in the event of a nuclear attack.[33] In order to best protect the American public, the CD first had to answer the question of what would happen to an average community in the United States if it were to be hit by an enemy's atomic bomb.

To ascertain this needed information, the CD was allowed to participate in the weapons-testing program at the Nevada site. Elaborate "Doom Towns" were constructed in the desert near ground zero. Full-scale homes were built and furnished with everything from brand-name foods in the refrigerator to current magazines on the coffee table. Late-model automobiles stood in carports and mannequins wearing the latest in ready-made fashions were strategically placed throughout in lifelike situations. During a blast, these "cities" were subjected to highly technical damage-effects tests that provided information on the ability of structures, foodstuffs, and other items of common use to withstand shock, heat, and radioactivity.[34] In addition, civil defense personnel participated in field exercises. Following a blast, they conducted an array of exercises in simulated situations, including mass feeding, sanitation, health, police, fire, rescue, and communications services.[35]

Despite seemingly elaborate precautions, accidents did occur at the Nevada Test Site (NTS, as the NPG was called after 1955) during the era of atmospheric testing. Several of these resulted in the exposure of civilian workers to higher than tolerable levels of radiation. On January 18, 1956, four workers were exposed to as many as twenty-eight roentgens of radiation when an atomic device detonated during a test to determine if simulated accidents could cause a nuclear reaction. The four men were examined by Dr. Ross Sutherland and reassigned to other jobs, upon which the AEC reported: "It is doubtful they will suffer any lasting effects."[36] Eight years later on June 6, 1963, twelve NTS workers engaged in re-entry work in the tunnel where an underground shot had occurred, suffered radiation overdoses when they inhaled gases which had escaped from the detonative chamber of the blast. The workers, whose radiation dosages to the thyroid ranged from 75 to 770 rads, were sent to Donner Laboratory at the University of California at Berkeley for testing. An AEC announcement on June 8 "indicated that radiation dosage level apparently was not serious and likened the amount received to a similar amount of radioactive iodine given many adults for diagnostic purposes in treating thyroid glands."[37]

Only one serious incident during these years involved people and animals outside the boundaries of the NTS. Its consequences have been consistently denied by the government ever since. In the spring of 1953, the AEC conducted a series of eleven shots code-named "Upshot-Knothole." The people of southern Utah were accustomed to taking certain precautions during testing, but this series, beginning on March 17 and ending on June 4, included three especially "dirty" shots: "Nancy," fired on March 24 with a yield of twenty-four kilotons; "Simon," with a yield of forty-three kilotons fired on April 25; and "Harry," detonated on May 19 with a yield of thirty-two kilotons. All released high levels of radioactive fallout over large sections of southern Utah. Exposed to the radiation were people living in the vicinity of St. George and several large flocks of sheep en route to their lambing sheds in Cedar City. Readings in St. George following the Harry shot were as high as six roentgens, and the townspeople were advised to remain indoors from nine o'clock in the morning until noon. Roadblocks were set up and many vehicles were washed down in an attempt at decontamination.[38] The AEC told area media that "radiation had not reached a hazardous level,"[39] while in Washington, Chairman Dean expressed concern to Test Manager Graves and urged that "everything be done to avoid another fallout over St. George."[40]

The human damage caused by this exposure was not to become evident until later, but the animals were affected immediately. Of the 11,710 sheep grazing in the contaminated zone 40 miles north to 160 miles east of the test site, 1,420 lambing ewes (12.1 percent of the total) and 2,970 new lambs (25.4 percent) died within weeks of the three shots.[41] Although the AEC had previously settled several claims for livestock damage, the practice had been to award compensation only for animals exhibiting external "beta" burns—internal damage allegedly caused by radiation was consistently denied.[42] When the Iron County sheepherders went to court in 1956 and sued the government for $226,000 in damages under the provisions of the Federal Tort Claims Act, they were unable to prove that the sheep deaths had been caused by radiation, and thus lost their bid for compensation.[43]

From 1951 to 1958, the Nevada Test Site was the scene of a hundred atmospheric tests of nuclear devices. Some seventy tests had been conducted in the South Pacific during the period since the war. There was a short-lived moratorium on testing, agreed to by the United States and the USSR, between November 1958 and August 1961, when the Soviets violated the agreement. Testing then resumed with 135 American detonations occurring over the next two years. When the Limited Test Ban Treaty was signed in Moscow on August 5, 1963, atomic testing at the NTS moved completely underground. Not only was testing banned in outer space, the atmosphere, and under the ocean, but limitations were also placed on underground testing which allowed venting of radiation over areas outside the boundaries of the state doing the testing.[44] This in effect eliminated the South Sea testing program and brought all the bombs home to Nevada. Since then over four hundred announced shots have been conducted underground at the NTS. These tests today are limited to a maximum yield of 150 kilotons under the Threshold Test Ban agreement signed by President Nixon in Moscow in 1974. Yucca Flat is still the site for most of the low-yield weapons detonations; the higher yield devices are tested at Pahute Mesa, some fifty miles further away from Las Vegas.[45]

In addition to the testing of atomic weapons for military purposes, a number of nuclear-related experiments have also been conducted at the NTS over the years. The first major experimental program was initiated in 1955 when the AEC chose Jackass Flat in the southwest corner of the test site as an area for developing and testing nuclear reactors for space-propulsion applications. This area, known as the Nuclear Rocket Development Station (NRDS), was administrated jointly by the AEC and the National Aeronautics and Space Agency (NASA). A $225-million plant, including the $50-million Engine Maintenance, Assembly, and Disassembly (E-MAD) building, was established at the site to house the space project. Employment at the test site greatly increased to meet the manpower demands of the new program.[46] Correspondingly, the narrow highway from Las Vegas to Mercury, known as the "Widow Maker" because of the high fatality rate from accidents along its sixty-five-mile stretch, was expanded to four lanes.[47]

A second nonweapons program was established by the AEC in February 1957 when a symposium at Livermore Laboratory yielded a recommendation for actually conducting nuclear explosions solely for peaceful purposes. By June, the suggestion had been formalized into a program and preliminary investigations into various possible applications quickly got underway. Four years later, the AEC formed the Division of Peaceful Nuclear Explosions and the first "Plowshare" test was conducted. Deriving their name from the biblical verse in Isaiah 2:4 which calls for men to beat their swords into plowshares, these tests investigated such varied peacetime uses of atomic power as control of underground water movement; tapping oil, natural gas, and other natural resources; exploding gigantic subterranean reservoirs; building highways; and digging canals and harbors. The first Plowshare test was not conducted until December 10, 1961. The shot, code-named "Gnome," was detonated in a salt formation near Carlsbad, New Mexico. Twenty-six additional Plowshare tests were conducted over the next twelve years; two were detonated in Colorado to fracture tight rock formations entrapping vast reserves of natural gas, but the rest were conducted at the NTS. Some of the specific projects included the "Sedan" shot on July 6, 1962, which created a crater 1,280 feet in diameter by 320 feet in depth; "Buggy" which simultaneously detonated five nuclear devices in a row to obtain data on digging canals; and "Carryall," a study by the AEC, the Atchison, Topeka, and Santa Fe Railroad, and the State of California Division of Highways which concluded that twenty-two nuclear explosions could cut a pass through the Bristol Mountains about eleven miles north of Amboy, California. The last Plowshare shot was conducted in 1973, and no active program exists today.[48]

A third major project was initiated in 1962 and involved the erection of the 1,527-foot BREN (Bare Reactor Experiment—Nevada) tower in Area 28. The tower, five hundred feet taller than the Eiffel Tower and 50 feet higher than the Empire State Building, was equipped with a small unshielded nuclear reactor mounted on a hoist car to emit radiation at various heights. Its original purpose was to expose houses of typical Japanese style and construction which had been built beneath the tower and thereby evaluate the doses of radiation received by survivors of Hiroshima and Nagasaki. During the midsixties, the tower was used in "Operation HENRE" (High Energy Neutron Reactions Experiment) to obtain scientific data on shielding against radiation, neutron activation in soil, and radiation dosimetry techniques. The tower was moved to Area 28 in 1966 and today is used for sonic boom and weather research.[49]

Additional programs at the NTS have included the "Vela Uniform" project initiated by the Department of Defense in 1963. Its purpose was to aid in the establishment of a reliable system of detecting, locating, and identifying underground nuclear explosions conducted by other countries which might be in violation of international agreements.[50] A bioenvironmental experiment farm was also established in Area 15 of the NTS by the Environmental Protection Agency (EPA) in 1965. A herd of approximately thirty Holstein and Jersey cows was studied to test the transport of radionuclides from the cows' food chain through their milk to humans. The herd grazed the ranges on the test site for more than two decades until the farm closed on December 30, 1981, and, according to Department of Energy (DOE) publications, no detrimental effects were ever detected.[51]

In more recent years, nonweapons research at the test site has focused on nuclear waste. After the NRDS space program was terminated in 1973, the E-MAD facility was transformed into a research and demonstration center for the handling and storage of highly radioactive, spent, unreprocessed reactor fuel from commercial nuclear plants. To date, three storage methods have been tested: a sealed storage cask on the surface, shallow dry wells located outside the building, and holes drilled in granitic rock fourteen hundred feet underground in one of the tunnels used in a weapons–effects test during the sixties. The results of this project, currently operated by the Westinghouse Advanced Energy Systems Division under contract to the DOE, will provide critical input into future decisions concerning nuclear waste disposal policies.[52]

As the AEC stepped up weapons testing and simultaneously conducted these various related projects, it became clear that operations at the NTS would require a full-time effort. Originally just a branch of the Test Division of the Albuquerque Operations Office, the Nevada Operations Office (NV) was created and assumed responsibilities for programs at the NTS on March 6, 1962. Today the Department of Energy is the primary authority at the test site. It provides support and assistance to the Department of Defense, which obtains its weapons from three laboratories: Los Alamos National Laboratory and Lawrence Livermore National Laboratory, both operated by the University of California, and Sandia National Laboratories, operated by AT&T Technologies, Inc. Additional contract arrangements are maintained between NV and various support, technical, and engineering organizations: Reynolds Electrical and Engineering Co., Inc. (REECo) provides maintenance, construction, and radiation safety services; Edgerton, Germeshausen, and Grier, Inc. (EG&G) is responsible for certain technical services, including fabrication and operation of timing, firing, and diagnostic equipment, and instrumenting tests and recording results; Holmes & Narner is the contractor for architect–engineer–management services; Fenix & Scisson, Inc. is the engineering consultant for drilling and mining activities; and Wackenhut Services, Inc. is responsible for security guard services at all NTS and DOE facilities.[53]

Currently, about 9 percent of the work force in southern Nevada is either directly or indirectly dependent on activities at the NTS. This includes some 240 federal employees, 7,100 private contractors, and 11,300 support jobs, for a total employment of 18,640. The DOE payroll in southern Nevada amounted to $301 million in 1985. Additionally, the test site is credited with providing one billion dollars annually to the economy of southern Nevada.[54] Should President Reagan's "Star Wars" program be pursued as he wishes or the high-level waste repository located at Yucca Mountain, these numbers will undoubtedly increase over the next decade.

For over three decades, the United States government has used Nevada as a testing ground for atomic devices of various kinds. A few experiments have been conducted in other states (three in Alaska, two in New Mexico, two in Mississippi, and two in Colorado),[55] but the bulk of atomic weapons development can be attributed to efforts at the NTS. And today, although American testing has ceased in the South Pacific and elsewhere, it continues at full throttle in Nevada. The success and stability of this program for over the past three decades are not the result of happenstance. On the contrary, the government has taken great pains to "sell the bomb" to the American public.

6 Selling the Bomb

Government Strategies for
Building Public Support

Throughout the thirty-five years of its existence, the Nevada Test Site and its operations have been assiduously promoted by the United States government. During the days of atmospheric testing, attempts to win support for the program were by necessity bold and brazen. Today, with testing underground and the general public more knowledgeable about atomic phenomena, these hard-hitting tactics are no longer appropriate or effective. Consequently, the DOE's public-relations approach has become more subtle and sophisticated. Nonetheless, a close look at policy over the last three decades indicates that while style has been altered to meet the times, few substantive changes have occurred.

Following three basic strategies, various presidential administrations have consistently sought to sell the American public on atomic weapons testing. First, the government emphasized the critical need for testing; playing on anti-Communist sentiments, officials maintained that weapons testing was essential for a strong national defense against the threat of confrontation with the Soviets. Second, politicians and bureaucrats alike stressed the additional nonmilitary benefits of the testing program, further justifying it in terms of its contribution to the development of peaceful uses of nuclear power. The third strategy has been to assure the citizens of this country that all testing is conducted under conditions reflecting the utmost concern for human health and safety. Together, these three strategies allowed the government to promote the weapons-development program by assuring the American people that the risks involved are minimal and as such are indeed a small price to pay for the preservation of democracy.

The government had little trouble convincing the American public of the need for initial testing in the South Pacific. Coming on the heels of World War II, the tests were acceptable for several reasons: Tired of fighting, the people were anxious to perfect a weapon that promised to make war obsolete; the tests were needed to gain additional scientific data that would speed this process. But it was not that noble aim alone which prompted support for early testing. The consensus also held that it was important for the United States to demonstrate to the world that the two bombs dropped on Japan were just a small part of an atomic arsenal being maintained in case of future need. Furthermore, the public was curious about this awesome new force which could level a city with one blow; press coverage of the tests allowed the man on the street to satisfy his curiosity and see for himself what a heretofore unknown atomic explosion was like. Finally, the tests were being conducted in a remote area far away from U.S. shores and consequently were not seen as threatening in any way.

In 1951, however, when testing moved to Nevada, the situation became more delicate. The decision to establish a continental test site was made in absolute secrecy and with careful calculation of the public reaction because, as President Truman wrote in his memoirs, he did not want to frighten people about "shooting off bombs in their backyards."[1] From that point on, the AEC became a public relations agency for atomic testing. Following the three strategies described above, the commission set out to promote the Nevada testing program and ensure its uninterrupted operation.

Selling the American people on the need for weapons testing and stockpiling as a defense against spreading communism was a relatively easy task after the Soviets detonated Joe One in the fall of 1949. In light of this event and other postwar international developments, it is little wonder that the public began to see Communists as a distinct threat to the American way of life. In 1948, Communists staged a coup in Czechoslovakia which replaced the existing government with one subservient to Moscow. That same year the Russians attempted to force Western Allies out of Berlin by blockading all land transportation routes into the city. In early 1949, forces led by Mao Tse-tung captured Peking and soon after established the People's Republic of China. Then in June 1950, armed conflict broke out between North and South Korea which brought American armed forces into combat with Communist troops.[2]

Attitudes towards the Communists, who just several years earlier had been viewed as useful if somewhat contentious allies in the fight against fascism, changed dramatically as McCarthyism pervaded American political culture. All three branches of government abetted this shift through their pursuit of policies which lowered the temperature of the cold war and institutionalized a suspicious attitude toward the Soviets. The government then took advantage of the climate it had helped to create to boost military appropriations and continue the development of bigger and better bombs.

Anti-Communist activities by Congress date back to 1934, when the House of Representatives set up a special investigative committee to look into un-American activities (HUAC). Although originally preoccupied with the right, by 1937 the committee, chaired by Democratic Congressman Martin Dies of Texas, had changed direction. Ignoring the actions of such extremists as Father Coughlin's Crusaders, the Citizens' Protective League, and the German-American Bund, the committee began to look to the left, labeling advocates of social change as Communists.[3] Two major cases, one involving the "Hollywood Ten"[4] and the other Alger Hiss,[5] are familiar hallmarks of the committee's activities throughout these years.

Meanwhile, Joseph R. McCarthy, an obscure Republican junior senator from Wisconsin, decided to stake his 1952 reelection bid on the issue of Communists in government. To that end, he launched a series of escalating charges against the Truman administration in a speech before the West Virginia Republican Club of Wheeling, West Virginia, on February 9, 1950. His bold charges of conspiracy and treason, given impetus by the gloomy international picture and the revelations of the Hiss trials, propelled McCarthy into the limelight and soon gave his name to the phenomenon of hysterical anticommunism. Following his reelection, he served as chairman of the Senate subcommittee on governmental operations from whence he led investigations of individuals, programs, and agencies he accused of being "pink." By the time of his demise in 1954, a result of the televised Army-McCarthy hearings, "Tail Gunner Joe" had contributed more than any other individual to creating a climate propitious to the selling of the atomic bomb.[6]

In addition to the investigative pursuits of specific committees and individuals in Congress, several laws were enacted during this period that reflected and reinforced the anti-Communist climate. As early as 1940, Congress passed the Smith Act, which made it a criminal offense to advocate the violent overthrow of the government or to belong to any group advocating such action.[7] Legislation of the postwar era was even more restrictive. Passed in 1950, the McCarran International Security Act required members of the Communist party to register with the Subversive Activities Control Board, whereupon they could be identified and thereby denied passports and employment in defense facilities.[8] In 1954, Congress passed the Communist Control Act with a vote of 79-0 in the Senate and 265-2 in the House. Drawn up by Hubert Humphrey, the bill made membership in the Communist party a felony punishable by fine or imprisonment.[9]

The federal courts further institutionalized strong national feelings of anticommunism. In a series of cases, the Supreme Court consistently upheld the constitutionality of congressional action aimed at suspected subversives.[10] The courts also provided a backdrop for several anti-Communist dramas which played during this period to tremendous audiences across the country. Certainly, the Alger Hiss case drew considerable attention in the late forties, but even more significant was the case of Julius and Ethel Rosenberg, who were convicted and executed for passing Manhattan Project secrets to the Russians during the war.[11]

The executive branch was likewise involved in fostering an atmosphere of suspicion and paranoia. Bowing to pressure from Republicans and the general public, President Truman in late 1947 named a special commission to study possible threats to internal security. On March 21, 1947, acting on the commission's recommendation, he issued Executive Order 9835 establishing a Federal Employee Loyalty Program. In May the FBI began investigating "disloyal and subversive" persons by conducting a "name check" of the two million people on the federal payroll. In addition, the bureau was responsible for checking the loyalty of the 500,000 annual applicants for government jobs. People were immediately terminated who were found to have "committed treason, engaged in espionage, advocated violent overthrow of the government, disclosed official confidence, or belonged to an association which the attorney general defined as subversive." Proof of these charges did not have to be absolute— "reasonable grounds for belief" of subversion were enough.[12]

When Eisenhower moved into the White House, he imposed an internal security program even harsher than Truman's. On April 27, 1953, he issued Executive Order 10450 under which the mere suspicion of treachery brought termination of employment. Other deviations deemed "inconsistent with the national security," such as drunkenness, drug addiction, participation in unusual sexual practices, mental illness, and unsanitary habits, were also cause for dismissal. The new regulation thinned employee rolls to such an extent that in his second State of the Union address, President Eisenhower boasted that the number of "security risks" eliminated from government service had risen to 2,200.[13]

The federal bureaucracy was also involved in fostering the political climate of paranoia. One government agency that played an especially significant role was the Federal Civil Defense Administration. The agency was created by Congress in response to public demands that arose out of fear of a Soviet attack.[14] It was not long, however, before the agency, in its attempt to soothe those fears, began to reinforce the climate from which they had sprung.

In addition to establishing community bomb shelters, the CD

sought to instruct citizens on self-protection against nuclear attack. Regularly scheduled air raid drills were held, and public meetings were called to teach preparedness and self-defense through such measures as assuming correct physical positions during impact, shielding one's eyes from the blast, and cleaning off radioactive fallout. As one official wrote, "To those who recognize the Russian threat and what it means . . . to those who see the atomic age for what it is, civil defense has become a vital part of their daily lives, because it offers the only training they can get which will insure their survival."[15]

To accompany these presentations, the CD distributed dozens of films to public schools and social organizations that were designed to expose the horrors of atomic warfare to citizens and attempted to impress upon them the need for self-protection. Their names alone tell the story: "Atomic Survival" (1951), "Survival Under Atomic Attack" (1951), "Survival City" (1955), and "Individual Protection Against Atomic Attack" (1958).[16]

The military, like Civil Defense, abetted the creation of an environment that it could use to its own advantage. During tactical maneuvers conducted at the Nevada Test Site throughout the fifties, the aggressor enemy in the war games was always portrayed as a Communist force. Soldiers were indoctrinated from the beginning with the belief that should another major war occur making the use of atomic weapons necessary, it would without doubt be fought against the Communists. Certainly this was reinforced by the ongoing conflict in Korea.[17]

The Atomic Energy Commission itself repeatedly reminded the American people of the dangers of communism. Numerous press releases issued during the fifties emphasized the perils of letting down U.S. defenses. In a typical statement delivered on April 15, 1955, before the Joint Committee on Atomic Energy, Lewis Strauss commented, "Soviet Russia possesses atomic weapons; there is no monopoly for the free world. Therefore, we have no alternative but to maintain our scientific and technological progress and keep our strength at peak level. The consequences of any other course would imperil our liberty, even our existence."[18] Similarly, in a public response to criticism from Dr. Albert Schweitzer, Atomic Energy Commissioner Willard Libby wrote in 1957: "Here the choice seems much clearer—the terrible risk of abandoning the defense effort which is so essential under present conditions to the survival of the Free World against the small controlled risk from weapons testing."[19] Edward Teller, "father of the H-bomb" and member of the AEC

General Advisory Committee, took this same anti-Soviet position in 1958: "But in our conflict with the powerful communistic countries which strive for world domination, it may be too much to hope for uninterrupted peace. If we abandon [weapons testing], we shall enable the Red bloc to take over one country after another, close to their borders, as opportunities arise."[20]

Not only did the AEC use scare tactics to garner support and funds for its programs but also to discredit its opponents. For example, when Oppenheimer publicly opposed the development of the H-bomb, the AEC charged him with having "fundamental defects in his character." The commission went on to say: "We find that his associations with persons known to him to be Communists have extended far beyond the tolerable limits of prudence and self-restraint which are expected of one holding the high positions that the Government has continuously entrusted to him since 1942."[21] As a result, Oppenheimer was stripped of his security clearance and denied access to restricted data. It should be remembered that Oppenheimer's early associations with Communists were known by General Groves when he was selected to head the Manhattan Project. They were not used against him, however, until ten years later when the AEC felt that it was expedient to remove him from a position of authority where he could possibly delay the desired development of thermonuclear weapons.[22]

The political climate that thus emerged in the United States after World War II lent itself readily to AEC endeavors to convince the public of the need for stepping up the atomic weapons development program. When Lewis Strauss stated, "We must not lose sight of the fact that our security and the security of the free world is dependent upon the nuclear tests," the American people believed him.[23] Congress fell quickly in line with annually increased appropriations for the weapons program, as did the chief executive with his approval of such projects as the establishment of the Nevada Test Site and the building of the hydrogen bomb.[24]

The U.S. government's portrayal of the Soviet Union as a mortal enemy persists today. Speaking on the thirty-third anniversary of the first test conducted in Nevada, NTS Manager Thomas Clark commented that the testing program was the key reason why a war between the United States and the Soviet Union had not occurred.[25] A month later, DOE spokesman Dave Miller told the press that testing at Rainier Mesa on the NTS was crucial to United States "Star Wars" defense; he claimed that this was where "America is learning how to knock out Russian satellites, how to make its own space hardware survivable for critical early warning of an enemy attack, how the MX and other missiles could take the Soviets' best shot."[26]

The AEC's second major strategy in its attempt to sustain public support for atomic weapons testing was to emphasize the benefits of the program over and above its contribution to American military superiority. This approach took several different but related directions. First, the AEC argued that the development of weapons was necessary not only to protect the United States in the possible event of war, but more importantly to discourage the Russians from attacking in the first place. As Captain James Russell, speaking for the AEC, told the American Legion in 1949: "I regard and I think you regard our present lead in atomic weapons as a tremendous power for preventing war."[27] Several years later, AEC Chairman Strauss told the JCAE: "The weapons which we test are essential, not only to our national security and that of the free world; they have and may well continue to be a deterrent to devastating war."[28]

A second argument can be summed up in further comments made by Strauss following the Bravo incident in 1954: "One important result of these [tests] has been the enhancement of our military capability to the point where we should soon be more free to increase our emphasis on the peaceful uses of atomic power—at home and abroad."[29] Third, the tests were justified on the grounds that "they provide vital data which can be obtained in no other manner, on which to build a sound and effective system of civil defense against the eventuality of an enemy attack."[30] Fourth, testing was presented as being a critical element in the search for radiological safety for it helped to "speed the development of weapons with greatly reduced radioactive fallout, that is to say, so-called clean weapons."[31] As the AEC reported in 1957, such tests produced much of importance not only from a military point of view but from a humanitarian aspect: "Success thus far has convinced us that widespread hazard from fallout is not a necessary complement to the employment of large nuclear weapons."[32]

The most persuasive argument along these lines, however, was that atomic testing was especially valuable because it provided "new fundamental data and a broader understanding" of the phenomenon of nuclear fission which could be applied to the development of peaceful uses of atomic energy. As early as 1947, Operation Sandstone was justified on these grounds, setting the precedent for a rationale which would be used commonly in the years to come.[33] The AEC maintained that, as Major General Percy Clarkson commented after the

Greenhouse series in 1951, testing allows the United States to develop nuclear energy for the defense of the free world while at the same time "pushing with wide and growing success its studies directed toward utilizing these energies for the productive purposes of mankind."[34]

This focus on the value of testing for development of peaceful uses of atomic energy received considerable impetus in December 1953, when President Eisenhower delivered his "Atoms for Peace" speech. The first half of the speech was devoted to a candid assessment of the American atomic stockpile, but more significantly, the second half expressed "hope" for the creation of an international "atomic pool." The president proposed that the nations capable of producing fissionable material contribute a sufficient amount of that substance to establish a pool from which all nations could draw for peaceful purposes. He hoped that the demand would be large enough to drain away material that might otherwise be used in the production of weapons. Toward this goal, he stated: "It is not enough to take this weapon out of the hands of the soldiers. It must be put into the hands of those who will know how to strip its military casing and adapt it to the acts of peace." He went on to claim that the creation of such a pool would make the "deserts flourish" and help "to warm the cold, to feed the hungry, to alleviate the misery of the world."[35]

A frenzy of public relations activity, directed by Eisenhower's speech writer C. D. Jackson, followed the address. Over 200,000 copies of a pamphlet containing the speech in ten languages were sent out by U.S. firms in their foreign mail, and some 350 foreign-language newspapers and related ethnic organizations launched a campaign to ensure that copies of the speech were sent by immigrants to their friends and relatives back in the "old country." The media were deluged with briefings and special follow-up feature stories. The United States Information Agency facilitated distribution abroad and the Voice of America carried the story on the radio waves of the world. Headlines at home read: "Nuclear Device in Fight Against Cancer," "Forestry Expert Predicts Atomic Rays Will Cut Lumber Instead of Saws," and "Atomic Locomotive Designed." Promotional films that examined the various possibilities were quickly produced; "Atomic Greenhouse," "Atomic Zoo," and "Atom for the Doctor" were among the most popular.[36] In addition, the JCAE provided a special film on the program to all members of Congress for showing in their home district or state.[37] The United States Post Office issued a three-cent stamp with the inscription "Atoms For Peace: To Find the Way By Which the Inventiveness of Man Shall Be Consecrated to New Life."[38] By February of 1954, Jackson declared that his efforts had met with tremendous success: "The President's speech . . . by focussing attention on the prospects for peaceful development of atomic energy [has] . . . captured the hopes of the common man and the interest of the scientific and intellectual classes."[39]

A month after his Atoms for Peace speech, the president followed up on this theme when, in his State of the Union address, he proposed that the United States share information on the tactical uses of nuclear weapons. Continuing along these lines, in his budget message on January 29, 1954, he called for amendments to the Atomic Energy Act to achieve three goals: allow the exchange of more classified atomic information with American allies, permit the transfer of fissionable materials to friendly nations for "peace-time atomic power development," and encourage wider participation in atomic power development by private industry. These objectives were further clarified in a special atomic energy message sent to Congress on February 17 which recommended fifteen specific changes in the original legislation.[40]

Congress responded to this directive by passing the Atomic Energy Act of 1954 which, as discussed previously, met the demand for international and commercial cooperation. During the next several years most of the attention paid to atomic energy policy in this country focused on these new activities pursued by the AEC. In November 1954 the president allocated the first hundred kilograms of U-235, highly fissionable uranium, to the program, followed six months later by a similar allocation for use under bilateral arrangements. In 1955, the first International Congress on Peaceful Uses of Atomic Energy was held, bringing together thirty-six hundred scientists, engineers, political leaders, and equipment salesmen to exchange ideas about using atomic energy for peaceful purposes. This conference led to the creation, in October 1956, of the International Atomic Energy Agency, which has grown steadily as an instrument of peaceful cooperation among its eighty member countries.[41]

Other Atoms for Peace projects conducted specifically by the AEC during this period received considerable attention. Nuclear reactor research projects were initiated in a number of countries including Japan, Portugal, Venezuela, Brazil, Denmark, Italy, Belgium, and Spain; "heavy water" was sold to Australia and Sweden; and an International School of Nuclear Science and Engineering was created at the Argonne National Laboratory in Illinois where, by January 1957, 214 scholars from forty-one different countries had attended symposia. In addition, atomic energy libraries were set up in friendly nations; two mobile radioisotope laboratories were presented to the

International Atomic Energy Agency; and observers from forty-seven nations, including NATO, SEATO, Inter-American Defense Board, and the Baghdad Pact, were invited to Nevada to witness the Plumb-bob series of shots in May 1957. The tests coincided with an inter-American symposium on the Peaceful Applications of Nuclear Energy which was attended by twenty countries. Such events were consistently reported in laudatory terms.[42]

In the long run, however, the United States became a victim of its own genius. The atomic pool never materialized and the American government was left having to promote the peaceful atom on its own through a series of bilateral agreements to transfer nuclear technology and fissile material to lesser developed nations. Furthermore, the Soviet Union accused America of sidestepping the key question of arms control through the diversionary tactic of promoting the advancement of nuclear energy. The worst consequence of all, however, was the inadvertent boost the program gave to the arms race. Ignoring the link between the peaceful and the warlike atom, a link ironically promoted by the AEC as part of its rationale for testing, the program provided for the dispersal of material and technology which could be used to make a bomb. No inspection or verification that such was not occurring was considered necessary; consequently, any hope of future control of weapons proliferation was illusory as long as the program existed.[43]

Nevertheless, the Atoms for Peace program was a tremendous success in terms of its public relations benefits for the AEC. A cold war propaganda triumph, the name of the program quickly became a "buzz phrase" in the best tradition of Madison Avenue. The imagination of the American people was fired by the numerous possibilities for using atomic energy; they were eager to unlock these secrets of nuclear technology and then use them to save the world. Correspondingly, they applauded the AEC's testing program which, in addition to protecting American national security, brought this dream closer to reality with every blast.

An offshoot of Atoms for Peace was the Plowshare Program initiated in 1961. Over the next decade, Plowshare experiments testing nuclear devices for possible peaceful applications were widely publicized as the AEC sought to capitalize on the positive benefits of testing in order to secure support for the Nevada operations center.[44] Although the Plowshare Program itself is no longer active, a tour of the NTS today includes a visit to several facilities where atomic research is currently being conducted on nonmilitary projects. These projects, most of which involve nuclear waste disposal, are promoted by the Department of Energy as valuable byproducts of the testing program.

The government's third strategy followed throughout the forty years of atomic testing has been to assure the American people that, first, there is little danger of exposure to radioactive fallout from testing, and second, should they be exposed, any problems can be easily remedied without harmful long-term consequences. This strategy was especially important during the days of atmospheric testing; a look at more recent policy, however, indicates that like the other original strategies, it too has continued.

Typical statements made during the fifties to reassure citizens—especially those living in the Southwest—that everything was being done to prevent their possible exposure to radiation can be found in Strauss's 1955 report to the JCAE:

> The American people can be assured that the rigorous safeguards which govern the tests are designed to prevent injury to the people of any community or city. . . . Rigid precautions are taken to hold the fallout from Nevada test shots to an absolute minimum. Suitable weather conditions are selected. . . . The Commission has an extensive network of monitoring stations in areas near the test site as well as throughout the United States and is able to measure the levels of radioactivity with extremely sensitive methods. . . . Radioactive fallout from the Nevada tests also is minimized by the manner in which the shots are fired. Most of the Nevada explosions occur well above the surface of the earth, with the result that only small amounts of earth are drawn up into the cloud.[45]

Likewise, references to safety precautions were included in all AEC press releases announcing the various shots during the era of atmospheric testing. In 1951, the AEC stated: "All necessary precautions, including radiological surveys and patrolling of the surrounding territory, will be undertaken to insure that safe conditions are maintained."[46] A similar announcement in 1957 began: "Safeguarding the public health and safety again will be a primary consideration in the Plumbbob series. . . . As a result of improved controls and procedures, radioactive fallout in the area around the Test Site is expected to be even lower than the levels which have resulted from previous tests in Nevada."[47] And in May 1958, a detailed plan on safety precautions taken at Eniwetok boasted: "Protection of health and safety is a primary consideration. . . . As in the past, test operations will be conducted in a manner designed to keep to as low as possible the public exposure to radiation arising from the detonation of nuclear weapons."[48]

Most impressive of the AEC's efforts during the period of atmospheric testing was the publication of a little green booklet entitled *Atomic Tests in Nevada*. Several thousand copies of the brochure were printed and distributed throughout Nevada and southern Utah in the midfifties. Under a section labelled "Potential Exposure is Low," the text read:

> The effects of a detonation include flash, blast, and radioactive fallout. Your potential exposure to these effects will be low. . . . The low level of public exposure has been made possible by very close attention to a variety of on-site and off-site procedures. . . . Every test detonation in Nevada is carefully evaluated as to your safety. . . . Every phase of the operation is likewise studied from the safety viewpoint.[49]

When testing moved underground in 1963, the problems of air blast, light and heat effects, and extensive exposure were virtually eliminated; nonetheless, the AEC and later the DOE continued to stress the numerous safety precautions taken with every shot. In a report issued in 1969, the manager of the NTS stated:

> We always prepare for the worst. Even when we are convinced that radiation will be entirely contained, we plan on the basis of the worst credible situation. Weather is watched for wind direction and speed. No detonation is approved unless conditions are such that if an unlikely and unexpected release of radiation should occur, there will be no hazard to the public. Similarly, our precautions in regard to blast, heat, ground shock, and other phenomena are based on maximum predictable effects.[50]

And, in the DOE's most recent public information handout, the heading reads, "Public and NTS Safety Is Paramount." The article beneath goes on to declare that "no test is permitted . . . unless conditions are such that even in the unlikely event of release of radioactivity the safety of people both on and off the Test Site can be assured."[51]

In addition to assuring the people that the government was taking every possible precaution, the AEC further advised citizens that exposure to the dangerous effects of a test blast "can be reduced still further" by following a few simple safety measures. The little green booklet warned people "to stay indoors for a few hours until the fallout had ceased. If you were outdoors during the fallout, you might be advised to bathe, wash your hair, dust your clothes, brush your shoes, etc." Potential observers were further cautioned about the effects of the flash: "Do not use binoculars or rifle scopes to look toward the Test Site at shot time. Do not look toward the test site at shot time unless you are wearing dark glasses." Precautions for dealing with shock waves were similar in scope. It was suggested that people "take simple measures such as opening windows and doors. Persons driving or sitting in automobiles should open the car windows. Another simple precaution is to stay away from large glass windows at shot time (windows usually break outward)." People were even advised that "fallout can be inconvenient, but your best action is not be worried about [it]."[52] The elementary nature of these safety measures further convinced people that the dangers of testing were indeed minimal. Even today with the general public much more informed on the dangers of radiation, Civil Defense films emphasize the "simple commonsense steps" that can be taken to guard against the problems caused by radioactive fallout. In reference to survival of a nuclear war, Thomas K. Jones, deputy undersecretary of defense, commented in 1981: "Dig a hole, cover it with a couple of doors and then throw three feet of dirt on top. . . . If there are enough shovels to go around, everybody's going to make it."[53]

Despite various precautions, however, there have been times when people were exposed to radioactive material. The government has dealt with this problem in two ways. First, the AEC claimed that the dosage levels received as a result of exposure to fallout from testing were far lower than would occur under normal circumstances in everyday life. Second, the commission issued dozens of scientific reports refuting allegations about the link between low-level radiation and such serious ailments as leukemia and genetic disorders.

Statements attesting to the low level of exposure abound in AEC press releases during the fifties. Strauss was especially adept at making such claims. Describing fallout from the NTS in 1955 he noted: "The highest actual dose of radiation at an off-site community has been estimated to be less than one-third of the greatest amount of radiation which atomic energy workers are permitted to receive each year under the AEC's conservative safety standards."[54] He pursued this argument before the JCAE:

> If we refer only to the current tests being conducted at the Nevada site we must speak—not of roentgens or even 1/10 of a roentgen—but of milliroentgens, that is to say, thousandths of a roentgen. During the Nevada test series the radiation exposure from fallout, outside the actual

testing area, has been well below the level that would constitute any actual hazard to the health of exposed individuals. Generally speaking, the exposure experienced by the American people from the current Nevada tests has been less than the radiation they normally receive every few days from natural sources.[55]

Commissioner Libby took the same position in his public response to Schweitzer: "It is very generally agreed, among those who have studied the question, that the radiation exposures from fallout are very much smaller than those which would be required to produce observable effects in the population. . . . We all carry in our bodies, and have in our surroundings, amounts of radioactivity very much larger than those derived from radioactive fallout."[56] Equally impressive are figures cited by the AEC's General Advisory Committee in 1959:

In order to place the hazard of fallout in proper perspective, it should be pointed out that the amount of total body external radiation resulting from fallout to date, together with future fallout in any part of the world from previous weapons tests, is:
  a. less than 5% as much as the average exposure to cosmic rays and other background radiation.
  b. less than 5% of the estimated average radiation exposure of the American public to Xrays for medical purposes.[57]

In a corresponding report issued that same year by Gordon Dunning of the AEC's Division of Biology and Medicine, it was estimated that the highest exposure level at any community as a result of testing in Nevada was only "about 6 roentgens."[58]

This official position concerning low dosage rates has been maintained throughout the years. Following the 1963 tunnel accident, the exposure of workers was compared to the amount of radioactive iodine used for diagnostic purposes in thyroid treatment.[59] And, in 1970, after the Baneberry venting accident (discussed in Chapter 8), the AEC was quick to report that the level of radioactivity traced beyond the test site boundaries was "very low" and "well within permissible levels for humans."[60] Recently commenting on the October 1984 accident at the Idaho National Laboratory when six workers inhaled radioactive air, an EG&G official stated: "It's not significant in terms of health effects on the employees [who] received internal radiation exposure estimated at a small fraction of the annual exposure limit."[61] In response to a number of negligence suits filed by downwind residents and test site workers, the Nuclear Defense Agency has conducted a series of highly technical, in-depth analyses of dose estimates for areas in the Southwest at the times of the different shots—they invariably conclude that levels of exposure were below the danger level.[62] And following the "Mighty Oak" tunnel accident in April 1986, during which two workers were exposed to xenon and radiation was detected outside the test site, DOE manager Tom Clark commented that the doses the workers received were "quite low. Those people are trained to work in those environments and these things can be expected. There are some people in this room who have been exposed to much higher levels [of radiation] and they look pretty healthy to me."[63]

Commenting on such action in an article published in *The Washington Monthly* in 1981, Colonel Raymond Brim, the federal officer responsible for monitoring off-site fallout from underground shots between 1966 and 1975, charged: "Just as the risk of fallout continues, so does the conscious government effort to cover up the situation. . . . Exactly as they did in the 1950s, officials refuse to reveal information necessary for those who live near radiation accidents to protect themselves."[64]

The AEC's second approach to dealing with the problem of exposure has been to deny that any damage could result from such low dosage levels. Hundreds of public statements consistently took the position that exposure below a certain "threshold level" does not cause permanent damage. Supporting the theory are two facts: human organisms are capable of some repair even when damaged by radiation, and the human race has existed for thousands of years in an environment bombarded by natural radiation.

Chairman Strauss summarized the government's position as follows: "The Commission's medical and biological advisers do not believe that this small amount of additional exposure [from testing] is any basis for serious concern. . . . There [is not] reason to believe that weapons testing programs of the United States have resulted in any serious public hazard."[65] Likewise, in a *U.S. News & World Report* article, Commissioner Libby told the country that based on "evidence" from AEC research, bomb fallout would "not likely be at all dangerous."[66] And in a 1957 article in *Science,* Austin Brues, the director of the commission's Division of Biology and Medicine, insisted that facts corroborated the existence of a threshold dose of radiation, below which no biological damage would occur.[67]

To substantiate these claims, the AEC commissioned dozens of scientific studies on the possible effects of radiation. While even critics concede that the AEC sponsored important research and published a great deal of valuable data on radiation effects, the scientific contributions of the commission are overshadowed by its tendency to gloss over the unknown and its failure to delineate the health hazards more frankly. Furthermore, the question of conflict of interest must be addressed. There was little doubt what the government scientists would find; indeed, the lesson of Oppenheimer's banishment was a profound one. As Dr. Karl Morgan, director of the Oak Ridge Health Physics Lab during that period, has stated: "It became unpatriotic and perhaps unscientific to suggest that atomic weapons testing might cause deaths throughout the world from fallout." Many of his colleagues consequently held onto "untenable and extremely shallow arguments . . ." in the face of contradictory evidence being presented by such prominent scientists as Linus Pauling, Herman Muller, and George Beadle.[68]

Current government officials and scientists continue to deny a conclusive link between radiation and cancer. For instance, in a 1979 letter to a former employee of the NTS, Walter Weyzen, the acting director of the Department of Energy's Division of Human Health and Assessments, wrote: "For your information, I would like to point out that, in spite of the extensive publicity on the association of adverse health effects and weapons testing, there are no scientific data in support of this."[69] Following the Salt Lake City decision in 1984 awarding damages to downwind residents, Dr. Marvin Rallison of the University of Utah, who is conducting a radiation study funded by the Department of Defense, noted to the press: "The conclusive scientific evidence is not there."[70] And in a recent address before the National Environmental Health Association, Billy Smith of Reynolds Electrical and Engineering Co. "contended there is no way to make a 'direct correlation' that exposure to moderate amounts of nuclear radiation caused a cancer."[71]

Despite current skepticism among the general public over the activities of the government during the era of atmospheric testing, it can be concluded that the three strategies followed by the AEC were successful. By contributing to the perpetuation of a political atmosphere of paranoia and anticommunism during the fifties, the government set the stage for a burgeoning arms race. Then, as an actor on the stage, the AEC gained public support needed for the program's success by promoting the nonmilitary advantages of nuclear weapons development and by assuring the people of this country that "fallout was much less dangerous than falling behind the Russians in the arms race."[72] It is not surprising that, in response to these official efforts, most people soon accepted the notion of living under a mushroom cloud and developed a positive attitude toward the testing program that still prevails today.

7 Living Under the Mushroom Cloud

The Public Response to Atmospheric Testing

With the explosion of the world's first A-bomb in 1945, the American public became fascinated with the mysteries and potentials of atomic power. Fanned by an ardent press, the fervor over atomic phenomena flourished and quickly permeated many aspects of everyday life in this country. Songs, movies, place names, and advertisements all reflected the new interest. By the end of the fifties, however, the general public had become fairly blasé about atomic weapons. The AEC's carefully conducted strategies had paid off. Convinced of the necessity of first-strike power and anesthetized by constant government assurances that they could be safe in the event of nuclear attack, people became accustomed to living with the bomb. In 1963, when testing moved underground, most soon forgot about the NTS altogether. Tacit acceptance of the testing program continued throughout the next decade, allowing the government even greater flexibility in its efforts to stockpile atomic weapons than it had enjoyed in the fifties.

Evidence of the American public's general support for the testing program can be found in survey and electoral data from the fifties and early sixties. Results from nationwide Gallup polls conducted during this era indicate that citizens: (a) feared a nuclear war with the Soviet Union, (b) advocated developing bigger weapons, (c) favored continued testing of weapons, and (d) expressed little concern over the dangers of radiation. In February 1950, 68 percent of those surveyed thought the Russians would use an H-bomb on the U.S. The following month, 40 percent of the people interviewed responded that "threat of war" was the most important problem facing the country. The next highest grouping was 15 percent who felt the economy was the greatest concern. Similarly, in December 1956, 66 percent of the sample responded that they thought it was likely that the U.S. would get into another war in their lifetime. And in November 1961, when asked if they thought Khrushchev was bluffing when he said he would agree to a test ban if it were part of a program for total disarmament, 79 percent said yes.[1]

As a result of their fear of the Soviets, the American people called for the development of bigger bombs and the continuation of testing. In January 1950, 73 percent of the people interviewed responded that the U.S. government should make a bomb which "might be a thousand times more powerful than the atom bomb"; the following March, 69 percent expressed specific approval of constructing an H-bomb.[2] With regard to testing, in April 1954, just after the Bravo incident and despite the news coverage of radiation damage, 71 percent of those surveyed responded that the U.S. should go ahead with the rest of the planned H-bomb tests in the Pacific. This feeling persisted in October 1956 when 56 percent disagreed with the proposal that the U.S. halt H-bomb tests. Likewise, in May 1958, 60 percent said the U.S. should not stop testing, and as late as March 1962, 66 percent said the U.S. should resume atmospheric testing, compared to 25 percent who responded negatively.[3]

Throughout this entire period the matter of dangerous fallout was not a major issue and, therefore, appeared only rarely in the form of a question in these surveys. On only two occasions is there evidence that Americans were concerned. In May 1957, 52 percent felt that fallout from testing was dangerous, and a year later in May 1958, 46 percent felt that continued testing could result in a "threat to the health of future generations." These figures changed in 1961, however, when the respondents were asked more specifically, "Do you think there is enough fallout in the air right now to be a danger to people or not?" Sixty-one percent said no. Although the people had some fear of radiation, they persistently endorsed the continuation of testing, a true testimonial to the government's success in selling the bomb.[4]

The 1956 presidential election, in which testing became a significant issue, sheds further light on public attitudes toward the program. That summer the dangers of fallout were televised nationwide from the Democratic National Convention, and Adlai Stevenson began his campaign with a promise to halt H-bomb tests. Over the next several months, considerable evidence was presented on the strontium 90 hazards and possible genetic damage resulting from atmospheric testing.[5] Nonetheless, in November the country went strongly for incumbent Eisenhower, a long-time proponent of the weapons-testing program. Nationally, the count was a landslide victory for Ike with 35,590,472 votes to Stevenson's 26,029,752; the electoral college split, 442 to 89, reflected Eisenhower's appeal in every section of the country.[6]

In the two states where concern over the dangers of testing should have been the greatest, the results were similar: 56,049 Nevadans voted for Eisenhower and 40,640 for Stevenson,[7] while voters in Utah cast 215,631 ballots for Ike and only 118,364 for his challenger.[8] More specifically, in Washington County, Utah, where the residents were frequently exposed to fallout from the NTS, the vote was an over-whelming 3,172 for Eisenhower and only 877 for Stevenson.[9] In Nye County, Nevada, the home of the test site, the vote was 946 or 55.8 percent for Ike, and 749 or 44.2 percent for Stevenson.[10] In Clark County, where most of the test site workers then resided, the vote was fairly evenly split, with Stevenson winning by 500 votes, 19,095 to 18,584. This does not contradict the supposition, however, that Eisenhower won votes away from Stevenson, given the fact that voter registration in Clark County was almost three-to-one Democratic, 30,184 to 10,737.[11]

The American people further demonstrated their support for atom-ic testing by returning men to Congress who consistently called for higher appropriations for the weapons-development program. This was especially true for delegates from states tied economically to the program. Henry "Scoop" Jackson, Democrat from Washington, an avid supporter of escalating development of atomic weapons and long-term member of the JCAE, was first elected to the House in 1941; he moved to the Senate in 1953 where he remained until his death in 1983. Clinton Anderson, Democrat from New Mexico, was another member of the JCAE who consistently promoted testing. Anderson served in the House from 1941 to 1945 and in the Senate from 1949 until 1972. Two long-term senators from Nevada also supported the testing program. Democrat Pat McCarran, who served twenty years in the Senate, was an early proponent of testing, and, later, Democrat Howard Cannon, who served four terms from 1958 to 1982, promoted the underground testing program from his posi-tion on the Armed Services Committee. Not only were these four men ideologically conservative in matters of national defense, but they also saw the testing program as a means for providing direct economic benefits to their states; they satisfied their constituents' needs and as a result were returned to Washington year after year.[12]

Acceptance of the bomb is also reflected in the large role played by atomic phenomena in American popular culture of the era. Within a short time, the mushroom cloud had truly become the symbol of a generation. Signs for "Atomic Cafe" and "Atomic Motel" were fairly common along major cross-country highways. A small town in southern Idaho near an AEC facility became known as Atomic City. Even Walt Disney got into the act, publishing a book for children entitled *Our Friend the Atom*.[13] The Boy Scouts created an atomic energy merit badge and by 1970 some 15,000 Scouts had qualified for the award.[14] The American Museum of Atomic Energy was established by the AEC at Oak Ridge, Tennessee, and soon became a popular stop for thousands of tourists. A similar museum that attracted many visitors from the West opened at the Los Alamos site of the Manhattan Project.[15]

In addition, several popular songs with atomic themes made the charts during this period. "Jesus Hits Like an Atom Bomb" by Lowell Blanchard and the Valley Trio equated the second coming of Christ with a nuclear detonation:

> Everybody's worried 'bout the 'tomic bomb
> But nobody's worried 'bout the day my Lord will come.
> When He'll hit! Great God Almighty! Like an atom bomb,
> When He comes, when He comes . . .[16]

The Slim Gaillard Quartet took a different approach in "Atomic Cocktail":

> It's the drink that you don't pour
> Now when you take one sip you won't need any more,
> It's small as a beetle, or big as a whale,
> Boom! Atomic cocktail.[17]

No less catchy was a tune released by Jackie Doll and His Pickled Peppers:

> There'll be fire, dust, and metal, flying all around,
> And the radioactivity will burn them to the ground
> If there's any Commies left, they'll be all on the run
> If General MacArthur drops the atomic bomb.[18]

Finally, Little Caesar compared his love to an atomic blast:

> Boom! Something exploded down inside,
> And rushed teardrops in my eyes,
> Oh yes,
> I have that funny feeling,
> I guess it's my atomic love, for you (ooooh) . . .[19]

Movies, as well as music, have traditionally reflected prevailing sentiments of society, and those of the fifties and early sixties were no exception. In addition to movies about subversion and battlefield confrontations with Communists, Hollywood also produced films that dealt specifically with atomic warfare. These generally took one of two basic forms: They either delivered the government's message realistically, in a straightforward, quasi-documentary fashion similar to the official government films, or they employed a more subtle approach by using fantasy and science fiction to create doomsday situations.[20]

The first motion picture to address the question of atomic power from a realistic standpoint was produced by MGM in 1946. *The Beginning or the End?* took its name from a quote by President Truman about nuclear development, and the movie was made with the complete cooperation and absolute approval of both the White House and the War Department. Starring Brian Donlevy as General Groves, Hume Cronyn as Dr. Oppenheimer, Joseph Calleia as Professor Enrico Fermi, and Barry Nelson as Col. Paul Tibbets, Jr., who flew the B-29 from which the bomb was dropped on Hiroshima, this film was highly touted as being of "unique value to all humanity." Allegedly the true story of the development of the atom bomb, the picture was described as "doing a definite good helping to inform the people of the destructive potentialities of the bomb." In the film, MGM took no formal side in the atomic polemic of the day, but did make it clear that the men who developed the bomb were American heroes. The producers also stated that the bombing of Japan was a necessary evil, less destructive than prolongation of the war. The picture ended with the implication that this new and vast potential must be put to the betterment of life for all peoples.[21]

The Atomic City, released in 1952 by Paramount, was the second realistic nuclear film to appear. It was the story of the FBI's successful efforts to foil a Communist kidnap attempt on the son of a famous American nuclear physicist. Directed by Jerry Hopper, who had previously worked only on army training films, it was done in psuedodocumentary fashion, in black and white, and bore great resemblance to the official reels being distributed by the government during the same period.

A third atomic movie, *Hell and High Water* (1954), was presented with somber documentary overtones so realistic that it has been compared to Orson Welles's radio version of *The War of the Worlds* for its seeming authenticity. Based on a 1953 AEC/White House announcement that a bomb of foreign origin had been exploded somewhere in the region between the northern tip of Japan and the Arctic, the movie began by claiming to be "the story of that explosion." A group of international scientists, played by Cameron Mitchell, Bella

Darvi, and Victor Francen, commissioned a high-powered submarine piloted by Richard Widmark to secretly carry them to the North Pacific to search for a suspected atomic arsenal being stockpiled by the Russians. There, they discovered that the Communists were about to drop an atomic bomb on North Korea, for which the United States would most certainly get the blame. The scientists shot down the fake B-52 which was carrying the bomb, and thus the mystery explosion occurred. Although private citizens rather than the government were involved in this atomic adventure, the message was the same: Russians were portrayed as perpetrators of evil who would stop at nothing, not even bombing their own allies, to gain control over the rest of the world. Atomic weaponry was not projected as being inherently bad, but, in the hands of the evil Communists, it could become deadly.

Much more popular with audiences than these realistic movies were the relatively new science fiction (sci-fi) films, a genre which rose to prominence during the fifties by capitalizing on the paranoia, loss of identity, and fear of the unknown which were the prevalent attitudes of people living under the mushroom cloud.[22] Some of the sci-fi films produced during this era merely used the circumstances of the Atomic Age as a backdrop against which to study human relationships.[23] The majority, however, followed the approach of realistic cold war films in propagating the government's pro-atomic-weapons line.[24]

One of the first progovernment sci-fi films about atomic war appeared in 1952. *The Atomic Kid,* based on a story by Blake Edwards and starring Mickey Rooney, was a sci-fi comedy which also reinforced the government's position on atomic weapons. Young Mickey was accidentally exposed to radiation during an atomic test blast. He then began to experience strange physical reactions, none of which were severe, only annoying: He ticked, he glowed, and his eyes spun around. When enemy spies tried to capture him for experimental purposes, the army became his benevolent protector. Mickey was saved and cured of his radioactive ailments, and the army was seen not as the cause of all his problems, but as his salvation.

Released the following year, *Invasion, USA* (1953) was an atomic war picture showing the invasion and subjugation of the United States by an unnamed but obviously Soviet army. It was almost totally composed of stock combat newsreel footage from World War II that had been edited to look like the future. Toward the end of the movie, the audience learned that war had really not occurred. The patrons of a local bar had been hypnotized by a television magician in order to teach them the lesson that the U.S. must be strong and prepared or its fate would be utter destruction.

A somewhat different approach was used in the 1956 film *The Amazing Colossal Man,* which starred Glenn Langan as an officer exposed to radiation at the Nevada Test Site. As a result of exposure, the officer's genes were knocked out of whack and he began to grow at the alarming rate of eight feet a day, eventually becoming a giant who terrorized Las Vegas. In the end, the army was forced to destroy the menace and save the community; Langan was shot down by bazookas and fell to his death from the top of Hoover Dam. As in the earlier Mickey Rooney comedy, the U.S. military was portrayed as the savior of society rather than as the cause of its problems—radiation was seen as the culprit for which the army could not be held responsible.

Produced by Val Guest in 1962, *The Day the Earth Caught Fire* was the story of what happened when the United States and the Soviet Union exploded simultaneous nuclear devices at the North and South Poles, thus throwing the earth off balance and changing its slant toward the sun. The basic incident in this movie was not atomic war, but rather a planned and carefully calculated test exercise. After much fire and general havoc internationally, the movie ended with the two enemy powers cooperating to set off additional atomic blasts in an attempt to push the earth back on its orbit and save the human race. The audience was left to wonder whether it worked or not, when, in the last scene, the camera panned in on two stacks of newspapers. The headlines of one read, "Earth Saved," and the other "Earth Doomed." Which set was to be delivered? Although this movie began by presenting the potential dangers of atomic testing, by the end, the audience had come to see that government leaders were wise and responsible men capable of compromise; such officials were portrayed as the world's only possible hope for survival.

Finally, *Panic in the Year Zero,* starring Ray Milland, Jean Hager, Frankie Avalon, and Marty Mitchell, was also released in 1962. This semirealistic film related the experiences of a typical middle-class American family fighting to survive following an atomic attack on southern California. This film could be described as a manual for the bomb-shelter generation; it told the audience how to get along after the initial panic had passed. The main themes confirmed accepted American values of the times. Preservation of the family was seen as sacrosanct, with the father portrayed as a savior of sorts. The movie ended on another familiar note: The family must come to realize the need for law and order—meaning government—if civilization is to survive.[25]

This invasion of the A-bomb into the popular culture of the times was even more evident in southern Nevada. It is only natural that the actual neighbors of the test site would be more attuned to atomic phenomena than the nation at large. Indeed, it was not long before the mushroom cloud was vying with the showgirl for top billing along the Las Vegas Strip. The "atomic hairdo," originally designed by GeeGee, hair stylist at the Flamingo Hotel, was a popular request for special occasions. The hair was pulled over a wire form shaped like a mushroom cloud and then sprinkled with silver glitter at a cost of only seventy-five dollars.[26] The "atomic cocktail" was also a big seller in bars along the Strip. Made from equal parts of vodka, brandy, and champagne, with a dash of sherry, the potent drink was served at breakfast parties following the predawn shots.[27] In the Desert Inn Sky Room, pianist Ted Mossman first played his boogie-woogie tune "Atomic Bomb Bounce," which soon had people swinging all over town.[28] Another local entertainer, Jackson Kay, billed himself as the "Original Atomic Comic."[29] And a musical group known as the "Atom Bombers" boasted that they were the "Detonators of Devastating Rhythm."[30] The Sands Hotel sponsored a Miss Atomic Bomb Contest which featured beautiful young contestants wearing puffy white mushroom clouds pinned to their bathing suits. One of the stage props was a small replica of a detonation tower labeled "Yuk Yuk Flats."[31]

Local merchants also capitalized on the atomic theme: Car salesman "Boob" Jones proudly advertised "Atom Drops on High Prices."[32] Allen and Hanson, Las Vegas haberdashers, placed a barrel full of broken plate-glass window fragments in front of their downtown store with a sign, "Atomic Bomb Souvenirs—Free." Within an hour the barrel was empty.[33] On March 13, 1953, Sheppard's Furniture Store advertised a "Great Atomic Bomb Sale" which "Starts the minute the 'St. Pat' atomic bomb is exploded." The ad went on to say, "We've blown our top-too." Free five-dollar gift certificates were promised to "the first ten customers to enter our store after the explosion."[34]

The gambling industry attempted to use the testing program as an additional draw for boosting the tourist trade in Las Vegas. The Chamber of Commerce provided tourists with up-to-date shot calendars so they could schedule their visits, and road maps pointing out several vantage points around the test site.[35] Many of the hotels packed box lunches for bomb watchers to carry to picnics at Angel's Peak, a mountain in the Charleston Range forty-five miles away, from which tourists could experience the blast and watch the rising mushroom cloud. One establishment even called itself the "Atomic View Motel" claiming that guests could witness the flash without ever leaving their poolside lounge chairs.[36] Although they promoted the tests as an additional attraction to Las Vegas, gambling establishments also devised certain precautions against the effects of the shots. Several casinos posted signs warning that if a tremor from a bomb blast caused dice to turn or roulette balls to jump from one slot on the wheel to another, the house ruling was final.[37]

The mushroom cloud was further institutionalized as a fixture on the Nevada cultural scene when it made its way into printed material. In the fifties the official Clark County seal, which today bears the picture of a Joshua tree, was designed around a large mushroom cloud.[38] The cover of the 1953 Las Vegas High School yearbook, the *Wildcat Echo,* also featured such a scene.[39] Likewise, the telephone directory for Clark County depicted a map of Nevada on its cover with a mushroom cloud emerging from the southern part of the state.[40] One of the best-selling postcards of the era was a color shot of "Glitter Gulch" with Vegas Vic waving in the foreground and a mushroom cloud rising over the Union Pacific Railroad station in the background.[41] And the feature story for the June–December 1955 issue of *Nevada Highways and Parks* was about the NTS with a "typical, mushrooming cloud of fire, smoke, sand, and radioactive particles" pictured on the cover.[42]

Nevada's fascination with the bomb did not go unnoticed. Several major nationally distributed publications also ran stories on Las Vegas and its reaction to the testing program. In 1952, Daniel Lang wrote a piece entitled "Blackjack and Flashes" for the *New Yorker* in which he described Las Vegas as "a shrill, restless resort town . . . in the throes of acute prosperity." According to Lang, "Governor Russell, Chamber of Commerce officials, and hotel people attribute the community's present [success] in large part to the publicity that the proving ground has given it."[43] A similar story by Samuel Matthews, "Nevada Learns to Live With the Atom," in a 1953 *National Geographic* began: "While blasts teach civilians and soldiers survival in atomic war, the Sagebrush State takes the spectacular tests in stride." The twelve-page piece ended on the same note: "To Nevadans, the atomic tests are only one more superlative in a State endowed with already spectacular history and scenery."[44] The famous postcard shot of Fremont Street in downtown Las Vegas was *Life* magazine's Picture of the Week in 1951. The accompanying story discussed the marriage of Marion Davies to Horace Brown and the voluntary closing of operations by thirteen bookies who refused to pay a 10 percent federal tax. The story concluded that in light of these events, "the residents of Las Vegas were hardly surprised on Thursday morning when a fleecy white atomic cloud drifted in toward the city."[45] A similar story, "Desert Capitol of the A-Bomb" by Gladwin Hill, appeared in the *New York Times* Sunday travel section in 1955. It advised readers on how to participate in "the non-ancient but nonetheless honorable pastime of atom bomb watching." Hill reported on accommodations provided by local facilities and promotional measures taken by the Las Vegas Chamber of Commerce. He reassured his audience that "there is virtually no danger from radioactive fallout" but cautioned against automobile accidents because "in the excitement of the moment people get careless in their driving."[46]

Other journalists came to Nevada during the fifties to cover these historical events. Invited by the government to photograph and report on various tests, dozens of well-known reporters regularly traveled the sixty-five miles from Las Vegas to the test site in order to witness the predawn blasts. Such noted journalists as Walter Cronkite, Dave Galloway, John Cameron Swayze, and Bob Considine perched on bleachers atop a small hill some ten miles from ground zero. From this spot, which came to be known as News Nob, they covered the awesome story for the American public.[47] Their accounts invariably focused on the visual effects of the shot with vivid descriptions of the aftermath of the blasts. They also consistently praised the government for its tremendous successes and parroted the AEC's line about the absence of radiation hazards.

The local Las Vegas newspapers were even more blatantly supportive of the testing program. From the start, news coverage was presented in optimistic terms. Headlines read: "Baby A-Blast May Provide Facts on Defense Against Atomic Attack,"[48] "Use of Taller Towers . . . Introduces an Added Angle of Safety . . . ,"[49] "Fallout on Las Vegas and Vicinity . . . Very Low and Without Any Effects on Health,"[50] "No Chance H-Bombers to Drop Death in Error,"[51] "Tunnel A-Bomb Test Gives New Hope to Oilmen,"[52] "A-Bomb Incident 'Proves' Safety,"[53] and "Radiation Danger in Vegas Nil."[54] The list goes on.

Local reporters, like their national counterparts, focused on the visual descriptive effects of the blasts and failed to question more serious potential hazards. This was especially true for coverage of civil defense tests which involved the elaborately stocked and furnished

"Doom Towns." Graphically describing the aftermath of such an operation, Archie Teague of the *Las Vegas Review-Journal* wrote: "People played by dummies lay dead and dying in basements, living rooms, kitchens, bedrooms. . . . A mannequin mother died horribly in her one-story house of precast concrete slabs. Portions of her plaster and paint body were found in three different areas. A mannequin tot . . . was blown out of bed and showered with needle-sharp glass fragments. . . . A simulated mother was blown to bits in the act of feeding her infant baby food." The gruesome account continues.[55]

In another firsthand account of a blast conducted in March of 1953, Robert Bennyhoff described the experience: "The dust cloud which swept across the trenches was choking and blinding. . . . It sounded like a dozen huge cannons firing all at once. . . . It was a horrible feeling to see that monster cloud, loaded with radiation, rising in an expanding ring virtually over our heads. But the scientists' calculations were correct; the cloud drifted directly away from us. We were safe from radiation fallout."[56]

Editorials from the years of atmospheric testing were also supportive of AEC activities at the NTS. On January 15, 1951, just prior to the first test blast conducted at the NPG, the *Review-Journal* reassured its readers that the furor regarding A-bombs at Indian Springs was "entirely uncalled for."[57] Shortly thereafter, on January 30, 1951, the *Las Vegas Sun* stated that "atomic experimentation must be carried on if we are to maintain our lead in the atomic and guided missiles field."[58] And in 1952, Joe McClain of the *Review-Journal* accused the AEC of "gyping its public: Time was when a nuclear detonation took place, people knew about it. . . . People seemed to enjoy the show. But the good old days . . . have passed. . . . We think it might be good for the town's spirit if the scientists would send a few effects down Vegas way. Just to keep people happy."[59]

In the spring of 1953, following the "Dirty Harry" shot, which sprinkled fallout on St. George, Utah Representative Douglas Stringfellow called for an end to testing in Nevada. In response, the *Review-Journal* again took the side of the AEC and warned Stringfellow to stay out of Nevada's business. It editorialized: "We like the AEC. We welcome them to Nevada for their tests because we, as patriotic Americans, believe we are contributing something in our small way, to the protection of the land we love."[60] Similarly, in 1955 when a Nevada state legislator from Eureka County, Republican E. C. Leutzinger, introduced a resolution to stop testing in Nevada, editorials appeared in both Las Vegas papers condemning the senator. The *Sun* reported the action as "another humiliation" and asked, "Who shall get out of Nevada, the AEC or the crackpot who makes such a suggestion in public?"[61] And the *Review-Journal* wrote: "More power to the AEC and its atomic detonations. We in Clark County who are closest to the shots, aren't even flickering an eyelid."[62]

This action by Leutzinger was certainly the exception and not the rule in terms of Nevada's official response to the testing program. In the twelve years of atmospheric testing, his resolution to "memorialize the AEC and other agencies to dispense with the exploding of nuclear weapons and devices in the state of Nevada in order to preserve the health and welfare of the Nevada citizenry" was the only measure introduced in the state legislature that attacked the federal government's testing policy. In his resolution, Leutzinger referred to both the Bravo and sheep death incidents as justification for ending the experiments, but his argument was insufficient. The bill was sent to the Committee on Public Health on February 17, 1955, and it died there at the end of the session.[63]

Other actions taken by the Nevada legislature during this period, although few in number, were without exception supportive. The first action did not come until four years after the testing program had begun. Assembly Bill 13, passed on January 19, 1955, granted the consent of the state of Nevada to the acquisition by the U.S. government of lands required by the Department of Defense or the AEC. This increased the size of the NTS from 640 square miles to 1,350.[64] Two measures adopted in Nevada in 1957, although only peripherally related to the test site, further illustrated the positive attitude taken by Nevadans toward nuclear power: Senate Joint Resolution 3 invited the AEC to build an experimental nuclear-power generating plant in Eureka County,[65] and Senate Joint Resolution 15 encouraged the Department of Defense to accelerate the integration of nonconventional weapons,[66] including nuclear, into the Naval Ammunition Depot at Hawthorne.

In addition to state legislators, other Nevada politicians supported testing activities in the state. Governor Charles Russell, for instance, frequently defended the NTS against criticism. Typical of his position was a statement made in 1952: "It's exciting to think that the submarginal land of the proving ground is furthering science and helping national defense. We had long ago written off that terrain as wasteland, and today it's blooming with atoms."[67]

Patrick A. McCarran, the powerful Democrat who represented Nevada in the U.S. Senate during the early days of this period, was likewise supportive of the testing program in his state.[68] Realizing McCarran's potential influence as a member of the Senate Appropriations Committee, AEC Chairman Gordon Dean paid him a special personal visit to inform him of plans to open the NTS before it was publicly announced. This "courting" helped insure McCarran's support and smooth the way for AEC activities in Nevada. McCarran consistently voted for increased funding for the AEC, praising the agency for its precision and care in making its tests: "The lead in development of this science is in the best interest of the United States, and we must maintain it. We have an avowed enemy who is developing atomic energy and we must keep ahead."[69]

A second senator from Nevada during the fifties, George W. Malone, wrote to a constituent in 1957:

> Qualified scientists who have knowledge of nuclear testing agree that radiation dangers are serious and must be guarded against and they say they are working it out. These same scientists also agree that this country must not discontinue testing until other nations agree to do likewise. . . . I am confident that every precaution is being taken to insure that these tests do not endanger the lives of our people or the health of future generations and the work of our own Atomic Energy Commission will be the best guidepost.[70]

Despite the overwhelming support for atomic testing exhibited both nationwide and within Nevada, it would be misleading to suggest that all Americans favored the testing program. By the late fifties with "red baiting" on the wane, the antinuclear movement picked up some momentum. A number of noted scientists consistently attacked the AEC's proposition that radiation exposure from testing was harmless. Herman Muller issued a paper in 1955 which assessed the worldwide fallout exposure to human gonads and the genetic damage it could cause, and in June 1957 Linus Pauling estimated that ten thousand persons had died or were dying from leukemia because of nuclear tests. Pauling's colleague E. B. Lewis issued a similar but more detailed report which refuted the AEC's "threshold" argument, concluding that there was no safe level of exposure.[71]

Some ordinary citizens also got involved in the antitesting movement. The National Committee for a Sane Nuclear Policy was founded in November 1957 and within one year had recruited 25,000 members.[72] Small-scale "Ban the Bomb" protests took the form of sit-ins at missile bases and refusals to participate in air-raid drills.[73] More dramatic incidents involved several attempts by activists to sail into the Marshall Islands testing zone. In the spring of 1958, a group of

Quakers aboard the thirty-foot ketch, the *Golden Rule,* attempted to sail from Hawaii to Eniwetok to protest the H-bomb tests scheduled for later that year. Referred to in the press as "atom lopers," these pacifists were seized by the U.S. Coast Guard two miles off Honolulu.[74] Another protest occurring in 1958 took the form of a lawsuit filed on April 4 by citizens of six nations seeking to end nuclear tests in the U.S. Named as defendants were Secretary of Defense Neil H. McElroy and all five commissioners of the AEC, including Lewis Strauss.[75]

Nevada too witnessed an increasing occurrence of protests as the years of testing continued. Most of these, however, were minor complaints concerning property damage from the blasts. Furthermore, they involved only a small percentage of the population and should be seen as the exception and not the rule. One especially disgruntled resident was Dan Sheahan, owner of the Groom Mine, located some thirty-eight miles north of the test site. Sheahan frequently complained to the AEC that he had to shut down operations during test blasts which was a great inconvenience and expense for his business. Ranchers filed complaints when their horses and cows grazing in the path of mushroom clouds suffered from beta burns. In order to minimize complaints, the AEC was always quick to reimburse local citizens for these minor property losses.[76]

In 1957, seventy-five residents of the Tonopah area signed a petition asking that "the atomic tests be suspended, or that some equally positive action be taken to safeguard us and our families." Copies were sent to President Eisenhower and the three members of Nevada's congressional delegation who took the matter under advisement.[77]

After testing moved underground in 1963, only one major local critic of the NTS arose—Howard Hughes, eccentric billionaire, big-time investor in Las Vegas, and ironically, the nation's largest defense contractor. Politically conservative, Hughes was not philosophically opposed to nuclear weapons; he only objected to their being tested near him or his hotels. He began a low-key campaign against the AEC in 1967, which escalated to a virtual war by the spring of 1968. Hughes contributed campaign funds to presidential candidates, lobbied the AEC, threatened to withdraw his investments from Las Vegas, and offered to pay any expenses which would result from delaying tests. He even wrote personally to President Johnson urging him to stop the testing program. Interestingly, although Hughes had had little difficulty lining up press support for most of his Nevada resort projects, he was unable to convince the local papers to side with him against the AEC.[78] Shortly thereafter, Hughes' mental and physical health deteriorated, and his interests turned elsewhere.

While it is true that a few local critics have emerged from time to time throughout the past thirty years, in the main, Nevadans have consistently supported the test site since its opening. Test site contractor EG&G described the cooperative attitude of the local community to prospective clients and personnel in a 1961 report: "There have been so many detonations of nuclear devices at the test site in the past ten years that the community [of Las Vegas] is completely accustomed to, and unconcerned about, radiation hazards from such operations."[79] Two years later, a 1963 public-opinion poll showed a majority of Las Vegans recommending continued atmospheric testing because they did not trust the Russians to uphold a test ban treaty.[80]

Although Nevada's representatives in the Ninety-seventh Congress were cosponsors of legislation to compensate "atomic victims," they made no sustained effort to actually get the bill passed into law and no mention was made of the issue during their 1982 campaigns. Nor did a nuclear-freeze question appear on the ballot in Clark County in 1982, although it was a major issue in many areas of the country.[81] On January 27, 1984, the thirty-third anniversary of the first atmospheric shot at the NTS, a protest in front of the Federal Building in Las Vegas drew only thirty demonstrators.[82] In March 1984, when presidential candidate Gary Hart announced that, if elected, he would call for a six-month moratorium on testing, southern Nevada labor union leaders were "aghast." Hart's campaign manager in Las Vegas first disavowed knowledge of the candidate's intentions and later declined to speculate on how this position would affect his campaign in Nevada.[83] Finally, in his column "Street Talk" in the *Las Vegas Sun,* Ken Jones asked Nevadans on June 29, 1984, "Does testing at the Nevada Test Site worry you?" Of the five responses printed, only one expressed concern.[84] Therefore, despite the absence of scientific polling on the question, one is led to believe that the majority of southern Nevadans still support the test site and favor its continued operation in the state. Interestingly enough, this support comes in the face of increasing evidence that activities at the NTS may have caused damage in the past. Furthermore, many of these same people who support continued testing oppose the construction of a high-level nuclear waste repository at the site because they feel it may be unsafe.[85]

Political Fallout from Above-Ground Tests

8

The Reemergence of an Issue

Between 1963 and 1976, public interest in atomic weapons testing subsided. This diminished attention can be attributed to several national and international factors. First, the aphorism "Out of sight, out of mind" seemed to describe the country's reaction to the conversion in 1963 to exclusively underground testing. Gone was the mushroom cloud on the horizon that previously had served as an ominous reminder of the testing program. Furthermore, many people felt that conducting the tests in underground tunnels eliminated the danger of radiation exposure which had been a primary objection of most of the program's earlier critics. On the international scene, the cold war of the 1950s was being replaced by a policy of détente between the two superpowers despite the ongoing conflict in Southeast Asia. And at home, the media turned their attention away from the seemingly mundane activities of the AEC to focus instead on civil rights, antiwar protests, and the antics of the flower generation.[1] Behind the scenes, however, several events took place during this interim period that were to have significant implications for atomic testing policy. In each case, the AEC's response was in keeping with its established practice of "duck and cover"; but by 1976, this approach was failing to satisfy the critics of atomic testing, and today's compensation issue was born.

The international agreement to move atomic weapons testing underground came after seventeen years of negotiations between the western Allies and the Soviet Union. By the time it finally went into effect on October 10, 1963, most tests in Nevada were already being conducted underground. Nonetheless, during the months preceding ratification, there was considerable debate in this country over the possible impact of an atmospheric test ban on American national security. Leading the proponents of a treaty was Dr. Linus Pauling, who later received the Nobel Peace Prize for his efforts. Pauling's arguments for a test ban were drawn from his scientific studies on the harmful effects of radiation exposure.[2]

In the U.S. Senate, supporters of a test ban treaty also focused on the problems caused by radioactive fallout from atmospheric testing.

While the legislators disagreed over the terms for a comprehensive test ban policy, many concurred on the dangers of radioactivity. Accordingly, on May 27, 1963, thirty-two senators from both parties joined Democrats Hubert Humphrey of Minnesota and Thomas Dodd of Connecticut in introducing a resolution, S. Res. 148, which urged the government to place "a ban on all tests that contaminate the atmosphere or the oceans."[3] Consideration of the resolution soon became moot when President Kennedy submitted his own treaty to the Senate on August 8.

Opposition to the treaty came primarily from the AEC and the military. Government scientists, testifying before various Senate committees during the ratification debates, argued against the treaty and claimed that radiation control should be a minor factor in its consideration. John Foster, director of Lawrence Radiation Laboratory, said: "From the technical point of view I believe it [the fallout question] has no bearing on the major issue."[4] Norris Bradbury, director of the Los Alamos Scientific Laboratory, declared his "regret that fallout from atmospheric testing has been so played up rather recently in public statements. I think this is an exaggerated situation far beyond the needs of the actual situation."[5] And Edward Teller stated emphatically: "I claim these two questions, the test ban and the fallout, are linked only by propaganda."[6]

A number of key witnesses from the military also opposed the treaty, disagreeing with the president's assertion that it would "assure the security of the United States better than unlimited testing."[7] General Thomas Power, commander in chief of the Strategic Air Command, argued that certain effects data which were critical from an operational point of view could be obtained only from testing in the atmosphere.[8] General Robert Booth, chief of the Defense Atomic Support Agency, testified that under the treaty he could not meet the requirements the services had placed upon him,[9] and General Nathan Twining, chairman of the group of technical experts who analyzed the Soviet test series and reported on them to the Department of Defense, declared unequivocally: "The Treaty will eventually weaken our military capabilities."[10] Generals Curtis Le May and Bernard Schriever and Admirals George Anderson and Arleigh Burke agreed.[11]

After hearing considerable testimony, the Senate Foreign Relations Committee reported the treaty out favorably on September 3 by a vote of sixteen to one. Democrat Russell Long of Louisiana was the sole dissenter. The Armed Services Committee, on the other hand, rendered an unfavorable report on September 9. The final vote for ratification, cast on September 24, was eighty to nineteen. The two senators from Nevada, Democrats Howard Cannon and Alan Bible, voted in favor; the Utah senators split, with Democrat Frank Moss voting aye and Republican Wallace Bennett nay. Overall, the vote against included eleven Democrats, all southerners except Frank Lausche of Ohio, and eight Republicans, all from west of the Mississippi except Margaret Chase Smith from Maine. Voting in favor of ratification were fifty-five Democrats and twenty-five Republicans.[12]

Although the desire to eliminate dangerous fallout was a concern in 1963, it was neither the primary impetus behind nor sole objective of the treaty. In a speech delivered before the United Nations on September 27, President Kennedy clearly outlined the political advantages to be derived from the treaty and the American motives for signing it. "Freeing the world from fears and dangers of radioactive fallout" is only one of four objectives mentioned. The president also saw the treaty as a means of reducing world tension, preventing the spread of nuclear weapons to nations not possessing them, and limiting the arms race.[13]

In retrospect, although the treaty is considered one of the most important diplomatic agreements of the twentieth century, it has failed to accomplish what it was originally intended to do. The treaty was not a successful deterrent to the spiraling arms race because soon after its enactment the Soviet Union and the United States changed direction in terms of defense technology and began developing ballistic and antiballistic missile systems which did not rely upon atmospheric testing for perfection. Nor did the treaty stop the proliferation of atomic weapons; since 1963, China and India and most likely Israel and South Africa have developed their own nuclear devices. Finally, the treaty also failed to eliminate the exposure of mankind to harmful radiation from test blasts. France and China refused to sign the treaty and have continued to test weapons in the atmosphere to the present time. Furthermore, venting from underground tests can release radioactive particles into the air.[14] In sum, it was simply, as President Kennedy proclaimed, "a symbolic first step" toward reducing world tension and resolving international conflict.[15]

Nonetheless, in 1963, with radioactive fallout supposedly contained in shafts and tunnels far below the earth's surface, any remaining fears about the dangers of testing were soon put to rest. Ironically, it was during this period that researchers began to look for the first time at the health of those most directly affected by the testing program. Analyzing the incidence of certain illnesses in parts of the Southwest, they were soon to discover that the move underground may have come too late for some. Unfortunately, the results of these studies were largely ignored by the AEC and did not receive the public attention they deserved at the time. Years later, however, they would be discovered and cited before Congress as evidence that the AEC for years had been aware of potential health problems being caused by the testing program, yet failed to take necessary safety precautions.

In January 1963, Dr. Harold Knapp, a scientist with the AEC's Fallout Studies branch of the Division of Biology and Medicine, reported that the original estimate of the internal hazard posed by radioactive fallout was drastically low. Testifying before Congress some ten years later, he detailed his earlier discovery: "For 11 years we had missed by a factor of 100 to 1,000, perhaps, the doses to the thyroid of infants and young children that drank milk from cows that were grazing downwind in the fallout areas down around the Nevada Test Site."[16] When Dr. Knapp recommended that the allowable dosage levels be revised, the AEC's immediate reaction was "to find . . . why [his] conclusions might not be true."[17] Nathan Woodruff, then director of the Division of Operation Safety, responded to Knapp's request with the following memo:

> We do not recommend any new radiation protection guides for nuclear weapons testing at this time. The present guides have, in general, been adequate to permit continuance of nuclear weapons testing and at the same time have been accepted by the public, principally because of an extensive public information program. To change the guides would require a re-education program that could raise questions in the public mind as to the validity of the past guides. Lastly, the world situation today is not the best climate in which to raise the issue. Therefore, we recommend the continuation of the present criteria.[18]

Shortly thereafter, testing moved underground and the problem was temporarily forgotten.

Two studies conducted by Dr. Edward Weiss of the United States Public Health Service in 1965 and 1967 met with similar results. In 1965 Weiss reported to the AEC that he had discovered, upon examining the leukemia death records for southwestern Utah from 1950 to 1964, an unusual increase in deaths for the years 1959–1960.[19] He recommended that a formal etiological study be conducted to analyze the deaths that occurred throughout Utah during this period and in addition proposed a formal review by the Public Health Service of the oral, dental, and medical characteristics of Utah schoolchildren for the 1950s.[20] Despite the serious health questions Weiss raised, the AEC advised against a formal investigation because of the potentially detrimental effect it could have on the testing program. Dwight Ink, then general manager of the AEC, clearly depicted the reasons: "Performance of the above U.S. Public Health Service studies will pose potential problems to the Commission. The problems are: (a) adverse public reaction; (b) lawsuits; (c) jeopardizing the programs at the Nevada Test Site."[21]

In 1967, Dr. Weiss issued a second report stating that thyroiditis increased twofold and thyroid cancer almost fourfold among Utah residents during the years 1948 through 1962. The abnormalities were observed in members of both sexes, primarily between the ages of twenty and twenty-nine and most notably in the 1958–1962 time period.[22] The Public Health Service and the Utah State Department of Health collaborated in the study. The final report again recommended further research to determine whether a true excess of thyroid cancer was occurring in Utah and, if so, to establish the genetic and/or environmental factors associated with it. Although Weiss recommended "long-term surveillance of the exposed population to accurately characterize the potentially adverse health effects of low-level radioactive fallout," federal funding for the project was terminated in 1970 before conclusive evidence could be compiled.[23]

The Center for Disease Control, in conjunction with the National Cancer Institute, both divisions under the Department of Health, Education, and Welfare, also conducted investigations of leukemia outbreaks in Arizona and Utah during the years 1965 through 1970. The communities studied included Fredonia in Arizona, and Kanab, Monticello, Parawan, Paragonah, Pleasant Grove, and Salt Lake City in Utah. While leukemia clusters were found in these areas, no conclusions were drawn as to the possible causes of their incidence. In fact, Dr. Donald Frederick reported that "it appeared possible that these case clusters were chance instances."[24] Later findings, however, indicate that "these clusters could be considered significant occurrences rather than mere 'chance instances.' "[25]

In addition to the release of these medical reports, another significant incident occurred during the period between 1963 and 1976. The AEC quickly resolved it in its usual fashion, but the ramifications of the event would be far-reaching in the years to come. On December 18, 1970, the "Baneberry" underground shot vented unexpectedly and sent a cloud of radioactive particles into the air. The fourth shot in three days, Baneberry, with a yield of less than twenty kilotons, was emplaced in an 86-inch diameter hole at a depth of 910 feet. The device was detonated at 7:30 A.M. Pacific time and at 3.6 minutes after detonation, a "dynamic venting commenced from a fissure that developed in a southwest direction between 60 and 375 feet from SGZ [surface ground zero]. The rate of release was significantly reduced by the surface collapse at 16.5 minutes after detonation, but continued for some twenty-four hours. The radioactive gases that escaped from the 315-foot-long fissure reached an altitude of some 8000 feet."[26]

The wind carried the cloud west over "Area 12" of the test site where nine hundred NTS workers were stationed. At 8:05 the AEC Test Manager issued an order to evacuate the personnel. When the evacuation was completed around 9:30, three hundred of the workers were found to be contaminated and twenty were sent to the AEC laboratory for further observation and testing. Nominal precautions, such as showering, changing clothes, and washing their vehicles were taken, but no one was found to need medical treatment.[27] The AEC reported that "the radiation presented no danger to human health or life and only the most minute traces of fallout were deposited on the ground."[28] Area 12 remained closed until after the New Year's holiday, but throughout the rest of the test site it was back to business as usual. No Nevada newspaper editorials or "letters to the editor" appeared criticizing the NTS and no official action was taken to interfere with its operations.

In the years following the accident, two test site workers developed leukemia that they alleged had been caused by their exposure to high levels of radiation from the venting. Harley Roberts, a test site guard, and William Nunamaker, a REECo shop foreman, filed suit against the government on February 2, 1972. They sought damages in excess of eight million dollars, charging negligence on the part of the defendants in the conduct of the Baneberry test.[29] Both men died in 1974, but their widows pursued the suits. Despite the concerted efforts of their Las Vegas attorney, Larry Johns, the case received little public notice as the court continually postponed its decision. It was not until ten years later that a judgement was made, and that is currently under reconsideration. The details of the court case will be discussed in the following chapter, but the significance of the Baneberry incident and its resulting suit must be acknowledged here. This episode truly marked the beginning of a new era in which the American people began to demand that government be held liable for its actions, even in matters of national security.

The harmful effects of radiation from weapons testing did not make the news again until late 1974 when Secretary of the Interior Rogers Morton interrupted the reconstruction and relocation process that had begun on Bikini Atoll. Although a 1967 AEC report had declared the island safe for rehabitation, subsequent surveys indicated that the remaining radiation levels were unsafe for human residence. The story soon slipped from the front page, however, as the problem disappeared into the bowels of the bureaucracy.[30]

Two years later, the domestic implications of atomic testing returned to the political agenda. This renewed interest came about by serendipity. By being in the right place at the right time, one former GI inadvertently launched a nationwide campaign to hold the government accountable for its actions during the conduct of atomic weapons tests. In February 1976, Paul Cooper, a retired army sergeant, was stricken with myelogenous leukemia and admitted to the Veteran's Administration hospital in Boise. Cooper had retired from the army at thirty-nine after having served in Korea and two tours in Vietnam. A member of the elite Green Beret Special Forces, he had led a number of dangerous missions in Southeast Asia for which he received the Bronze Star, the Air Medal, the Republic of Vietnam Medal, and the Soldier's Medal. After retirement, Cooper joined the Idaho State Police. He was married and had two sons and a daughter.

Shortly after Cooper's leukemia was diagnosed, he was moved to a hospital in Salt Lake City where he was examined by Dr. Thomas Cosgriff, a physician formerly with the U.S. Center for Disease Control (CDC) who had experience working with radiation victims from Hiroshima and Nagasaki. When Dr. Cosgriff questioned Cooper about possible exposure to radiation, Cooper recalled his participation as a member of the 82nd Airborne Division in the 1957 "Smoky" shot at the NTS. Dr. Cosgriff filed with the VA for service-connected disability for Cooper stating that "the disability since Mr. Cooper's exposure is well within those limits observed for previous cases of radiation-induced leukemias."

J. C. Peckarsky, the VA compensation officer in the central office in Washington, denied the claim, saying, "The likelihood that the veteran developed leukemia as a result of radiation in 1957 is remote to the vanishing point." Cooper then wrote to the Department of the Army for his complete medical records, which he submitted with a second claim. When it too was turned down, he filed for a third time. Upon its rejection, Cooper, embittered by the government's failure to help, turned to the Disabled American Veterans (DAV) for assistance and decided to go public with his story. He appeared first on the Salt Lake City television station KUTV, interviewed from his hospital bed by reporter Sandy Gilmore. The story soon attracted national attention in June 1977 when *Parade* magazine ran it as a feature.

After a long struggle, the DAV was able to convince the Board of

Veterans' Appeals to reverse Cooper's third claim and pay him service-related benefits of $820 per month; the board never did admit, however, that the disease was caused by radiation from testing. Paul Cooper died two years later, in February 1978, but not before he had started in motion a drive to learn the truth about what really happened during the days of atmospheric testing and to hold the government accountable for its actions.[31]

In response to Cooper's case, the Center for Disease Control petitioned the Pentagon for data on the Smoky test and its participants. Although the few extant records were fragmentary and incomplete, Dr. Glyn Caldwell at the Center was determined to investigate the matter in order to ascertain whether there were leukemia clusters among the former Smoky soldiers. Preliminary results of the study, which did not appear until 1980, showed a significant increase, from 3.5 to 9, in the number of expected cases of leukemia occurring among the 3,224 participants. This led Dr. Caldwell and his associates to conclude that either the soldiers had received a greater dose than originally estimated or there was a greater effect of radiation on humans per rem at low-dose levels than had been previously acknowledged.[32]

The Department of Defense responded to the publicity of the Cooper case by setting up "a full program to fulfill the government's responsibility to the people involved." The first action was the establishment of a toll-free "hot line" in December 1977 that included six telephone lines through which former military personnel who had participated in the atmospheric testing program could call in for additional information. Within the first two weeks, over ten thousand calls were received and the phone bank had to be extended to twenty lines. The Pentagon's follow-up plan also included pulling together for the first time the names of all soldiers who had participated in the testing maneuvers, reexamining the data on each test and calculating with modern computers the probable radiation dosage at various distances from ground zero, seeking to locate "those who have gotten a high level of exposure," and providing the CDC with all available information on the Smoky veterans.[33] Despite these grandiose gestures by the Pentagon, atomic veterans filing claims for benefits through the VA met with little success.

During this same period, another Smoky veteran, Donald Coe of Tompkinsville, Kentucky, also learned that he had leukemia. Again, coincidence was to play a key role in bringing this issue to the government's attention. Coe's congressman was Tim Lee Carter, a country doctor who was then the ranking minority member of the

House Subcommittee on Public Health and the Environment, of the Committee for Interstate and Foreign Commerce. Having lost his own son to leukemia, Congressman Carter became outraged over the possibility that thousands of soldiers might have contracted the disease because of government negligence: "I am mad as hell about the way the government has treated veterans who were exposed to nuclear radiation. Congress should investigate, and I am going to do my best to see that it is done!"[34]

Working diligently on the problem, Congressman Carter was instrumental in setting up three days of hearings in January 1978, during which extensive testimony on the matter of participation by military personnel in the nuclear testing program was recorded. Although over the years at least fifteen congressional panels had concerned themselves with radiation and health questions, the 1978 hearings organized by Carter and chaired by Democrat Paul Rogers of Florida represent a milestone in the evolution of a radiation compensation policy. For the first time, government officials, representing both the military and the AEC, admitted that errors had been made during the atmospheric testing period. Their testimony alerted the general public to the possibility of government negligence, and placed the issue on the government's active agenda at a time when it could not be covered up.[35]

The political climate made the public receptive to the information revealed by Congressman Carter's hearings, and what began as health problems for two soldiers was soon transformed into a matter of national interest. By 1978, after Vietnam and Watergate, the American people were in no mood to tolerate secrecy. Their demand-to-know attitude was further encouraged by several 1974 amendments to the Freedom of Information Act. The original Freedom of Information Act, passed in 1966, had required the federal government and its agencies to make available to citizens upon request all documents and records except those specifically excluded such as classified material, internal personnel records, and law-enforcement-investigation findings. Problems with the statute soon became evident, because obstacles to public access were erected by the federal bureaucracy, which had opposed the measure from the start. People seeking information often faced lengthy bureaucratic delays and excessive charges imposed by the agencies for retrieving certain data; in addition, few citizens could afford the high cost of bringing suit to force disclosure by the government.

In 1974, PL 93-502 was passed as an amendment to the 1966 act. President Ford vetoed the bill on October 17, but the Congress overrode his decision on November 21. Under the revised law, deadlines for response are imposed on government agencies. Now a federal judge can rule on a decision by the government to classify certain material and can review "in camera" classified material which is relevant to the case; furthermore, he can assign the government to pay attorney fees and court costs for plaintiffs who win suits brought for information.[36] These changes were to prove quite helpful to subsequent radiation litigants.

By the spring of 1978, public pressure had increased to such an extent that the chief executive got personally involved with the issue. In May, President Carter appointed his own task force, under the directorship of Peter Libassi, to investigate the effects of low-level radiation. Libassi, general counsel for the Department of Health, Education, and Welfare, was joined by representatives from the Departments of Energy, Defense, and Labor, and from the Environmental Protection Agency, the Nuclear Regulatory Commission, and the Veterans Administration. The task force was instructed to "coordinate the formulation of a program covering (1) research on the health effects of radiation exposure, (2) public information on radiation, (3) care and benefits for persons adversely affected by radiation exposure, and (4) steps to reduce adverse radiation exposure."[37]

The group's final report, issued in June 1979, proposed a research agenda that could "provide some answers to questions about the effects of low-level radiation" and made recommendations for facilitating the research. It also outlined a public-information program, advanced suggestions for improving "systems that deliver care and benefits to those who may have been injured by exposure to radiation," and offered recommendations for taking steps that "might reduce unnecessary radiation exposure in the future."[38] The report stopped short, however, of linking leukemia and other ailments to radioactive fallout from testing: "The Task Force's Science Work Group . . . concluded that existing knowledge is insufficient to provide an unequivocal answer to the low-dose question. The Group also concluded that inherent methodological problems may prevent scientists from ever finding a definitive answer."[39]

The president created a second, more specifically defined task force on July 20, 1979, "to study and recommend alternatives for compensation of persons who may have developed radiation-related illnesses as a result of exposure to radiation from nuclear weapons tests." Representatives from the same seven agencies served on the board, with the addition of a member from the Justice Department. This group went a step further than its predecessor. In its first report, issued on February 1, 1980, the task force concluded: "It is well established that fallout exposed the population to ionizing radiation and that radiation exposure can increase the risk of many forms of cancer. Accepting the no-threshold hypothesis, we may reasonably assume that at least some additional cases of cancer in the downwind population resulted from atmospheric test fallout."[40] The group went on to state, however, that, based on its findings, "the overall health risk to downwind residents from fallout appears to be small."[41] The report concluded with possible recommendations for compensating victims "without also benefiting other, undeserving claimants."[42] The recommendations included adding amendments to the Federal Tort Claims Act, making litigation easier, and establishing an administrative remedy program similar to existing VA benefits.[43]

Congress also got into the act. On November 9, 1978, Congress passed P.L. 95-622, amendments to the Community Mental Health Centers Act. In Part E, sections 2 A & B of the statute, provisions are made for the establishment of a "comprehensive program of research into the biological effects of low level ionizing radiation" and the conduct of comprehensive review of currently existing federal programs of research in the area. These activities were to be carried out by the secretary of the Department of Health, Education, and Welfare.[44]

Meanwhile, residents living near the test site (in the tristate area of Nevada, Utah, and Arizona) organized themselves into the Committee of Survivors. Aided by former Secretary of the Interior Stewart Udall, they began filing damage claims against the government for cancer and other health conditions that they believed were caused by radiation from the tests. Twenty-four of these "downwind residents" filed suit in Federal District Court in Salt Lake City (*Allen et al. v. United States*) in August 1979. The trial, which would eventually affect some twelve hundred claimants and prove to be a landmark in the history of federal tort settlements, began on September 20, 1982. It lasted nine weeks and involved 6,600 pages of testimony and twenty crates of evidence. Judge Bruce Jenkins deliberated for another seventeen months before announcing his decision on May 10, 1984.[45]

Concurrently, two other pressure groups were being formally organized. The National Association of Atomic Veterans (NAAV) was founded in April 1979 by former sergeant Orville Kelly, who has since died of cancer. Kelly was commander of Japtan Island at Eniwetok Atoll where he witnessed twenty-two nuclear blasts during the "Hardtack" series conducted in the summer of 1958. Kelly's illness was diagnosed in 1973 and he spent the next six years fighting to gain official government acknowledgement that veterans who participated in the test blasts had been exposed to harmful radiation. The organization, based in Burlington, Iowa, has continued to grow and operate as a lobby group since Kelly's death on June 26, 1980. His widow Wanda serves as its current director.[46]

A second organization was formed in Las Vegas to represent civilians involved in the testing program. In 1978 Bennie Levy, an ironworker, quit his job after twenty-five years at the NTS and began gathering data on the health of people with whom he had worked. Levy had originally constructed steel towers upon which the bombs were perched for atmospheric tests; after the detonation he and fellow workers would retrieve the instrumentation from ground zero. After 1963, he took part in drilling tasks for underground shots. By compiling lists of test site workers who had died of cancer, Levy determined that 18 men out of 3,100 construction-trade employees working in the highly contaminated forward areas of the test site had died of leukemia, a rate of approximately five times the normal.[47] In 1980 he organized the survivors and other test site workers currently suffering from alleged radiation-related illnesses into the Nevada Test Site Radiation Victims Association, headquartered in Las Vegas. By 1981, the association had assisted workers in the filing of 263 suits seeking compensation from the government. The group also has actively lobbied Congress to include workers in their consideration of compensation for downwind residents.[48]

A more broadly based organization which cuts across all these lines was founded in 1982. Established "to provide medical, legal and mutual support to veterans, civilians, and others who were exposed to ionizing radiation," the National Association of Radiation Survivors has joined in a collaborative effort with the aforementioned groups as well as with the Committee of Atomic Bomb Survivors (Hibakusha) and the Uranium Miners Association. Together they have generated scientific studies on radiation effects, appeared in the media on behalf of their cause, testified before Congress, sponsored conferences for concerned parties, and filed tort claims for radiation illness in state and federal courts. The groups have also set up a computer data-bank service for victims seeking additional information on dosage levels, and established a quarterly information newsletter with medical, legal, and legislative updates.[49]

Efforts to gain political support for the alleged victims of atomic testing received an unexpected, and unfortunate, boost when an accident occurred on March 28, 1979, at the Three Mile Island nuclear power plant near Harrisburg, Pennsylvania. In the plant's Unit II a balky valve malfunctioned and set off an intricate chain of mechanical and human failures. The reactor was shut down, but not before some radioactive steam was leaked into the environment. During the early hours, there was concern that a "meltdown" might occur. If that were to have happened, the core could have melted its way through the walls of the reaction vessel, penetrated the floor of the containment structure, contaminated the soil, or hit a water pocket and sent up lethal gushers of radioactive steam.

Potentially, the accident was the most serious ever to occur in the United States. Pennsylvania Governor Richard Thornburgh closed nearby schools, ordered pregnant women and preschool children within five miles to leave, and advised people within ten miles to stay indoors. Plans were made to evacuate from 200,000 to 300,000 residents, but fortunately this action did not become necessary. Although the government and the power company, General Public Utilities, quickly assured the public that amounts of radiation released to the environment were too small to cause concern, the accident got dramatic publicity for several weeks. The extensive media coverage inundated the public with information on low-level radiation and its long-term effects on health. Dr. George Wald, Nobel Prize laureate in biochemistry, and professor emeritus at Harvard, told the world: "Every dose of radiation is an overdose."[50] The accident notably increased the activity of organizations critical of nuclear power and made nuclear safety a common topic of discussion in many American households. As people followed the events of Three Mile Island, they began to question whether there was any difference between this radiation and that from atmospheric testing.[51] Over the next several years, this question would be asked repeatedly in the courts, in Congress, and in the press.

9 *More Likely Than Not*

The Courts' Changing Posture

In the late 1970s, upon learning that they suffered from ailments possibly caused by radiation from weapons testing, many people began to turn to the courts for redress. Their resort to litigation was a relatively new phenomenon on the American political scene. Although the court traditionally has been the accepted arbiter of questions involving negligence, in cases where the government itself is alleged to be responsible for damages the judicial process has not always been available to private citizens seeking compensation. It was not until the passage of the Federal Tort Claims Act (FTCA) in 1946 that Congress granted the people the right to sue the government in tort cases. While this waiver of immunity represented a major concession by the government, certain limitations and exclusions were written into the statute that work in favor of the sovereign state and against the claimant.

The United States inherited the principle of sovereign immunity, or government exemption from suit, from the English common law maxim that the king can do no wrong. As Blackstone described the doctrine in his commentaries on English law, "Whatever may be amiss in the conduct of public affairs is not chargeable personally on the king, nor is he, or his ministers, accountable for it to the people."[1] This proposition was formally recognized in the United States as early as 1821 when Chief Justice Marshall stated in *Cohens v. Virginia:* "The universally received opinion is, that no suit can be commenced or prosecuted against the United States."[2] It was extended in 1869 in *Gibbons v. United States* when the court stated that incorporation of the doctrine perpetuated a historical tradition that "[n]o government has ever held itself liable to individuals for misfeasance, laches, or unauthorized exercise of power by its officers and agents."[3]

As government activities expanded during the twentieth century both in numbers of people and aspects of life affected, arguments were raised against the doctrine of absolute immunity. Some began to feel that the government's denial of consent to be sued, especially in tort, "constitute[d] a patent injustice to bona-fide claimants."[4] Concurrently, others expressed alarm over the mounting work load being placed on Congress to provide, through the passage of private relief bills,

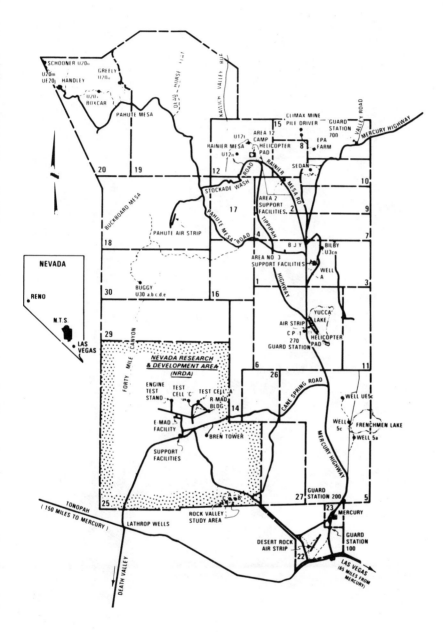

The Nevada Test Site. (Department of Energy map)

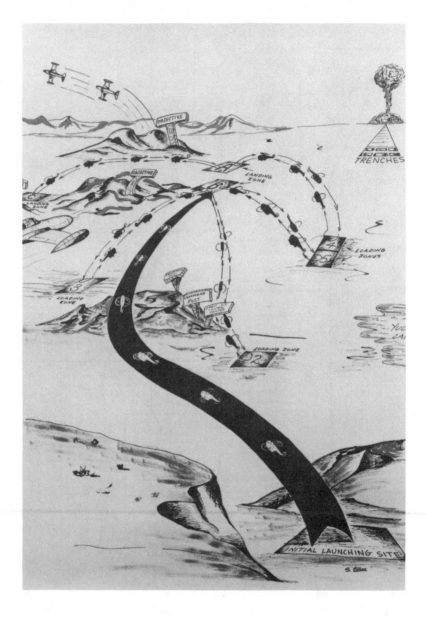

Marines' atomic–maneuvers map, mid 1950s.
(Las Vegas News Bureau)

Soldiers at the Nevada Test Site brushing off
fallout with a broom, March 2, 1955. (Las
Vegas News Bureau)

The press corps observing the twentieth det-
onation from News Nob at the Nevada Test
Site, August 16, 1957. (Las Vegas News
Bureau)

Typical mushroom cloud from an atmospheric
test in the mid 1950s. (Nevada Historical
Society)

An atomic cloud as seen from downtown Las
Vegas. This photograph was picture of the
week in *Life* magazine for November 12, 1951,
and a version of it became a popular postcard.
(Las Vegas News Bureau)

Atomic cloud as seen from the Last Frontier
Hotel on the Las Vegas Strip. (Las Vegas
News Bureau)

Preparing mannequins from Penney's depart-
ment store for use in civil-defense Doom
Town maneuvers, April 4, 1958. (Las Vegas
News Bureau)

Miss Atomic Bomb, selected at the Sands
Hotel, Las Vegas, 1957. (Las Vegas News
Bureau)

Reports about "Geiger counters . . . going crazy . . . may worry people unnecessarily. Don't let them bother you." (From the U.S. Atomic Energy Commission's 1957 book, *Atomic Tests in Nevada*)

"Do not look toward the test site at shot time unless you are wearing dark glasses." (From the U.S. Atomic Energy Commission's 1957 book, *Atomic Tests in Nevada*)

"Our Little A-Bomb," a first-place winner in
the 1953 Western Parade, St. George, Utah.
(From Lions Club souvenir book)

Clark County's official seal during the 1950s,
reflecting the importance of atomic testing at
the time. (From the cover of the Clark County
Budget for 1958–59)

individual remedy for an increasing number of cases; this method of granting compensation was not only inequitable but burdensome and excessive both in cost and delay.[5]

Such concerns led eventually to the enactment of the Federal Tort Claims Act.[6] After previous attempts in 1929, 1940, and 1942, the FTCA was passed by the Seventy-ninth Congress as an integral part of the Legislative Reorganization Act of 1946.[7] A general waiver of government immunity, the law satisfied the two primary criticisms of the existing system: First, it limited the principle of sovereign immunity and provided access to justice for those who had suffered injuries or losses through negligent acts of government employees; second, and more pragmatically, it relieved Congress of having to dispense the only source of relief available to such injured parties.[8]

These objectives were accomplished by granting to the federal district courts, sitting without a jury and subject to the Federal Rules of Civil Procedure, exclusive jurisdiction over claims against the United States for injuries negligently caused by government employees acting within the scope of their employment. The act further provided that the law of the place where the incident occurred would prevail, and that the "United States shall be liable in respect of such claims to the same claimants, in the same manner, and to the same extent as a private individual under like circumstances." It also banned congressional consideration of private bills on any claims recognizable under the statute.[9]

In addition to these provisions, the government was careful to include twelve specific exceptions to the waiver of immunity which it determined necessary for protecting itself from "undue judicial interference." These exclusions listed in section 1346(b) of the statute include losses involving postal matter, claims arising from the assessment or collection of any tax or customs duty, any claim relating to suits in admirality against the United States, and any claim caused by imposition of a quarantine. Also excluded are claims for damages caused by the fiscal operations of the treasury, arising out of combat, originating in a foreign country, or resulting from the activities of the Tennessee Valley Authority and the Panama Canal Company. Other exceptions to the waiver include claims arising under the provisions of the Trading with the Enemy Act and from actions by investigative or law enforcement officers such as false arrest or imprisonment.[10]

The most significant of the exceptions for radiation cases is, however, the "discretionary function" exclusion which relates to claims based upon "the exercise or performance or the failure to exercise or perform a discretionary function or duty on the part of a federal agency or an employee of the government, whether or not the discretion be abused."[11] Its primary purpose is to maintain separation of power among the three branches of government and thereby prevent judicial evaluation of and interference with administrative activities. The exclusion stands even if such activities by a private individual might give rise to liability, or if the statute or regulation authorizing the activity later proves to be invalid. This exception is at once the most sweeping and least definite because its scope depends primarily upon interpretation. Unfortunately, the courts' decisions in cases involving the discretionary function exception have been less than harmonious, leaving the concept poorly defined and with few guidelines for application.[12]

In a number of cases arising since 1946, federal judges have attempted, albeit with little success, to formulate a comprehensive definition of discretionary function. In *Dalehite v. United States* (1953), a class action suit was filed under the FTCA to recover damages resulting from an explosion of fertilizer being produced by the government; three hundred claims amounting to some $200 million were represented.[13] The district court awarded judgement to the plaintiffs, the Fifth Circuit unanimously reversed the decision, and the Supreme Court then upheld the action of the circuit court. The Supreme Court ruled that the negligence that had resulted in the explosion did not subject the government to liability because injuries arose from the exercise of a discretionary function. While the court did not precisely define discretion, it did hold that it included more than the decision to initiate programs and activities and could extend to determinations made by government employees in establishing plans, specifications, and schedules of operations. As Justice Reed stated in the majority opinion: "Where there is room for policy judgement and decision there is discretion. It necessarily follows that acts of subordinates in carrying out the operations of government in accordance with official discretions cannot be actionable."[14]

Two years later, however, in *Indian Towing Co. v. United States,* the Supreme Court modified its position.[15] In this 1955 case, which involved the Coast Guard's negligent operation of a lighthouse, the court ruled that once the government made the decision to operate a lighthouse "and engendered reliances on the guidance afforded by the light, it was obligated to use due care to make certain that the light was kept in working order."[16] By finding that the exercise of discretion by the government ended with the decision to operate the lighthouse, the court clearly limited the broad language in *Dalehite* which had previously extended the scope of discretion to all aspects of a project.

The distinction among kinds of activities included under the exception was further delineated in the 1964 case *United Airlines v. Weiner,* where the Ninth Circuit Court drew up a catalog of discretionary and operational activities.[17] For instance, firefighting is a discretionary judgement while negligence by firefighters is not immune from liability, admitting a patient to a hospital is discretionary whereas treatment is an operational activity subject to suit, and where discretion is involved in establishing air traffic control towers at airports, negligent conduct by controllers is not protected by the exception to the FTCA. In sum, the court was upholding *Indian Towing Company* and attempting to more clearly draw the line between "planning" and "operational" stages of policy-making.

Another caveat was added in 1973 when the Supreme Court ruled in the case of *Doe v. McMillan* that in the consideration of discretionary function cases, there must be a pragmatic judicial balancing between public and private interests. In each case, judges must weigh the harm suffered by the individual against the threat the suit places on effective government.[18] The court determined that in such cases, one must "look beyond the words [of the law] to the context in which a particular person may have been hurt to determine if in that context the cost of that hurt to that person should be borne alone by that person or shared by all for whose benefit the hurt may have been inflicted."[19] While this ruling offered a new guideline by which to consider discretionary function exclusions, at the same time it exacerbated the problem by requiring judges to assess each case *de novo.*

The difficulty of defining the discretionary function exclusion has greatly affected the outcome of atomic testing cases over the years. In the 1956 case *Bulloch v. United States,* District Judge Sherman Christensen upheld the distinction between "planning" and "operational" activities.[20] The Bullochs, a family of sheep ranchers in southern Utah, brought action against the federal government for injuries to their livestock. They argued that the damages were caused by radioactive fallout resulting from negligence by the AEC in exploding atomic weapons near the area where their sheep were grazing. The government argued that employee negligence did not cause damage to the sheep, and that if there were any damages, there could be no recovery in any event as they would be in consequence of the exercise of a discretionary function.

Christensen denied the government's motion to dismiss. He ruled that even though the determination of how and when nuclear tests were to be conducted was within the exception, the government's failure to give notice of an impending detonation to local ranchers could not be excluded:

> That the Government may be liable for the negligence of its agents in failing to warn herders in an area of anticipated fallout of planned detonations known to involve substantial danger to them or their property, I entertain no doubt. Not unmindful of the vital importance of nuclear experimentation to the welfare and safety of our country there yet has been established nothing here that would justify the intentional or negligent endangering of lives or property in the course of the tests. To seek to do so would seem to compromise fundamental human rights for the protection of which our governmental policy is designed. Indeed, while reluctant to broadly concede the point, it was not disputed by counsel for the Government that its responsibility was to so conduct the tests as not to intentionally, wantonly or negligently endanger human lives or private property. Certainly, there was no evidence from which it might be inferred that to do so was within the discretion vested in any officer or agent of the United States.[21]

In 1957, however, the Ninth Circuit Court, using the discretionary function exclusion, barred a claim based on the alleged negligence of a government employee who inaccurately determined the radius of a blast prior to detonation of a nuclear weapon. In this case, *Bartholomae v. United States,* the plaintiff corporation was alleging damages to its buildings located some 150 miles away from the point of the blast.[22] Denying government liability, the court stated that nuclear weapons testing was a program authorized at the highest level for the public benefit, and furthermore, all of the important decisions, from preparation to final detonation, were made at that level.[23]

A similar decision was reached in the 1964 case *Blaber v. United States,* which involved an AEC contract with an independent company to perform experiments using thorium.[24] The claimants, employees of the contractor, were injured when the material exploded while being handled in their laboratory. They charged that the government was responsible for the accident because the AEC had failed to promulgate and enforce adequate safety requirements. The Second Circuit Court disagreed and ruled the government immune for its nonfeasance because the activity of engaging independent contractors was authorized by the enabling statute of the AEC and was thereby within the scope of the discretionary function exception.[25]

By 1967 the court's position had again changed. In *Kuhne v. United States,* the plaintiff brought action against the government for the death of her husband, allegedly caused by the negligence of the AEC while the decedent was working as a civilian electrical engineer for an independent contractor engaged in the production of atomic weapons.[26] The court found that at the time of his employment, the project had advanced beyond the planning to the operational stage and therefore that the government was liable for damages. While an employer is generally not liable for injuries arising from a contractor's behavior, the court stated that in this situation, the government should have a "non-delegable duty of care because of the intrinsically dangerous nature of the activity."[27]

Likewise, in more recent atomic testing cases, the lower courts have ruled that activities at the NTS are not immune from suit under the discretionary function exclusion. Although government lawyers have invariably begun their defense by asking for a dismissal based on this exclusion, district judges have refused to comply. In *Roberts v. United States* and *Nunamaker v. United States* (the Baneberry case), Judge Roger Foley justified his position by referring to the earlier *Bulloch* case. Citing Christensen, Judge Foley wrote in his conclusions of law:

> Thus, the fact the nuclear testing is at the heart of this action does not give rise to any different application of the FTCA. . . . "To hold the Government responsible for certain acts or omissions occurring in the course of nuclear tests would not necessarily visit the Government with novel or unprecedented liabilities contrary to the intent of Congress."[28]

Judge Bruce Jenkins also denied the government's motion to dismiss in the downwind residents suit, *Allen, et al. v. United States.* While Jenkins agreed that the government's decision in 1951 to conduct atmospheric tests in Nevada was a discretionary choice made as "a matter of power and as a matter of right," the conduct of the tests was not:

> The manner in which the tests were conducted, carefully or carelessly, was also a matter of choice but was not a matter of discretion because such operational conduct was subject to a standard, a limitation. That limiting standard to conduct, due care, reasonable care under the circumstances, is called a duty. The person to whom a duty is owed is said to have a right. . . . The duty limits choice and thus denies discretion or its exercise.[29]

Jenkins went on to argue that another reason underlying the government's liability for negligence in this case is that it had a deliberate, publicly stated policy on safety which it did not uphold:

> At no time has the defendant ever asserted that as a matter of conscious choice it deliberately adopted a policy of not warning, not measuring and not educating the populace at hazard.
>
> The United States simply did not make such a conscious choice. At the highest levels of government, in Congress, in the Executive Office, and in the Atomic Energy Commission, public safety was a stated government objective. There was no official policy of indifference to safety.[30]

Finally, citing an AEC internal document dated September 23, 1953, Jenkins pointed out that the commission itself referred to its various safety and public relations activities as "operational." This classification is in contrast to the way the government has characterized such action for purposes of current litigation. In an attempt to have the atomic testing cases dismissed, the government is now claiming that all decisions involving atomic weapons were policy decisions made at the top and should therefore be exempt from challenge under the discretionary function exclusion.[31]

Establishing liability is only the first of several hurdles that atomic litigants have faced under the FTCA. A second is the restrictive statute of limitations written into the law: "A tort claim against the United States shall be forever barred unless it is presented in writing to the appropriate Federal agency within two years after such claim accrues."[32] Atomic plaintiffs did not know the cause of their injuries until relevant information became available during the late 1970s. Furthermore, ailments caused by exposure to low-level radiation can have latency periods of up to thirty years. Therefore, the question for them is when to start the statute-of-limitations clock.

Despite government arguments to the contrary, Judge Jenkins ruled in *Allen* that the clock "commences to run from the point at which the plaintiff's knowledge of his injury and its cause is sufficient to fairly justify placing the burden of inquiry upon him as to its legal consequences."[33] Basing his argument on the 1979 decision in *United States v. Kubrick*, which involved medical malpractice,[34] Jenkins held that "a cause of action accrues [under the FTCA] when the plaintiff knows of the facts of his injury and its cause."[35] In cases such as this in which the injury does not manifest itself until years later, the principle underlying statutes of limitations, discouraging litigation of "stale claims," is not relevant. The claim is not stale; it merely took time to accrue, and according to Jenkins, "Genuine concern about lost evidence, fading memories, and the passage of time are subordinated to a greater concern that legal wrongs be remedied at the first practical opportunity."[36]

Jenkins conceded that the plaintiffs knew in a general way about the ongoing test program at the NTS, that they were somewhat aware of a phenomenon called radiation, and that some may have been cognizant of possible links between radiation exposure and illness. He concluded, however, that beyond these general impressions and suspicions, hard evidence was not readily available. Press coverage of the testing program was positive, AEC reports were reassuring, and scientific opinion was divided and inconclusive. Furthermore, the relationship between cancer and radiation is so complex that Jenkins doubted "whether any layman could reasonably be said to have the requisite knowledge of the causal relationships—particularly during the years prior to the commencement of this action."[37]

The third and most serious barrier to compensation for "atomic victims" under the FTCA is having to establish "proof of causation," showing that radiation "more likely than not" caused their illnesses. Litigants have been fairly successful in demonstrating negligence on the part of the government *(Bulloch, Baneberry)* but proving that damages actually resulted from that negligence has been extremely difficult. Professional commentary has consistently criticized general tort law for failing to recognize and accommodate the unique nature of radiation injuries. In the past, attention focused primarily on the problems of filing claims against private industry, but the difficulties of proving causation are the same for nuclear power plant workers, uranium miners, or today's victims of atomic testing. Exposure to radiation is very different from most tort situations, such as a car collision or a broken ladder, where the cause of injury is more direct, more immediate, and readily observable. It is impossible to establish absolutely a causal connection between radiation exposure and a given case of radiogenic cancer because the clinical features of radiogenic cancer are indistinguishable from the features of other cancers. Modern science cannot isolate a person with radiation-induced cancer from the much larger number of persons who develop cancer for other reasons.[38]

As a result of this difficulty in proving direct causation, claimants are forced to rely on epidemiological evidence to statistically establish that the rate of cancer which occurs among radiation-exposure victims is greater than that which would occur otherwise. There is extensive disagreement within both the scientific and legal communities regarding the validity of epidemiological approaches. Some argue that such evidence merely establishes an association in time and place and "will never give 100 percent proof."[39] Another point of debate is that risk estimates for low dose levels of radiation depend heavily on extrapolation of observable cancer rates corresponding to higher dose levels. Furthermore, epidemiological research is very expensive and time consuming because extensive data must be gathered on a claimant's medical history, employment, genealogy, and possible exposure to other cancer-causing elements; the difficulties are compounded if a long time has elapsed since exposure and/or if the victim is deceased.[40] Faced with such uncertainties, the court is often forced to decide cases by weighing the prospective harm to human health against the social and economic value of the program in question. Such a difficult decision can only be compounded by the fact that the policy in question is one which greatly affects national security.

The decisions reached in both *Bulloch* and *Baneberry* demonstrate the difficulty plaintiffs faced in proving causation. In *Bulloch*, after reviewing voluminous testimony and numerous exhibits, Judge Christensen recognized that the government had indeed been negligent and chastised the AEC for not taking greater precautions:

> There were no advance warnings given or other precautions taken to safeguard the herders or their sheep. There was no suggestion in the evidence of any unexpected developments. Any variables with reference to direction or velocity of winds aloft would seem immaterial since the agents of the Atomic Energy Commission did not attempt to ascertain the location of the sheep with or without reference to any prospective pattern of fallout dependent upon winds. Damage, if any, which did occur from the blasts could well have been anticipated by those in charge of the tests for aught the evidence discloses.[41]

Nonetheless, Christensen ruled against the sheepherders because the government produced evidence indicating that the sheep deaths were not caused by radioactive fallout, but "were the natural result of unprecedented cold weather during the lambing and shearing of sheep, inadequate feeding, unfavorable winter range conditions, and infectious diseases of various types." Lacking evidence to the contrary, which the sheep ranchers were unable to provide because most of it had been classified by the AEC, the judge ruled: "The great weight of evidence indicates, and I find, that the maximum radioactive doses, were well within the permissible maximums for human or animal body tolerance." The action was dismissed on the merits.[42]

Some thirty years later, after evidence had been uncovered during congressional hearings about AEC activities during the period of atmospheric testing, the plaintiffs asked the court to set aside the earlier judgment. Still on the bench, Christensen heard testimony in May 1982 on the case that led him to conclude that the government had used "improper means" that were "unacceptable as part of the judicial process" and that "clearly and convincingly demonstrate a species of fraud upon the court for which a remedy must be granted even at this late date." He vacated the 1956 judgment, ordered the government to pay court costs of about $120,000, and scheduled a new trial.[43]

The Tenth Circuit Court in Denver heard the case in the fall of 1983 and struck down Christensen's finding. The court stated: "We have considered this carefully . . . and must conclude that nothing was demonstrated which would constitute fraud." They further accused Christensen of "abuse of discretion" and suggested that the ranchers' defeat in 1956 was perhaps more attributable to their own attorney than to any government misconduct. According to the court, reports that may have assisted their case were available at the time of the original trial. It was also noted that the only thing that had changed since 1956 was the growing public awareness of the dangers of radiation and in the court's determination, this was no reason to overturn the previous decision.[44] Nonetheless, six months later in April 1984, the Tenth Circuit granted a reargument of the case before the whole bench. Almost a year passed before the arguments were again presented on March 14, 1985. Unfortunately for the ranchers on May 22, 1985, the court, by a vote of five to two, once again ruled in favor of the government. The plaintiffs filed a petition for *certiorari* before the United States Supreme Court, but the court refused to hear the case, thereby upholding the Tenth Circuit's ruling.[45]

The problem of causation also prevented the *Baneberry* plaintiffs from receiving any damage payments from the government. After years of postponement, their trial began in January 1979. Represented by Larry Johns, the claimants relied heavily on epidemiological evidence and expert testimony from the scientific community to establish a link between exposure to radiation from the venting accident and subsequent death from leukemia. Judge Foley ruled on June 8, 1982, that the government had indeed been negligent on two accounts—in the manner in which persons were evacuated from Area 12 after the accidental venting occurred, and in the attempts to decontaminate persons who had been exposed to radiation.[46]

The plaintiffs' victory was short-lived, however. Seven months later on January 20, 1983, Judge Foley ruled against granting compensation to the widows. Referring to their epidemiological evidence as "experimental, speculative, and lacking in credible medical support," he stated: "The burden of proof relative to dose and causation is upon the plaintiffs to establish by a preponderance of evidence that the dose of radiation received did, to a reasonable degree of medical certainty, cause the leukemias from which Roberts and Nunamaker died. Plaintiffs have not met this burden of proof."[47] On May 4, 1984, the claimants filed a motion to either reopen the case or hold a new trial to allow them to present additional evidence about radiation doses which became available as a result of the *Allen* decision. Judge Foley refused to modify his earlier decision, again stating that the dosage levels were too low to have resulted in leukemia.[48]

Judge Jenkins also grappled with the difficult causation problem in the *Allen* case. From the beginning, he acknowledged that "the factual connection singling out the defendant as the source of the plaintiff's injuries and deaths is very much in genuine dispute . . . complicated by the nature of the injuries suffered, the nature of the causation mechanism alleged, the extraordinary time factors and other variables involved in tracing any causal relationship between the two."[49] He went on to state, however, that although "the injury is not specifically traceable to the asserted cause on an injury-by-injury basis," this does not end the injury:

> That the court cannot now peer into the damaged cells of a plaintiff to determine that the cancer or leukemia was radiation-induced does *not* mean (1) that the damage was not in fact caused by radiation; (2) that the radiation damage involved did not result from the defendant's conduct; or (3) that a satisfactory factual connection can never be established between plaintiff's injury and defendant's conduct for purposes of determining liability. Experience and the evidence in the record indicate that indeed it can.[50]

Jenkins defended his argument by citing previous cases in which the plaintiff successfully established "factual connections" rather than direct proof. In *Bolger v. Chris Anderson Roofing Co.,* a New Jersey court ruled in favor of a claimant who was occupationally exposed to fumes from tar, pitch, asphalt, and asbestos in "large and intense volume" over a period of years. Noting that the chemicals were known carcinogens, the court found that exposure had contributed to the injury, notwithstanding the fact that the claimant had also smoked cigarettes.[51] Likewise, in *Smith v. Humboldt Dye Works, Inc.*, a Workmen's Compensation award was affirmed on the basis of "substantial evidence that the plaintiff's twenty-five years of exposure to known carcinogens was factually connected to his papillary tumors in the bladder."[52] In *Bressner v. Walter Kidde Nuclear Labs*, the court again affirmed a Workmen's Compensation award, ruling in favor of the physicist who had contracted acute myeloblastic leukemia after working in a laboratory near cobalt 60 sources from which he received radiation exposure.[53] In the most recent case, *Krumback v. Dow Chemical Company*, the Colorado court remanded to the state industries commission a claim in which compensation had been denied to an employee of the Rock Flats nuclear weapons plant. The commission reviewed the case and reversed its decision, concluding that "said radiation was the proximate cause of the cancer of the colon which resulted in death."[54]

While Jenkins presented an elaborate argument in behalf of relying on factual causation in such cases, he did not presume a causal relationship from the government's negligence. To the contrary, he noted that "in these cases, the factual details of the immediate environment out of which the case arose must be shown with considerable particularity." It will then be up to "the finder of fact—this court—to draw the most appropriate inference using the court's own best judgement, experience and common sense in light of all the circumstances."[55]

Doing just that, Jenkins ruled in favor of only ten of the twenty-four litigants. He held the government liable for eight cases of leukemia, one of breast cancer, and one of thyroid cancer, and awarded $2.66 million to be distributed to the claimants in sums depending on their particular losses.[56] "As to the remaining plaintiffs of the bell-weather group of 24, this court concluded as a matter of law that the evidence is insufficient in each instance to demonstrate with the requisite weight that the defendant's negligence proximately caused the conditions of which each complains."[57] In response to Jenkins's ruling, the government appealed the case to circuit court, and a decision is expected in summer of 1986. Until a final decision is reached, no compensation can be awarded.

Originally, test site workers faced a fourth barrier to compensation not encountered by the downwind residents.[58] A "sweetheart agreement" between the federal government and the state of Nevada signed in 1956 provided that any employee claims for radiation injury arising from activities at the NTS would be considered by the Nevada Industrial Commission (NIC); if payments were rendered, they would be reimbursed by the AEC. This in effect denied test site workers access to the courts as a means of seeking redress because under Workmen's Compensation law, the *quid pro quo* for employers who contribute to the fund is immunity from suit. The responsibility for initial deliberation of employee claims is transferred from the court to a specially created administrative body, in this case the NIC.

This arrangement was recently negated by a ruling from Judge Foley in the case of *Prescott v. United States* when the claimant sued REECo, an AEC contractor, for damages. The case involved Keith Prescott, an operating engineer who worked at the test site from 1961 to 1968 and subsequently contracted cancer of the bone marrow. On September 9, 1981, Judge Foley denied REECo immunity from suit and ruled that the original sweetheart arrangement between the AEC and the NIC was invalid. According to Judge Foley, the contract was "void under Nevada Revised Statute 617.190 which prohibits modification or waiver of liability and did not constitute voluntary acceptance of coverage as provided in Nevada Revised Statute 617.200." Because no contributions were ever made by the AEC or REECo to the state Workmen's Compensation fund, Foley ruled that there was no coverage for radiation injuries provided by the NIC during the period of Prescott's employment; therefore, he had a right to sue both his immediate employer and the federal government for damages.[59] This decision, upheld by the Ninth Circuit Court of Appeals in San Francisco on April 25, 1984, would allow test site workers to sue AEC contractors and have their claims heard in the courts before a jury rather than "going through the almost hopeless workmen's compensation hearings."[60] However, Congress has subsequently taken action which overrides Judge Foley's rulings, as will be discussed in Chapter 10.

The difficulty of gaining compensation is even greater for soldiers exposed to radiation from atmospheric testing than for either civilian workers or downwind residents.[61] The *Feres* doctrine, a precedent set by the Supreme Court in 1950, interprets the FCTA exclusion of claims for damages arising out of combat as precluding the government from liability for "injuries to servicemen when the injuries arise out of or are in the course of activity incident to service."[62] The *Feres* doctrine resulted from three cases which were consolidated because all three involved a serviceman or his representative seeking recovery for injuries sustained while on active duty and caused by the negligence of others in the armed forces. In *Feres v. United States,* the negligence alleged was that the Army had failed to maintain adequate fire protection and had quartered the deceased in barracks which were unsafe because of faulty heating devices.[63] *Jefferson v. United States* involved a plaintiff who underwent abdominal surgery while in the army; still having problems eight months later, he underwent a second operation during which the surgeon removed a towel marked "Property of United States Army" from his stomach. The plaintiff alleged that the towel had been left there negligently by the army surgeon.[64] And in *Griggs v. United States,* unskilled medical treatment by an army surgeon which resulted in death was the action in question.[65] In all three cases, the Supreme Court denied recovery under the FTCA.

Scholars and politicians alike, including Democratic representative Emanuel Celler of New York, who drafted the FTCA, have argued that this strict interpretation was not the intention of Congress. Instead, the law was meant to exclude claims by soldiers only for injuries arising out of wartime combat. Nonetheless, the court established and has continued to uphold this doctrine based on three main rationales. First, it has been argued that the doctrine is necessary because the relationship between soldiers and the government is "distinctly federal in character" and should not be hampered by the application of varying state tort laws. Second, the courts have stressed that judicial interference in such matters would undermine critical military discipline. Finally, the doctrine has been justified in terms of the existence of a comprehensive system of benefits and compensation already available to servicemen through the Veterans Administration.[66]

Although the rationale for the doctrine is questionable, the court has reaffirmed *Feres* as recently as 1977.[67] Consequently, servicemen and veterans have been forced to develop new legal theories by which to overcome the problem of military immunity. One strategy followed by atomic veterans has been to circumvent the FTCA and bring a cause of action against individual officers and Defense Department officials alleging that these individuals denied them their constitutional rights by exposing them to dangerous substances without notice. This approach, however, has been unsuccessful. In the 1979 case, *Jaffee v. United States,* it was alleged that the plaintiff, along with other soldiers, was ordered to stand in an open area near the explosion of an atomic bomb without any protection against radiation exposure.[68] The plaintiff further alleged that the explosion caused the soldiers to be exposed to massive doses of highly dangerous radiation which government officials realized but nonetheless deliberately compelled the soldiers to endure without their consent or knowledge of the danger. Finally, the plaintiff charged that because of his exposure he had developed cancer. This, Jaffee contended, was a deliberate violation of his rights guaranteed by the first, fourth, eighth, and ninth amendments to the Constitution.[69]

Although Jaffee did not bring his action under the FTCA, the court still based its conclusion on the *Feres* doctrine. Denying recovery under the Constitution, the court stated that this basis for recovery would interfere with the jurisdiction and procedure of the VA and the important military function of protecting the country. In sum, the doctrine of sovereign immunity barred relief. The case was then remanded to the district court for consideration of Jaffee's personal monetary claims against specific officials. Again, the court ruled in favor of the government, noting that the protection of *Feres* extends to individual officers as well as the government at large.[70]

Veterans have also attempted to overcome military immunity by using the postservice tort, which involves a claim for injuries which were "caused after" discharge even though the original injury occurred during service.[71] The first case to allow recovery for such a claim was *Brown v. United States* in 1954.[72] Brown was injured while on military duty and later, after his discharge, treated at a VA hospital. The VA doctor negligently harmed Brown during the surgery, for which Brown sued the government. The Supreme Court ruled in favor of Brown, allowing him to recover for the injuries caused by the doctor after discharge even though the injury that had precipitated the surgery occurred during active military duty. The court also ruled that Brown could collect both VA benefits for this inservice injury and damages in tort under the FTCA for injuries caused by the government's negligence which occurred after his discharge.[73]

The first nonmedical malpractice claim to apply the postservice tort was *Thornwell v. United States* in 1979.[74] Thornwell, an army private stationed in Germany, was injected with LSD for the purpose of determining the utility of the drug in interrogations. Since that time, he has suffered severe mental illness and physical pain. Thornwell did not learn the details of the experiment until seventeen years later, at which time he filed suit against the government for failing to provide followup medical treatment and to inform him after his discharge that he had been given LSD. The court ruled in favor of Thornwell, recognizing a cause of action for this separate tort of failure to warn.[75]

Since *Thornwell*, several veterans have attempted to use that decision as a precedent to recover for injuries caused by exposure to radiation. The courts' responses have been varied, and the current state of the law remains undefined because most of the relevant cases have yet to reach the appellate stage. In *Lombard v. United States,* the Eighth Circuit Court distinguished between intentional, such as in *Thornwell,* and nonintentional actions and denied recovery to a veteran because his exposure to radiation was in the course of duty and not part of an intentional experiment.[76] But, in *Lasswell v. Brown,* the Eighth Circuit Court expressly rejected the postservice tort using the *Feres* doctrine. Lasswell, during service in the Navy, was stationed at Eniwetok where he witnessed three atomic explosions and later built an airstrip less than a mile from ground zero. He alleged that he was exposed to radiation that resulted in Hodgkin's disease.[77] Likewise, the district court in Pennsylvania denied recovery in *Kelley v. United States.* In this case, the court did not reject outright the notion of a postservice tort but ruled instead that there was no separate tort for the failure to warn. The court found no difference between the failure to warn Kelley before he was exposed to radiation from testing in the South Pacific and the failure to warn him after he was discharged.[78]

In two more recent cases, the courts have allowed for possible recovery for atomic veterans using the postservice tort approach. In *Everette v. United States,* the plaintiff brought charges against the government for her husband's wrongful death allegedly caused by exposure to radiation when he was forced to march through a nuclear blast area less than one hour after detonation.[79] The court admitted the possibility that the purpose of the maneuver was to determine the effect an atomic explosion could have on troops and, as in *Thornwell,* held that the failure to inform Everette of his exposure and its possible consequences was a separate tort for which he could seek recovery.[80] The Ninth Circuit Court took a different approach in the 1981 case *Broudy v. United States.*[81] The complaint filed by Major Broudy's widow alleged that his participation in atomic maneuvers resulted in cancer. The court held that Mrs. Broudy could recover damages only if she could prove that the military learned of the dangers of radiation after her husband was discharged and that the military's failure to warn him caused further injury.[82]

Another potential victory was won by atomic veterans on May 7, 1986, when U.S. District Judge Marilyn Patel in San Francisco certified a "class" of atomic veteran plaintiffs to challenge a $10 limit on attorney fees in veterans' disability claims. Judge Patel had declared the 1864 law that established the fee limitation unconstitutional in June 1984, but her decision was overturned by a Supreme Court vote of 6 to 3. This time around, rather than attacking the fee cap as unconstitutional on its face, the plaintiffs alleged it to be unconstitutional as applied specifically to atomic veterans because of the complexity of their claims. Judge Patel agreed. Assistant U.S. Attorney George Stoll commented, however, that the decision would create mounds of what could become needless work: "Everyone will have to diddle with class discovery when so far no one has established any right to relief."[83]

Regardless of which strategy a veteran follows in his attempt to overcome the precedent of military immunity, it must be remembered that winning the right to sue the government is merely the first step. Like all atomic litigants, he must also meet the challenges of a giant opponent in the courtroom. From the outset, claimants suffer disadvantages in gathering information upon which to base their claims. Much of the needed data on weapons testing remains classified and thereby unavailable to the public. Even under the provisions of the 1974 amendments to the Freedom of Information Act, the process of acquiring such material is both difficult and time consuming. Furthermore, there exists a distinct conflict of interest problem in that most of the studies of radiation effects and all the records of dosage levels upon which the claimants are forced to rely are compiled by, and must be obtained from, the very agency, or one of its subsidiaries, which is the opponent in the case.

Finally, the government has much greater resources available with which to build a case than do the plaintiffs. Scores of lawyers have been hired to research and represent the government's position, and an information clearinghouse has been established by a DOE contractor in Las Vegas to consolidate archival data and provide the government with needed material for its case. The Justice Department's head lawyer on the *Baneberry* case, William Elliott, told a newspaper reporter when asked how much the government was spending to defeat the plaintiffs, "As much as it takes to win."[84] Consequently, citizens have begun to seek help through channels other than the courts.

Time to Build 10
a Monument

Legislative Approaches to
Compensation of Alleged Victims

In recent years, frustrated by delays and unfavorable rulings from the courts, many atomic-victim groups have turned to Congress for assistance. Their lobbying efforts are directed toward two goals: first, they want official recognition that the government made mistakes; and second, they seek either to modify the Federal Tort Claims Act so as to remove barriers to successful prosecution of their suits, or to establish a new administrative compensation program similar to the VA's. As is its wont, Congress has responded by calling for further investigation into the matter. Accordingly, several sets of special hearings were conducted during the Ninety-sixth and Ninety-seventh Congresses in an attempt to gather more data on the activities of the AEC during the era of atmospheric testing. These hearings eventually led to the introduction of various compensation bills, most of which died in committee. There have been a few minor successes, however, which, while falling short of providing outright compensation, have chipped away at the government's claim to immunity.

The first response of Congress to the question of atomic compensation involved hearings conducted by the House Subcommittee on Public Health and the Environment in January 1978. These hearings, discussed in Chapter 8, were spearheaded by Congressman Tim Lee Carter, and dealt specifically with the participation of American soldiers in atomic testing maneuvers at the NTS. The information revealed was shocking and soon prompted other committees to look further into the many questions being raised about exposure to radioactive fallout.[1]

Perhaps the most significant of these additional inquests was held during the spring and summer of 1979 before the House Subcommittee on Oversight and Investigation of the Committee on Interstate and Foreign Commerce, chaired by Democrat Bob Eckhardt of Texas. Four days of hearings were conducted: on April 19 in Salt Lake City, April 23 in Las Vegas, and May 24 and August 1 in Washington, D.C. The first hearing was conducted jointly with the Senate Subcommittee on Health and Scientific Research of the Committee on Labor and Human Resources and the Committee on the Judiciary. As chairman of both these Senate bodies, Democrat Edward Kennedy of Massachusetts soon became heavily involved with the issue. Based on detailed testimony and the examination of complex scientific data never before revealed, the subcommittee reached several important conclusions which virtually reversed the previous position of the government in this matter.[2] These conclusions have formed the basic arguments for all subsequent radiation-compensation legislation introduced in Congress.

First, the subcommittee concluded that the federal government had been negligent during the atmospheric testing of nuclear weapons at the Nevada site. During the hearings, numerous in-house AEC memos demonstrated that, although its members were aware of potential health hazards, the AEC perceived its primary goal as the development of atomic weapons, and that its actions reflected that priority. It was shown that the AEC failed to give residents living downwind from the test site adequate warning regarding the dangers of radioactive fallout, sufficient notification of upcoming test blasts, or necessary information on how to protect themselves from radiation exposure. The subcommittee also found that the radiation monitoring system used during testing was deficient for accurately measuring estimates of exposure dosages, and furthermore, that the government had falsely interpreted and reported the radiation exposure rates it recorded in order to give a lower assessment of the hazards of fallout.[3]

Second, the subcommittee concluded that exposure to fallout from the atmospheric tests in Nevada was, more likely than not, the cause of adverse health conditions suffered by many downwind residents. Reviewing the findings of a number of recent scientific studies, including the CDC report on Smoky veterans,[4] and Dr. Joseph Lyon's study of children living in southern Utah during the fifties,[5] the subcommittee found significant evidence of higher-than-normal incidence of leukemia and thyroid cancer among the radiation victims. Testimony from the scientific community also pointed out that symptoms of radiation damage can take up to thirty years to appear.[6]

Third, it was concluded that the deaths of some 4,400 sheep lost in Nevada and Utah during the summer of 1953 were attributable to nuclear fallout from the Upshot-Knothole test series, and that, therefore, the ranchers should be compensated for their losses. Substantial documentation from the files of AEC veterinarians assigned the task of investigating the sheep deaths in 1953 revealed that the government not only disregarded data linking the losses to radioactive fallout, but also fabricated the agreement between the AEC and various health officials which discounted radiation as the cause of the deaths.[7]

The fourth and perhaps most important conclusion reached by the subcommittee was that some type of legislative compensation program was needed, because, as discussed in the previous chapter, the existing avenues for seeking compensation for radiation exposure under the Federal Tort Claims Act are fraught with legal difficulties.[8]

Although the subcommittee's conclusions were fairly extensive, they failed to address several crucial aspects of the fallout issue. In the first place, they were limited in geographic scope; they focused only on atmospheric testing at the Nevada site, with no investigation into the test blasts in the South Pacific, nor any discussion of the postbomb cleanup operations in Japan. The hearings were also restrictive in that the subcommittee was concerned only with fallout from atmospheric testing, excluding any consideration of the potential danger of radiation leakage from venting during underground testing after 1963. Finally, the hearings dealt primarily with the problems of downwind residents who lived near the test site; no attention was paid to either civilian test site workers or troops who participated in training maneuvers during the tests.

In the meantime, however, on June 20, 1979, the Senate Committee on Veterans Affairs, under the chairmanship of Senator Alan Cranston of California, held its own hearing on veterans' claims for disabilities from nuclear weapons testing. Testimony was received from representatives of such groups as the military, the AEC, the VA, and the NAAV, as the panel looked more closely into the questions raised by Congressman Carter a year and a half earlier. Shocking accounts of troops marching to ground zero within an hour of a test blast were recorded, as well as reports that many soldiers wore no radiation measurement badges or protective gear of any kind. It was also pointed out that soldiers face an even greater difficulty than civilians in charging the government with negligence in radiation cases because of the *Feres* doctrine.[9]

Despite general acknowledgement by these various congressional committees of the legal obstacles facing atomic victims, the national legislature, like the courts, has done little to provide them with alternate routes to compensation. In the past, Congress has deliberately avoided action which would expand environmental law beyond prevention to include compensation. While Congress has enacted numerous laws mandating the elimination or control of pollutants believed to cause illness, in only a few cases has it acknowledged that environmental agents created abnormal, compensable conditions. In 1964, Congress appropriated $950,000 to be distributed among those Marshall Islanders who developed thyroid cancer as a result of being exposed to radiation from the 1954 Bravo-test blast,[10] and in 1969, Congress established a compensation fund for coal miners afflicted with "black lung."[11] In 1976, the Senate approved a third compensation program, for Michigan residents exposed to PCBs in their food following a 1973 incident in which livestock feed was contaminated, but that program never passed the House.[12]

Similarly, in the matter of nuclear power, Congress in the past has been willing to impose certain regulations on the employment of radioactive materials but, with the exception of the Bravo incident, it has failed to consider the needs of individual victims. Originally, the matter of safety was left specifically to the AEC to determine and regulate. Then in 1957, Congress passed the Price-Anderson Act as an amendment to the Atomic Energy Act of 1954, establishing a compensation and indemnification program for financing public liability claims against the nuclear power industry "in the event of a catastrophic nuclear accident."[13] Basically, the act provides for three sources of compensatory funds: First, liability insurance for up to $160 million is available; second, each licensed nuclear power plant will be assessed a $5-million retrospective fee for each nuclear accident; and third, government indemnity of the nuclear industry in an amount currently limited to $50 million is also mandated. Renewal of this act and adjustment of its provisions to meet the demands of high-level waste disposal are currently under consideration by the Ninety-ninth Congress.[14]

The compensatory provisions of the Price-Anderson Act, however, are undermined by its other stated objective, "to protect the nuclear industry against unlimited liability if such an event were to occur."[15] In the absence of a catastrophic event, plaintiffs must sue under common tort law in order to obtain recovery. Even for plaintiffs harmed as a result of an "extraordinary nuclear occurrence," the act fails to resolve many of the problems they will face in seeking compensation. Plaintiffs must demonstrate cause in fact and their claims are limited to only those ailments which become evident within twenty years after exposure. Furthermore, certain problems such as genetic injury and shortening of life, which have been scientifically linked to radiation exposure, are "presently [in]adequately cognizable in American courts as giving rise to liability."[16] Finally, the statute refers only to damages caused by accidents in the privately owned nuclear power industry; there is absolutely no coverage provided for people harmed by radiation from government-sponsored atomic weapons testing.[17]

Compensation programs for environmentally induced health disorders have been rare for several reasons. First, there are evidentiary problems unique to alleged cases of environmental illness. Many such illnesses may result from multiple factors, or they may have decades-long latent periods between exposure and illness; consequently, victims have difficulty in proving a direct cause-and-effect relationship. A second problem is cost; compensating an unknown number of victims could run into billions of dollars, and the government is no more anxious than industry to shoulder such a burden. Finally, in the past, compensation programs have lacked a unified base of support; environmental groups have usually regarded prevention and cleanup as more urgent priorities than compensation programs, which they have often considered "parochial" issues. Powerful industrial lobbies, on the other hand, have consistently been a formidable opponent to such programs.[18]

Despite recent concerted efforts by various victims' groups to overcome these obstacles, Congress has maintained its position of leaving the business of compensation to the courts. For instance, in 1979 under the direction of President Carter, Congress enacted P.L. 96-510 which created a "superfund" to clean up toxic contaminants spilled or dumped into the environment. Congressman John LaFalce, Democrat from New York's Love Canal district, led a movement to extend the scope of the bill to include compensation for victims injured by chemical accidents, but the final version contained no such provision.[19] In a similar action, Congress passed P.L. 97-72, amendments to the Veterans Health Care, Training and Small Business Loan Act of 1981. This act provided medical care eligibility for Vietnam veterans exposed to herbicide defoliants and authorized the VA to expand its epidemiological study of the health effects of Agent Orange. No compensation package per se was included, however; instead, the statute leaves it to the VA to determine, on an individual-case basis, whether the veteran's ailment was caused by exposure to the chemical.[20]

It is not surprising, then, that although several members of the Ninety-sixth Congress introduced atomic compensation bills in the wake of these special hearings, none became law. In the House, Democrat Gunn McKay of Utah introduced H.R. 4766 on July 12, 1979, to "amend title 28 of the U.S. Code to make the United States liable for damages, arising from certain nuclear tests at the Nevada Test Site, to individuals residing for a year or more in the affected area and having cancer, to individuals present at the test site during a particular blast, and to certain sheep herds."[21] Edward Kennedy introduced a companion bill in the Senate, S. 1865, which also included uranium mine workers. Both bills acknowledged government liability for damages, but they did not establish a compensation program per se—they simply required that the courts waive the "cause in fact" requirement when hearing radiation cases under the Federal Tort Claims Act. Neither bill received much attention, and both bills died in committee at the end of the session.[22] During this same period, Congressman Carter introduced H.R. 8278 on October 2, 1980. This bill called for an amendment to Title 38 of the U.S. Code to make certain veterans eligible for wartime disability compensation for ailments attributable to exposure to atomic radiation during their period of active service. It too died in committee.[23]

The question of compensation of atomic testing victims became an even greater issue during the Ninety-seventh Congress. Although Congressman Carter did not return for another term in the House, his atomic veterans bill was reintroduced on February 5, 1981, by Democrat Norman Mineta of California.[24] Several other bills relating specifically to atomic veterans were also introduced but failed to pass out of committee before the end of the session.[25] One substantial gain was made for atomic veterans, however, when Congress passed P.L. 97-72. In addition to providing medical eligibility for Vietnam veterans exposed to Agent Orange, the bill contained an amendment introduced by Senator Cranston which recognized the potential problems of veterans exposed to fallout from atmospheric testing. The amendment extended medical care eligibility under the VA to veterans "whose disabilities could be linked to service-connected exposure to nuclear weapons test radiation."[26] This in effect eliminated the requirement that, in order to be eligible for benefits, soldiers must place their claims for service-related injuries within one year of the time they leave the service.

When the amendment was first introduced, the Department of Defense expressed opposition. In a letter dated September 4, 1981, William Taft, general counsel for the department, wrote to the chairmen of the Committees on Veteran Affairs in the House and Senate: "The amendment . . . creates the unmistakable impression that exposure to low-level ionizing radiation is a health hazard. This mistaken impression has the potential to be seriously damaging to every aspect of the Department of Defense's nuclear weapons program." Senator Cranston's response was entered into the *Congressional Record* on October 16. Noting that there are some eighty thousand published articles on the cancer risks of low-level radiation exposure, the senator concluded: "For the record, therefore, let me state clearly that these suggestions in the Department of Defense letter are, in my view, absurd!"[27] The passage of the Cranston provision was significant because it reflects official congressional recognition that soldiers may have been seriously injured during their participation in atomic testing maneuvers. Nonetheless, the value of the legislation itself remains primarily symbolic. Under the law, the VA maintains the authority to make the final determination in radiation injury cases and it has proven to be less than sympathetic. Of several thousand claims submitted to date, fewer than twenty have been awarded.[28]

A more encompassing radiation compensation bill, S. 1483, was introduced on July 14, 1981, by Republican Senator Orrin Hatch of Utah.[29] Playing on the public's emotions, he announced the bill's introduction in highly dramatic terms:

> A great wrong was committed by the Federal Government in exposing thousands of Americans to radioactive fallout while simultaneously conducting a massive campaign to assure the public that no danger existed. . . . There are now many innocent suffering victims of the mistakes made by government officials over two decades ago. . . . We must make sure that it does not happen again, and make certain that those who have suffered, and those who still suffer, will receive just compensation.[30]

Over the next four years, Hatch would continue to receive considerable publicity for his efforts to push a compensation program through Congress.

A revised version of Senator Kennedy's bill from the previous Congress, Hatch's new Radiation Compensation Act of 1981 required the secretary of Health and Human Services, within sixty days of enactment, to publish a list of types of cancer that may be related to radiation exposure. It also mandated the development of epidemiological tables reflecting the statistical probabilities that various doses of radiation caused a given cancer; this was to be completed by the Department of Health and Human Services within a year of enactment. The bill further authorized suits for damages against the federal government by individuals (or their heirs) with radiation-related cancer diagnosed after January 1, 1952. To assist in these suits, the bill provided for the release of federal records related to the testing program in Nevada, permitting private examination by the court of the still-classified materials. Finally, S. 1483 authorized payment of damages to anyone who could demonstrate a "probability of causation" of at least 10 percent that his cancer was caused by fallout from the Nevada testing program. This payment was to range from $50,000 to $500,000, with the amount prorated to reflect the individual's probability figure.[31]

Overall, S. 1483 called for a legislative compensation program which departed from existing court approaches in two controversial ways. First, it recognized radioepidemiological evidence as proof of "cause-in-fact" that a plaintiff's ailment had resulted from radiation exposure. And, second, the bill provided for the compensation of anyone with an "attributable risk" factor of 10 percent or higher, thus setting a much lower figure than the standing legal definition of causation, which is 51 percent ("more likely than not").

As chairman of the Committee on Labor and Human Resources, Senator Hatch conducted three sets of hearings (on October 27, 1981, March 12, 1982, and April 8, 1982) at which testimony from all sides was heard. Speaking on behalf of S. 1483 were frustrated victims, who felt that the government has a moral responsibility to admit its error and try to amend it, and members of the scientific community, who attested to the validity of epidemiological research. Opposition to the bill came primarily from the administration, especially the Departments of Energy and Defense and the VA, whose arguments were reminiscent of AEC statements from the previous decade. Their reasons for opposing S. 1483 included: (1) the need for further research into the health effects of low-level radiation; (2) the increased financial burden that would be placed on the federal government by this type of compensation program, for which so many could qualify; (3) the dangerous precedent being set for further negligence cases; (4) the replication of benefits which were already available through the VA; and (5) the threat to national security.[32]

Despite the administration's opposition, S. 1483 cleared the Labor Committee on April 20, 1982, by a vote of fourteen to one, with Republican Senator Dan Nickles from Oklahoma casting the sole negative vote.[33] It was then referred to the Committee on the Judiciary, chaired by conservative Republican Senator Strom Thurmond of South Carolina who had replaced Ted Kennedy when the Republicans won control of the Senate in 1980. No action was taken on the bill, and so it died there at the end of the session. Republican Congressman Dan Marriott of Utah introduced a companion bill, H.R. 6052 in April 1982. It too died in committee.[34]

The fate of S. 1483 was not surprising. Even if this radiation compensation bill had been passed out of the committees, it was not likely to have been enacted into law before Congress adjourned its

Ninety-seventh session. Not only did S. 1483 need more time, but it lacked a strong, consolidated base of support. Despite strong sentiment in Congress that the government had been negligent and should compensate victims of atomic testing, there was almost no agreement on how this should be accomplished. Furthermore, it was an election year, and many legislators seeking another term opted to duck the controversial issue.

With the primary exception of Senator Hatch, there was little Republican endorsement of the bill, because it contradicted presidential policy in two ways: Funding a special project to benefit a relatively small number of people conflicted with the "Reaganomics" approach to fighting inflation through the reduction of federal expenditures, and criticizing the Pentagon's nuclear testing program appeared to undermine the administration's defense policies.

The Democrats, on the other hand, were typically divided over the issue. Some saw S. 1483 as Hatch's bill, and therefore did not support it for partisan reasons. Others felt that S. 1483 was too limited—it had been restricted to such a point that few people would actually be compensated, it did not include soldiers or workers exposed to radiation from "venting" during underground testing after 1963, and it did not cover possible radiation-related illnesses other than certain specified cancers. "Bollweevils," conservative Democrats who generally vote Republican, followed the president's line, and still others saw the bill merely as a pork barrel program which did not affect them or their constituencies to any great extent.

Those legislators who did support the measure—including several representatives from the "affected area"—for the most part merely signed on as cosponsors, without actually pushing for the bill's passage or making it a major campaign issue back home. This was certainly true of senators Paul Laxalt of Nevada and Jake Garn of Utah, both Republicans. Democratic Senator Howard Cannon of Nevada was placed in a somewhat different position. He supported the measure on moral grounds as evidenced by his remarks in the *Congressional Record* following its introduction: "The individuals exposed under the Radiation Exposure Compensation Act of 1981 are no less deserving [than the victims of the Bravo shot in 1954] of some compensation for the tragedy, illness, and death caused in large measure by the cavalier attitude of the Atomic Energy Commission."[35] On the other hand, he was conservative in matters of defense and had been a long-time supporter of the testing program. Furthermore, his political strength was based in southern Nevada, which continued to have strong economic ties to the test site. Consequently, his actions concerning the bill were mixed; while doing little to push for the bill's enactment, he was successful in getting test site workers added to the bill's list of eligible recipients of compensation.

The question raised by the defeat of S.1483 was why the government had been willing to compensate the Marshall Islanders and the Japanese fishermen but not its own citizens who were also exposed to radiation during testing in the South Pacific and later in Nevada. The government's steadfast response to this repeated query has been two-fold. First, the unique nature of the Bravo incident is emphasized: The accident involved only one test shot rather than a series of tests over an extended period of time, it affected a specific isolated population, all of whose members could readily be identified, and it presented a problem of one-time, high-level exposure as opposed to long-term, low-level dosage, the consequences of which are less well known. Second, government scientists argue that the immediate connection between radiation exposure and thyroid illness, the malady affecting most of the Bravo victims, has been more clearly established by the medical profession than the link between radiation and other cancers or birth defects, which many of the current litigants are alleging they have today as a result of exposure.

There are other reasons, although not officially articulated, for the government's seeming inconsistency in the matter of atomic compensation. In 1954 the United States was under much greater international pressure to compensate the Bravo victims than it is today to compensate its own citizens. Under the stipulations of the trust agreement the United States was legally obligated to provide for the health and security of the islanders. With regard to Japan, the United States was already in an awkward position, having bombed the country in 1945. This new tragedy, again involving a *pikadon,* as the Japanese called the atomic bomb, revived the anguish of Hiroshima and Nagasaki and aroused spontaneous, universal indignation.

It should also be noted that the government was able to compensate these first (and only) acknowledged victims quickly, quietly, and relatively inexpensively. The $2 million given to the Japanese in 1954 received little news coverage at home, as did the Bikini Compensation Act of 1964, which was passed during a time when attention was focused on urban riots, the Democratic National Convention, and the Vietnam War. Enacting a similar compensation program today to include civilians and soldiers alike would be extremely difficult: It would attract considerable attention, would involve thousands of people and could cost the government millions of dollars, and it would be highly controversial. It could also open the door for victims of other harmful environmental agents employed by the government, such as Agent Orange.

Although S. 1483 failed, one small portion was salvaged when Senator Hatch attached it as a rider to the Orphan Drug Act, which was subsequently passed by the lame-duck Congress on December 17, 1982. The amendment required the Department of Health and Human Services to develop statistical tables on the occurrence of various kinds of cancer among different groups of people exposed to fallout from atomic tests. These epidemiological tables were to be completed and turned over to Congress in January 1984.[36]

The Ninety-eighth Congress made little attempt to compensate the downwinders, supposedly awaiting the results of the mandated study. Few held much hope, however, that the tables would resolve the controversy which was by now a highly political matter rather than simply a scientific debate. Ron Preston, top aide to Senator Hatch, commented that the "Jane Fonda nuclear scientists" on the side of the victims would consider the figures too restrictive, while the "mainstream scientists" working for the government would find them too lenient.[37] Nonetheless, Hatch reintroduced the bill (S. 921) on March 24, 1983.[38] Now referred to as the Radiogenic Cancer Compensation Act, the proposal was submitted to the Judiciary Committee where no action was taken pending the release of the tables. In the end, the tables were not completed until after the session closed, so Hatch's bill again died in committee.

The same Congress took other actions, however, which had a major impact on the fate of alleged atomic victims. One was decidedly negative, the other two positive. The adverse action came as the result of a little-noticed provision inserted by Republican Senator John Warner of Virginia as an amendment to the Defense Department authorization bill signed by the president on October 19, 1984. At the request of the administration, the amendment made the government, rather than defense contractors, the sole defendant in all pending and future lawsuits involving atomic weapons testing:

[Suit against the federal government] shall be exclusive of any other civil action or proceeding for the purpose of determining civil liability arising from any act or omission of the contractor without regard to when the act or omission occurred. The employees of a contractor . . . shall be considered employees of the Federal Government . . . the civil action or proceeding shall proceed in the same manner as any action against the United States . . . and shall be subject to the limitations and exceptions applicable to those actions.[39]

In effect, this amendment did two things. First, it left veterans with no one to sue. Unlike the Agent Orange veterans who could sue the chemical companies that manufactured the dangerous substance, under Warner's amendment, atomic veterans have no comparable fallback position.[40] Under the *Feres* doctrine, they cannot sue the government, and now they cannot sue any of its contractors involved in the atomic testing program. When questioned about his amendment, Senator Warner claimed, "I would not have done this if I hadn't been assured by the Departments of Justice and Energy that veterans who can show a link between cancer and atomic tests are being compensated through the administrative process."[41]

The second negative implication of Warner's amendment is that it negated Judge Foley's *Prescott* ruling which allowed test site workers to sue AEC contractors under ordinary civil proceedings. Civilian employees, like downwind residents, were now back to square one in their fight against the inherent difficulties of the Federal Tort Claims Act. There was talk of challenging the constitutionality of the amendment on the grounds that it is *ex post facto* in two respects: It includes pending as well as future cases, and it retroactively extends protection to all actions regardless of when they occurred.[42]

Meanwhile, Congress moved in the opposite direction with the passage of P.L. 98-558 in October 1984.[43] This bill, primarily aimed at extending programs under the Head Start Act, contained a provision to appropriate funds to "establish cancer screening and research facilities for people who lived in the path of fallout from open-air atomic weapons tests." More particularly, the bill allocated $6 million to be used to establish a cancer screening clinic in St. George and up to $4 million in federal matching funds to pay for a cancer research center at the University of Utah in Salt Lake City.[44] When the president signed the bill into law on October 30, Senator Hatch told the press: "Finally the government is making real progress to help out the people who took the fallout from a hundred nuclear tests. For more than three decades, U.S. presidents had failed to aid these patriotic Americans."[45] Interestingly enough, Ron Preston, when commenting the previous year on the unlikelihood of getting an atomic compensation bill through Congress, observed, "It's time to build a monument."[46] Certainly these cancer research centers represent such a monument. Establishing the centers is a positive act in the sense that the government is finally doing something to recognize and help atomic victims, but it may prove to be negative in the long run if it serves, as monuments often do, to substitute symbol for substance and preempt the drive for direct financial compensation.

In late 1984, Congress also passed P.L. 98-542, the Veterans' Dioxin and Radiation Exposure Compensation Standards Act. Designed primarily to assist veterans exposed to Agent Orange in Vietnam, the measure also provided benefit payments specifically for veterans who could show they suffered from certain ailments as a result of exposure to ionizing radiation in connection with above-ground nuclear weapons tests and with the American occupation of Japan.[47] The regulations promulgated in accordance with the act, released September 25, 1985, set out the criteria that must be met by claimants in order to establish a service-connected disability; these included providing evidence of exposure to at least five rads of radiation. The soldier's gender, family history, and age at time of exposure, in addition to the extent to which other factors, such as smoking, might have contributed to the development of the disease, were also considered in determining eligibility. Twenty-two diseases, mostly cancers, were recognized as radiogenic for the purposes of compensation.[48] But in *Combee v. Brown* in 1994, the court ruled that the VA did not have the authority to adopt an exclusive list of radiogenic diseases.[49] In response, the bill was amended in 1995 to allow consideration of any disease; if the disease is not on the list, however, the veteran must submit scientific evidence that it is radiogenic before consideration is given to his or her claim.[50]

The mandated Health and Human Services study was finally released in late February 1985. A 355-page report, it contained data on fourteen types of cancer possibly linked to radiation. Extensive tables showed the percentage of likelihood that cancer victims of all ages exposed to various doses of radiation could link the cause to fallout. Prefacing these tables, however, was a disclaimer that "even after cancer has developed, we cannot state with certainty whether it was caused by radiation."[51]

Little of consequence occurred in the Ninety-ninth Congress. Hatch announced that he would hold special hearings to go over the HHS report, but no action was taken. Indeed, Preston's earlier fears that the HHS findings would do little to change the position of any of the parties involved on either side of the issue were confirmed. Once again, political and personal concerns prejudiced interpretations of the scientific evidence in this debate over government culpability. Accordingly, Hatch continued to reintroduce his compensation bill while the various administrative agencies—VA, DOE, and the Department of Defense—continued to oppose its enactment.

Similarly, a new atomic veterans' relief bill, sponsored by Senator Paul Simon and Congressman Lane Evans, both Illinois Democrats, made little headway. Introduced on February 18, 1985, S. 707 would have expanded the list of illnesses for which radiation-exposed veterans could file for health assistance. It would also have extended VA health insurance to cover "genetically damaged" children of atomic veterans. The VA opposed the bill, arguing that no conclusive proof exists to link the diseases with the nuclear tests.[52] Meanwhile, the House passed a measure in May 1986 that would have overturned Warner's amendment denying individuals the right to sue private contractors who conducted the nuclear tests, but it died in the Senate.[53] This lack of progress was not surprising, however, given the Republican-controlled Senate, a conservative promilitary mentality dominating the political scene, and a personally popular president leading the opposition.

The failure of Congress to enact relief legislation during this session, after nearly a decade of considering the matter, was a major setback for atomic victims. While there were too many forces at work for the issue to disappear, time was clearly on the side of the government. As the years passed, many victims had begun to lose hope or simply die off; sympathetic lawyers eventually looked for more lucrative cases; interest groups ran out of steam; and plaintiffs' families ran out of money. Continuing the struggle against an opponent with unlimited resources seemed a daunting task at best as the country looked ahead with uncertainty to the next decade.

The nineties can be characterized as a period of transition, for the world at large and for the Nevada Test Site. The dramatic shift in the international balance of power that occurred during the last decade of the twentieth century brought with it a corresponding transformation of American atomic policy, both at home and abroad. When the threat of communism ceased to exist, the U.S. found itself with no archenemy and no challenger left standing at the end of a forty-year arms race. And the NTS, long a key player in that race, was suddenly faced with new challenges that meant major adjustments if it were to survive.

These imperatives arose rather quickly, set off by a chain reaction of events in the Soviet Union that no one could have anticipated. In 1985, Premier Mikhail Gorbachev instituted two new policies, glasnost and perestroika, which opened his nation's society and economy to outside influences. By the time of the Soviet legislative elections in 1989, many new faces were in power and the communists were on the run. Within two years, the old Soviet Union had ceased to exist, having broken apart into fifteen republics. On December 8, 1991, the treaty founding the Soviet Union was dissolved, and on December 25 Gorbachev resigned, leaving Boris Yeltsin as president of the Russian Federation. The old Soviet arsenal was dispersed among four republics—Russia, Belarus, the Ukraine, and Kazakhstan.[1]

The American foreign policy response to these developments included two major actions directly related to the Nevada Test Site. First, the United States entered into an extensive weapons agreement with the four nuclear republics. START I, or the First Strategic Arms Reduction Treaty, reduced the U.S. inventory of intercontinental nuclear bombs and missiles from more than 12,000 to fewer than 9,000 and downsized the combined former Soviet force from 10,000 to some 6,500. The U.S. Senate ratified the treaty by an overwhelming vote of 93 to 6 on October 1, 1992.[2]

START II, based on a subsequent agreement between Presidents Bush and Yeltsin, was ratified on January 26, 1996, by a similar vote of

87 to 4. It would further reduce nuclear arsenals to 3,500 warheads each in the United States and in the four former Soviet republics combined, and would eliminate ICBMs with multiple warheads by the year 2003. Russian lawmakers finally approved the treaty on April 14, 2000, by a 288 to 131 vote. This action marked a victory for newly elected President Vladimir Putin and his centrist majority in the Duma. In his announcement, Putin commented that Russia did not want to be dragged into a new global arms race, but he warned that the country would withdraw from all existing agreements if the United States attempted to amend the 1972 Anti-Ballistic Missile Treaty to allow limited missile defense systems.[3]

During the same period, Congress also passed legislation suspending nuclear weapons testing. Motivated by statements from Boris Yeltsin reiterating his country's commitment to a testing moratorium, the 102nd Congress suspended testing until July 1993. They allowed for up to five tests per year after that point, with testing to be halted altogether on September 3, 1996. The bill began in the House under the leadership of Les Aspin (D-Wisconsin), chair of the Armed Services Committee. The vote there, taken on June 6, 1992, was 198 to 168, with most of the opposition coming from Republicans. Likewise, when the Senate voted on August 8, the Republicans opposed passage; of the 68 senators in favor, only 17 were from the GOP, although one of the moratorium's most vocal champions was Mark Hatfield (R-Oregon).

The entire Nevada delegation, three Democrats and one Republican, voted against the measure. Although their arguments were couched in terms of national security (Senator Reid stated that testing was needed to deter Third World nations from developing their own nuclear weapons), their primary concern was over the potentially detrimental impact that a moratorium could have on the state's economy.

The Bush Administration had opposed a moratorium from the start, but the president was prevented from vetoing it by public opinion at home and political events abroad. When it finally reached his desk, in the form of an amendment to the Energy and Water Development Appropriations Act (P.L. 102-377), he signed it on October 2, 1992.[4] The last critical test conducted in Nevada was "Divider" on September 23, just days before START I and the moratorium went into effect. Preparations for "Ice Cap" and "Mighty Uncle," tests planned for the summers of 1993 and 1995, respectively, were put on hold, despite millions of dollars already expended.[5] After Bill Clinton was elected president, he announced on July 3, 1993, that he would continue the moratorium through September 1994 as long as no other nation tested. On March 15, 1994, he extended the moratorium again through September 1995 and eventually held it in place throughout his eight-year administration. During this time, he pushed for the conversion of the military to an appropriate post–Cold War machine and the adoption of a comprehensive test-ban treaty.[6]

Against the backdrop of these international developments, various victim groups continued to pressure Congress for recognition and compensation. Finally, after decades of denying culpability, Congress began to respond with the enactment of provisions that went beyond the symbolic to provide substantive relief. As Representative Wayne Owens (D-Utah), a former lawyer for the downwinders, commented, "It seems so appropriate as we have watched and wondered over the demise of the Cold War that we compensate the victims of the Cold War."[7]

Over the years, dozens of compensation bills have been introduced. The movement was led primarily by representatives from Utah, home of most downwinders, but it also involved lawmakers from Nevada whose constituents included Test Site workers; Representative Morris Udall (D-Arizona), whose brother, former Secretary of the Interior Stewart Udall, was the attorney for the uranium miners; and a number of veterans' advocates, including Representative Lane Evans (D-Illinois) and later Senator Paul Wellstone (D-Minnesota).

A major step was finally taken on the eve of the new decade when Congress passed P.L. 100-321, effective May 1, 1988. It is not surprising that the measure applied to veterans only, because the precedent for compensating them had already been set in 1984 and the political need to take care of our fighting forces was naturally more acute than the need to address the alleged problems of a handful of civilians. Known as the Radiation-Exposed Veterans Compensation Act (REVCA), the bill, introduced by a physician, J. Roy Rowland (D-Georgia), resulted from numerous complaints by veterans that it was extremely difficult, if not impossible, to prove a service-connected disability under the 1984 law. REVCA, as amended and broadened in two subsequent sessions, establishes a presumptive link between veterans' exposure to radiation and the subsequent development of any of fifteen types of cancer. Claimants no longer have to prove that they were exposed to a sufficient amount of radiation to cause disease; with the presumption of a service-connected disability, they only have to demonstrate exposure to ionizing radiation as a result of participating in the nuclear tests in the South Pacific and Nevada or in the U.S. occupation forces in Japan.[8]

The House vote on the original bill was 326 to 2. It met stronger opposition in the Senate, where Strom Thurmond (R-South Carolina) commented that it "sweeps too broadly." Senator Tom Daschle (D-North Dakota) responded, "How long will we wait . . . ? Will we wait until all these veterans are dead?" The vote on April 25 was a close 48 to 30; those voting in favor included 38 Democrats and 2 Republicans, while 28 Republicans and only 2 Democrats were opposed. Of those absent, 8 were Republicans, making President Reagan's threatened veto potentially override-proof. In the end, however, the president signed the bill on May 20 after colon cancer, a commonly occurring illness, was removed from the list of compensable diseases.[9]

The VA reports that as of April 1998, 19,885 veterans and survivors had filed radiation-related compensation claims. Of those, grants had been awarded to 1,408 atomic veterans, including 1,057 soldiers involved in atmospheric testing and 351 GIs in Japan, including prisoners of war.[10] Because the number receiving compensation is relatively low, subsequent bills have been introduced by Wellstone (S. 1385 in 1998) and Evans (H.R. 1286 in 1999) to expand the list of diseases covered by the presumption to include lung, bone, skin, ovarian, and rectal cancers, among others.[11] Currently, veterans with these illnesses are eligible for compensation under the 1984 law, but they must prove causation by "dose reconstruction estimates."

The VA opposes expansion of automatic coverage and argues that "blanket presumptions . . . would be vastly over-inclusive. . . . The more responsible policy is to afford claimants case-by-case determinations based on the individual merits of their unique cases." Advocates, however, counter that accurate records were not kept; files have been lost; and access to classified information was denied, thus making it impossible for veterans to pursue their claims effectively. "Our nation failed to keep the records of the exposures of our atomic veterans," said Representative Evans. "They should not suffer for that neglect."[12] At the end of the century, Evans's bill was still being debated and seemed unlikely to pass the 106th Congress.

A critical shift occurred in 1990 when Congress moved beyond its focus on veterans to acknowledge that civilians too had been harmed by U.S. nuclear policies of the past. After more than a decade, Senator Hatch succeeded in pushing the Radiation Exposure Compensation Act (RECA) through Congress. Although initially opposed to this policy, President Bush signed the bill into law with little fanfare on October 15, 1990, as he traveled on board Air Force One to Dallas to campaign for Republicans. His released statement further reflects his general lack of enthusiasm for the bill: ". . . [it] will fairly resolve the claims of people who believe they contracted cancer. . . ."[13]

RECA created a compensation program administered by the Justice Department through which lump-sum payments were to be awarded to two distinct atomic victim groups. Uranium miners who had worked in underground mines between 1947 and 1971 and had developed lung diseases were eligible for $100,000 each. Down-winders—people living in specified counties downwind from above-ground testing at the Nevada Test Site in the 1950s and early sixties who had developed certain types of cancer—could receive payments of $50,000 each. If the victim had since died, his or her survivor was entitled to the compensation payment. In addition, the law apologized to the victims on behalf of the country, conceding for the first time that the U.S. government had been negligent in its actions.

The law was amended just days later, on October 26, to include on-site workers who had participated in the above-ground testing program. The amendment resulted from a compromise negotiated by Representative James Bilbray (D-Nevada), a member of the House Armed Services Committee. The Justice Department strongly opposed Senator Harry Reid's amendment to the Defense Authorization bill repealing the 1984 Warner amendment, passed in the wake of the *Prescott* ruling, which had extended sovereign immunity to protect private weapons contractors from suit. The administration argued that repealing the prohibition would create a "bottleneck of cases." By agreeing to leave the Warner amendment in place, Bilbray was able to gain support for adding certain Test Site workers to the compensable groups recognized in RECA.[14]

The Justice Department developed appropriate regulations for administering the program, and the first appropriation of $100 million was authorized in late November 1991. Commenting on the relatively low lump-sum payments, Representative Owens stated, ". . . the settlement is really more of a compassionate payment rather than a payment for damages." As such, it did little to assuage grief, placate anger, mete out justice, or restore a community's faith in Washington. As one reporter summarized the views of downwinders, the money was "too little, too late, and too grudgingly given to fill the void left in their lives by the deaths of parents and children whose only sin was to be in the wrong place at the wrong time."[15]

Since the enactment of RECA, the Justice Department has approved 3,135 claims worth nearly $232 billion. The program has been criticized, however, for its "burdensome" procedures and "excessive regulatory hurdles," making it "easier to compensate a dead miner than one living with disease." This led western senators Hatch, Ben Nighthorse Campbell (R-Colorado), Pete Domenici (R-New Mexico), Jeff Bingaman (D-New Mexico), and minority leader Tom Daschle to introduce amendments to the 1990 law (S. 1515). Their proposal would streamline and expedite the application process as well as broaden the list of compensable diseases to mirror those covered in REVCA. It would also add those sickened by working in open-pit uranium mines to the list of individuals eligible for compensation and establish a $20-million grant fund for state, local, and tribal outreach programs to identify and assist radiation victims. It is estimated that the cost of the change would be $1 billion over the next twenty-one years. These amendments passed the Senate on November 19, 1999, and the House on June 28, 2000, making more than nine thousand additional downwinders eligible for compensation.[16]

As the House considered the RECA amendments in the spring of 2000, the Clinton Administration made a dramatic announcement. On April 12, Secretary of Energy Bill Richardson unveiled a proposal to compensate all of the men and women who had fallen ill as a result of exposure to radiation and toxic substances while working to build America's nuclear defense. This reversed a decades-old government practice of opposing workers' claims that their illnesses resulted from hazards associated with designing, testing, and building nuclear weapons. The program, which requires approval of Congress, would compensate more than three thousand workers from DOE facilities at Hanford, Oak Ridge, Savannah River, Nevada Test Site, Rocky Flats, Pantex, Lawrence Livermore, Los Alamos, and Paducah, Kentucky. It would provide a lump sum benefit of $100,000 or a package of benefits including lost wages, medical expenses, and job retraining. And of great significance is the proviso that if adequate information about the amount of radiation that workers were exposed to is not available, the DOE will assume that they were exposed to the highest amount of radiation associated with the tasks they performed.[17] A bill to implement and fund the proposal was introduced in Congress on May 9 by Senator George Voinovich (R-Ohio) with Nevada Senators Reid and Bryan, among others, listed as cosponsors. The program is estimated to cost $120 million annually over the first three years, declining to about $80 million per year as the backlog of claims is reduced. A companion bill was introduced in the House by Representatives Ed Whitfield (R-Kentucky) and Ted Strickland (D-Ohio).[18]

There is considerable support for these measures, and rhetoric abounds about their passage being a heroic step in the right direction. Senator Reid, however, cautioned that it will be difficult to move the legislation through the Congress before adjournment. "It's late in the session and a lot of things can come up," he said. This is especially true in an election year. Nonetheless, on June 8 the Senate added the measure as an amendment to the 2001 defense authorization bill, increasing the lump-sum payment to $200,000. The defense bill is expected to pass, but it is being slowed by fights over campaign finance, health care, and other unrelated issues. Meanwhile, in the House, the Republican leadership sought to substitute a nonbinding resolution urging members "to tackle the problem" instead of voting on the actual bill because of disagreements over who should pay for the plan, the DOE or the DOD. Congresswoman Shelley Berkley (D-Nevada) criticized this maneuver, commenting, "We are duty bound to protect the workers who are now suffering horrific illnesses because of services they performed for their country."[19] Although it may take a while to enact the program, it will be impossible for the government to reverse its position acknowledging what nuclear workers have alleged since the *Baneberry* case.

Meanwhile, following the precedent set by Congress with REVCA and RECA, the Nuclear Claims Tribunal of the Marshall Islands, established in accordance with Section 177 of the 1985 Compact of Free Association, developed its own presumptive approach to compensation. The tribunal was originally authorized to issue regulations establishing criteria for medical conditions that are irrefutably presumed to be the result of the nuclear testing program. However, numerous officials and experts during the early years advised the tribunal against making any such presumption; instead, they recommended that the tribunal follow the precedent set by the courts in radiation-damage cases by requiring proof of causation or, at least, a demonstrated probability that a compensable medical condition was the result of an individual's exposure. Unfortunately, the only reliable information about exposure levels forthcoming from the U.S. government was for those whom the U.S. had admitted exposing on Rongelap and Utrik atolls during the "Bravo" shot of March 1, 1954. This left thousands of islanders with no proof of exposure and no hope for compensation.

Once REVCA and RECA passed, the tribunal likewise changed its personal-injury compensation policy. The presumptive approach was seen as both filling the need for an efficient, simple, and cost-effective program and recognizing the difficulties of individual proof of causation. Drawing from the downwinder legislation, which covered some fifteen counties totaling more than 83,000 square miles in Nevada, Utah, and Arizona, the tribunal decided there was ample justification for including all the Marshall Islands and atolls in the program's "affected area." Furthermore, the total yield of the tests conducted in the Marshall Islands was approximately 93 times the total of the Nevada atmospheric tests, making the likelihood of damage from radiation that much greater.

The new compensation policy was implemented in August 1991 and included twenty-five specific diseases. In late 1993, two more conditions were added to the list. Another review of the list was conducted during 1995–96. Based largely on findings by Dr. Edward Radford, former chair of the National Academy of Sciences Committee on the Biological Effects of Ionizing Radiation, in a study on the incidence of solid cancer, the tribunal added seven new presumed medical conditions in 1996. Bone cancer was added in 1998, bringing the total to thirty-five, considerably more than recognized by REVCA or RECA. As of April 30, 1999, the tribunal had made net awards of $67.7 million to, or on behalf of, 1,613 Marshall Islanders.[20]

When the atomic victims finally achieved a measure of justice, relief came in the halls of Congress, not through the courts. But it can certainly be argued that it was litigation that let the genie out of the bottle. The atomic cases put the issue on the national agenda; made the public aware of the situation; opened doors to heretofore secret information; presented arguments that were too credible to be ignored; and, in defeat, gave Congress the justification it needed to overturn precedent and compensate the victims. These litigants and their attorneys truly laid the groundwork that allowed Congress to act.

As discussed in chapter 9, the court for years sided with the federal government in atomic cases, with only a few exceptions, based either on sovereign immunity or lack of proof of causation. These decisions were usually handed down rather tersely with little editorial comment from judges. That began to change in the 1980s, however, as overwhelming and irrefutable evidence of damages began to mount up. When Stewart Udall lost the *Begay* case involving uranium miners in federal court in Phoenix, Judge Copple admitted that the case clearly called out for compensation to be provided to the victims, but that in this instance, the government could not legally be held liable.[21] Upholding his decision in August 1985, the Ninth Circuit Court stated, "We agree with the district court that this is the type of case that cries out for redress, but the courts are not able to give it; Congress is the appropriate source in this instance."[22]

Similarly, in the Tenth Circuit's reversal of Judge Jenkins's *Allen* decision in April 1987, Judge McKay gave Congress the additional ammunition it needed. He recognized that indeed "the people who designed the downwind safety program deviated from optimum practices based on the best available scientific knowledge" and that such deviations "would clearly support liability for injury under standard test analysis." He also conceded that the departures were "the proximate cause of suffering and death from cancer in many of the plaintiffs." Nonetheless, he concluded that the discretionary-function exclusion "put compensation for injury ... beyond our power to order." He went on to say, "while we have great sympathy for the individual cancer victims who have borne alone the costs of the AEC's choices, their plight is a matter for Congress."[23]

This set the stage for Congress to intervene on behalf of the victims. Advocates could now argue that the government had undeniably brought harm to its own citizens who, having exhausted all other possible remedies, had nowhere to turn but Congress. This admission of guilt, which is always difficult for any government, was made more palatable for some members by the winding down of the Cold War and the decline of the nuclear imperative. Such action also fit with the national penchant for righting old wrongs, which seemed to pervade Washington during this period. In the summer of 1988, for example, Congress also passed H.R. 442, which awarded $20,000 each to approximately sixty thousand surviving Japanese Americans who had been placed in internment camps during World War II.[24]

Specific aspects of other atomic cases are reflected in the various compensation bills passed by Congress. Both the *Baneberry* and *Prescott* cases can be credited with bringing the problems of Test Site workers into the equation, as well as for expanding the list of illnesses for which compensation could be granted. Both cases lasted for over a decade and kept the issue on the agenda. The *Baneberry* case, which involved a 1970 venting, went to court in 1979 and was finally resolved in 1995 after the two victims, their widows, presiding federal judge Roger Foley, and a primary witness, Shields Warren of the AEC, had all died.[25]

When asked how it felt to be a hero in this long battle for compensation, the lawyer for the two Test Site–worker cases, Larry Johns, responded modestly, "Every group needed its champions. The miners had Udall; the downwinders had Dale Haralson; and we were just there for the Test Site workers. We did it because we care about this community. We have lived here since the days of atmospheric testing. We remember it, as witnesses and residents."[26] His brother and partner in the cases, Alan Johns, added, "I always say that we won. We forced the government to lift the cloak of secrecy, to open up a lot of records. Although the courts did not decide in our favor, much of what we were trying to accomplish has been put into place. It's just unfortunate that it took so long and that so many people had to die along the way."[27] A *Las Vegas Sun* editorial following the Ninth Circuit's final ruling in the *Baneberry* case agreed with Johns's assessment: "But the families [of Nunamaker and Roberts] can take some satisfaction in knowing that, without their patient efforts, the dangers of fallout and other radioactive exposure would not be public knowledge."[28]

Indeed, during the last twenty years of the century, as a result of these court cases, the claims of victims' groups, and the legislation itself, the American public became increasingly aware of the dangers of radiation and more interested in the country's nuclear history than ever before. Not since testing went underground in 1962 had atomic bomb stories so dominated the news. Just as the initial detonation of the A-bomb shook the foundations of our belief system and drastically impacted our culture, spawning books, movies, songs, and fashions, the previously untold stories of the atomic victims quickly captured and held the public's attention through the eighties and into the nineties. Their influence was certainly less dramatic and less pervasive than that of the bomb itself, but they are worthy of note because they revived the nation's interest in "atomorabilia" and reflected a general shift in attitude from support to suspicion of the country's atomic policies.

During the early days of the atomic victims movement, in addition to the barrage of press coverage, a rash of popular books appeared, written primarily by journalists and victims themselves chronicling the activities of the AEC during the era of atmospheric testing. These authors also made the talk-show circuit, often recounting tales of horror about their personal atomic experiences. Such stories, with their combined elements of intrigue and tragedy, captivated the American public and press.[29]

Later, scholars grew interested in the topic and produced more balanced, better researched, less sensational works that appealed to a more limited audience. DOE itself sponsored two "official" histories, one on safety within the Manhattan Project and the other on the story of the Hanford facility.[30] A conference devoted to "The Atomic West" drew historians to the University of Washington in September 1992, where they read papers on western communities' close and often secret relationships with the federal government. Likewise, the Nevada Humanities Committee sponsored a 1995 lecture series entitled "Nevada in the Nuclear Age." Both events culminated in edited publications.[31]

Fiction writers also capitalized on the public's renewed interest in nuclear themes. Martin Cruz Smith's spy novel, *Stallion Gate,* and Joseph Kanon's provocative murder mystery, *Los Alamos,* both set in New Mexico in the 1940s, became best sellers. Pulitzer Prize–winning author Robert Olan Butler also used Los Alamos as a backdrop for his novel, *Countrymen of Bones.* Less well known was *Golden Days* by Carolyn See, which *Time* called "an adventuresome blend of feminist fiction and nuclear apocalypse fantasy set in California." And Umberto Eco even published a nuclear children's book, *The Bomb and the General.*[32]

Several movies produced during these years also built on atomic settings. Unlike many of their predecessors, however, they were often critically acclaimed but did not become big box-office hits. *Desert Bloom,* starring Jon Voight and JoBeth Williams, juxtaposed a young girl's loss of innocence with that of a nation as both watched the mushroom cloud on the horizon. *Nightbreakers,* starring Martin Sheen, a frequent protester at NTS, told the story of an atomic veteran stationed in Nevada during the fifties, as did *Blue Sky,* with Tommy Lee Jones and Jessica Lange, but from the lonely wife's perspective. *Atomic Café,* a popular documentary that played at art houses around the country, featured a collage of old newsreel clips and civil-defense film excerpts played against a soundtrack of atomic songs from the forties and fifties. *Mulholland Falls,* with a cast led by Nick Nolte, used protection of radiation secrets at the Test Site as a motive for murder. *Testament,* starring Jane Alexander, was an admirably understated drama about a small town contending with nuclear holocaust, and *Fatman and Little Boy,* named for the two bombs dropped on Japan, featured Paul Newman as General Leslie Groves and fairly accurately depicted life inside the Manhattan Project.

Nor was television left out of this atomic revival. The television movie *Day One,* based on the book by Peter Wyden and starring Brian Dennehy as General Groves, offered a less theatrical, more documentary-like look at the Manhattan Project than its big-screen counterpart. *The Day After,* about the chilling after-effects of the fictional nuclear bombing of Lawrence, Kansas, was probably the most controversial television movie of its time; written by Edward Hume, it played to large viewing audiences and became a newsworthy event itself. *Trinity and Beyond,* produced by Peter Kuran, the animator for *Star Wars,* aired on the Discovery Channel; this 95-minute documentary, narrated by William Shatner of *Star Trek* fame, featured previously classified film stock only recently released by the DOE. And a modernized remake of the classic movie *On the Beach* aired on HBO in June 2000, starring Armand Assanti and Rachel Ward.

Other artists were also drawn once again to atomic themes. Peter Goin, an NEA Artists Fellow and professor of photography at the University of Nevada, Reno, produced *Nuclear Landscapes,* a book of photographs taken with DOE permission at the NTS. Carole Gallagher's book *American Ground Zero* is a similar photographic essay with pictures, not of places but of people. Photographer Robert Beckman took a slightly different approach in his show, "The Body of a House," which featured slides from movies of civil-defense tests conducted at the NTS during the fifties. And a number of personal scrapbooks of pictures from Los Alamos appeared, including one compiled by Enrico Fermi's granddaughter.[33]

In the music world, the eighties and early nineties brought a virtual explosion of atomic references.[34] Not only did dozens of groups take names laced with nuclear imagery (Atomic Gods, Atom Kraft, Smithereens, Overkill, Megadeth, Nuclear Assault, Ned's Atomic Dust Bin, and Nuclear Test Band), but the theme was found in many different types of music, including pop, folk, punk, new wave, reggae, ska, and heavy metal. Popular artists, as well as little-known niche groups, released nuclear songs: Prince in "1999" seems resigned to nuclear war; Sting took up the theme in "Russians" and "Walking in Your Footsteps"; Robbie Robertson wrote "Showdown at Big Sky"; Culture Club released "The War Song"; REM addressed the subject in "It's the End of the World as We Know It"; and the Dead Kennedys had several nuclear songs, including "Kill the Poor" and "When Ya Get Drafted." Other atomic songs from this era include "Civil Defense" by the FUs, "Nuclear Future" by Cryptic Slaughterhouse, "The Last Test" by Atomic Gods, "Atom Bombs" by KIX, "Atomic Tan" by the Clash, "Nuclear Attack" by Greg Lake, "No Nuclear War" by Peter Tosh, "Manhattan Project" by Rush, and "Christmas at Ground Zero" by Weird Al Jankovic. Even dancing seemed to reflect the new nuclear culture; one observer noted, "People throw themselves wildly at each other like atoms, then ricochet like dynamic clusters of light-emitting diodes in a human video game."[35]

By the mid-nineties, most of the hoopla surrounding the victims of atomic weapons testing had died out. As Jonathan Schell wrote, "In the first years of the post Cold War period, the nuclear peril seemed to all but disappear from public awareness."[36] The Cold War was over; our nuclear arsenal had been reduced and a moratorium placed on testing. Furthermore, REVCA and RECA were in place to compensate the victims of testing, so in effect their story was over. That is not to suggest that the public was not still concerned about government cover-ups and the dangers of radiation, but rather the focus of their attention had shifted. There was a new set of victims to read and exclaim about: records released in 1993 by DOE Secretary Hazel O'Leary in an attempt to be more open with the public indicated that thousands of individuals had been used by the government over the years as guinea pigs in radiation experiments, including pregnant women in Utah, retarded children in Massachusetts, and prisoners in Oregon.[37] Coincidentally, as Congress continued to fight over how and where to build a high-level repository, nuclear waste began to replace nuclear weapons as a more relevant and therefore more salient issue for alarm.[38]

The end of the nuclear arms race impacted weapons facilities across the country. As Congress, with the DOE's cooperation—albeit reluctant at times—moved to close doors and make amends for actions of the past, other doors were being forced open. The new, daunting challenge was how to adapt the nation's nuclear weapons facilities to a post–Cold War world. On the one hand, politicians were hesitant to possibly let down their guard by dismantling a national security system that could be credited with winning the Cold War; they feared mothballing the plants lest they be needed again. As Senator Richard Bryan (D-Nevada) commented, ". . . we should not be blinded by euphoria . . . we must be vigilant."[39]

On the other hand, the government recognized that the world had changed and the days of nuclear brinkmanship were over. Restructuring the economy for the challenges of the new millennium became the critical priority. This clearly meant identifying alternative ways to utilize the infrastructure, technology, personnel, and other resources developed over the years in the manufacture and testing of nuclear weapons. By doing so, the nation could realize an additional return on its long-term investment in nuclear deterrence. While important to the U.S. economy overall, reinvestment and conversion were even more crucial for the thousands of defense industry workers who would no longer be needed and for the communities that had relied so heavily for decades on the economic input of local nuclear facilities.

This conversion task was exacerbated by the fact that before anything else could be done, the imperative of cleaning up fifty years of radioactive contamination, initially estimated to cost a staggering $100 billion, had to be addressed. In 1989 the Bush Administration developed a separate program within the DOE to consolidate the department's efforts to clean up environmental problems caused by defense nuclear waste. Subsequently, Congress created the Defense Environmental Restoration and Waste Management Account under the Energy and Water Development Appropriations Act for FY 1992 to specify the amount of funding reserved for this program. The initial appropriation was $3.68 billion. Additional accounts created in 1998 and 1999 provide funds for expediting the cleanup and closure of certain nuclear facilities and for privatizing cleanup projects at the DOE's defense environmental management sites.

A total of 113 sites were identified where the production of atomic materials used in weapons construction had led to contamination and need for remediation. By the end of FY 1998, the DOE reported that 65 of those sites had been cleaned up. The goal is to clean up an additional 38 sites by the end of FY 2006. The remaining 10 sites, which include the largest and most severely contaminated, will require long-term remediation activities estimated not to be completed until FY 2070, at an additional cost of $147 billion. This puts the extent of the environmental damage in these "national sacrifice zones," which include Hanford, Oak Ridge, Rocky Flats, and the NTS, in some perspective.[40]

While some nuclear weapons facilities are moving toward closure, the NTS will remain a primary site for operational readiness and stockpile stewardship; accordingly, the DOE will retain oversight and management of the facility for the "foreseeable future." Furthermore, because of the nature of the contamination of some surface soils and subsurface areas, which can never be sufficiently repaired so as to be restored to unrestricted use, the DOE will exercise "institutional control and monitoring responsibility" over the existing boundaries of the site "in perpetuity." As Bob Bangerter, manager of the DOE's Underground Test Area Project, commented, "Our plan is just to leave it there and monitor and develop action plans in the event contamination is detected off site." Nevertheless, some cleanup efforts, referred to by the DOE as paying its "environmental mortgage," are under way, especially in the southwest portion of the NTS Complex where there is considerable interest in several private economic-development ventures.

To assist in the cleanup project, a Test Site community advisory board (CAB) was created by federal mandate in the mid-nineties. This board, comprised of volunteers who meet on a monthly basis, is designed to foster interactive public participation and help set goals for the decontamination and restoration effort. During its tenure, an environmental impact study for the Test Site was completed in 1996, followed by a resource management plan in late 1998 and a long-range planning document, entitled "Accelerating Cleanup: Paths to Closure," which set specific deadlines for projects to be completed by the end of 2006. This document outlines corrective actions for some 800 former underground sites and 100 above-ground test locations at an estimated cost of $7 billion. The plan was approved by the Nevada Environmental Protection Division in September 1999.

The planned corrective activities are divided into four categories. Within the underground test area project, the primary concern is groundwater; scientists are monitoring the level of contamination of the water and its migration patterns, with the goal being containment within the boundaries of the NTS rather than elimination of the hazard. The industrial sites project includes locations that supported historic testing activities, such as disposal wells, muck piles, spill sites, drains and sumps, and ordinance sites. After undergoing characterization, contaminated sites may be closed in place; may be destroyed and removed; or, if the contamination is excessive, may require excavation and subsequent monitoring. Off-site projects include characterizing, cleanup, and monitoring in four other states where testing was conducted—Alaska, Colorado, Mississippi, and New Mexico—as well as two non-NTS sites in Nevada. The soils project identifies and characterizes contaminated sites, excavates certain areas, disposes of any waste, removes hot spots, and continues to monitor the areas.[41]

A side-bar to this cleanup process is the evaluation of historic Cold War structures on the Test Site in accordance with the National Historic Preservation Act. In 1992 the DOE contracted with the Desert Research Institute to begin an inventory of the buildings, structures, and objects that are potentially eligible for inclusion in the National Register of Historic Places. These include a railroad bridge, the Mosler bank vault, a Japanese-style village, and various reflector towers. Preservation is difficult as the DOE struggles to maintain a balance between the natural deterioration of the properties and the preservation of the attributes of destruction from nuclear testing. It is somewhat ironic that sites are being preserved in an area to which so few visitors will ever have access, although it has been suggested that perhaps someday the Test Site "could be a tourist destination."[42]

While the DOE moved ahead with its atomic cleanup operations, Congress tackled the problems of downsizing and restructuring the country's nuclear weapons facilities with the 1990 passage of the Defense Economic Adjustment, Diversification, Conversion, and Stabilization Act. Congress appropriated $100 million for existing programs in the Commerce and Defense departments to help communities plan how to take up the economic slack when a local business loses a large defense contract or a federal facility is closed. An additional $100 million was earmarked in an amendment by Representative Nicholas Mavroules (D-Massachusetts) for aid to displaced defense workers.[43]

The following session, Congress continued along these lines and passed the DOE Defense Nuclear Facilities Work Force Restructuring Plan on October 23, 1992. To accommodate the reconfiguration of defense nuclear facilities with the least possible economic upheaval, the act called for the creation of committees comprised of local stakeholders to draw up an appropriate work-force conversion plan for their own communities. These committees were referred to as community reuse organizations (CROs). One of the stated objectives was that the plan "should be accomplished, when possible, through the use of retraining, early retirement, attrition, and other options that minimize layoffs." Congress appropriated some $1.4 billion for the program, but President Bush opposed the bill and declined to spend the funds.[44]

In March 1993, however, President Clinton announced his Defense Reinvestment and Conversion Initiative, which outlined a plan for spending the $1.4 billion and called for an additional $300 million for FY 93. The package included four major areas of new investment: worker training and adjustment; community development funds for hard-hit locales; dual-use technology and commercial-military integration; and conversion opportunities in new civilian technology investment. A DOE Task Force on Worker and Community Transition was formed, and guidelines for the program were adopted whereby local impact assistance could be provided to affected locales. CROs were established at the local level in affected sites across the country with a reasonably representative cross-section of public and private interests; and restructuring got under way.[45]

In Nevada, Governor Bob Miller appointed the Economic Adjustment Task Force in March 1993 to develop a plan of action for the future of the NTS. The group released its recommendations in June 1994. In March 1995 the task force became Nevada's CRO at the request of the DOE, which granted the new organization $20,000 to continue its work. The CRO, in turn, gradually evolved into the NTS Development Corporation under the leadership of Tim Carlson, former Director of Economic Development for the state. Recognized officially in July 1995 as a nonprofit economic development organization, the NTSDC became an official vehicle through which DOE funds could be channeled to southern Nevada. In its first five years of operation, it received some $8.5 million.

The NTSDC board of directors consists of presidents and CEOs of major corporations, elected officials, labor representatives, business owners, economic development specialists, university officials, and scientists. Its stated mission is "to facilitate the development of sus-

tainable commercial activities in science and technology which max-
imize utilization of DOE resources, support on-going DOE missions,
expand non-government opportunities, and add long-term value to
the regional economy." To further this goal, the organization designs
programs to attract private investment and foster the development of
technological industries in the counties around the NTS.[46] Although
the relative economic impact of the NTS is much less today than it
was earlier, because of the tremendous growth of gaming and tourism
in southern Nevada, it is still significant, prompting Senator Reid to
state, "As the mission of the Test Site changes, we need to market the
resources at the facility and create new opportunities for business and
jobs."[47]

One of the subsidiaries of the NTSDC is the Nevada Innovation
Center, a science and technology incubator that works with entrepre-
neurs to commercialize their technologies. Some of the companies
that have taken advantage of the incubator services are Next Generation Power, a waste water treatment and alternative-power generator;
NRG Technologies, the developer of a hydrogen-enriched lean burn
process; Cryo-Live, Inc., which uses "Blue Bottle" technology to re-
capture and recycle ozone depleting substances; FMJ Technologies,
which manufactures cloth consisting of 100 percent pure oxidized car-
bon; and Hasting's Chariots, which is developing rockets for micro-
gravity testing.[48]

The NTSDC has also assisted the rural counties of Nye, Esmeralda,
and Lincoln that were perhaps hardest hit by the downsizing. Under
the Nevada Test Site Redevelopment Act (AB 528) passed by the
1999 state legislature, these counties can partner with the NTSDC to
develop industrial parks. Assistance has also been provided to Nye and
Esmeralda counties to develop an advanced telecommunications network along U.S. 95 from Pahrumph to Tonopah; this route is called
the Nevada Science and Technology Corridor and is designed to attract industries that contract with the Test Site for various projects. A
grant from the NTSDC provided seed money to the Community
College of Southern Nevada to open a high-tech learning center in
Pahrumph. The NTSDC is also making arrangements to develop
Desert Rock Sky Park, a commercial industrial park in a vicinity of
the Test Site known as Area 22. Potential users are businesses with
safety, security, and encroachment issues that would benefit from the
remote location, security, and extensive infrastructure provided by the
Test Site.

The lynchpin of this development effort, which gave the NTSDC
instant credibility, is Kistler Aerospace, which hopes to house its K-1

reusable space vehicle launch-and-recovery operations at the Test Site. A location for the project has already been identified within Area 18 of the NTS; a 12,000-acre tract was withdrawn by the DOE and is being held by the NTSDC for subleasing to Kistler. The permit allowing this unprecedented arrangement was signed by Energy Secretary Federico Peña on August 18, 1997. If the necessary financing and the needed government permits and licenses are acquired, launch could occur within a few years.[49]

The Kistler arrangement has added to Nevada's clout in the ongoing bid for Venture Star as well. Lockheed Martin is in search of a place to locate its lucrative new spaceport, home of a space shuttle project that is predicted to provide two thousand jobs and have an economic impact of $3 billion annually. One of seventeen sites vying for this project, Nevada hopes to become "the Cape Canaveral of the future." Toward this end, the NTSDC is doing all it can to convince Lockheed Martin that the Test Site would be an ideal location for the new spaceport. Not only does the Test Site offer a dry, sunny climate and air space the size of New Jersey, but according to NTSDC President Tim Carlson, "Nevada is also known for cutting through bureaucracy when needed."[50]

While the NTSDC seeks to attract private investors and high-tech industries to the Test Site, the DOE is independently pursuing a number of its own non-weapons-related programs. The HAZMAT Spill Center, for example, is a unique facility built to conduct hazardous-materials testing and training under controlled conditions; containing a wind tunnel, spill pads, and a tank farm, it can be used for training purposes or to develop emergency planning. The NTS also now houses the National Exercise Test and Training Center for Counter-Terrorism, where exercises are conducted dealing with potential nuclear, biological, and chemical crises; these exercises are described as "realistic, hands-on, multi-team, multi-agency events based on threat-driven scenarios." And the Nevada Seismic Testing Center at NTS provides engineering researchers worldwide with "repeatable strong ground motion for structural and lifeline testing," contributing greatly to our understanding of earthquakes. Working with the DOE on these projects is the Nevada Alliance for Defense, Energy, and Business, originally formed in 1992 as the NTS Contractors Association. The group's goals are to preserve the current missions of the NTS and to bring new and expanded economic activities to the facility.[51]

Two additional projects initiated during the 1990s came as the direct result of efforts by Nevada's two senators. Richard Bryan was instrumental in getting a $3 million DOE grant in 1995 to start up

CSTRR, the Corporation for Solar Technology and Renewable Resources, a not-for-profit group created to facilitate the commercialization and deployment of solar and renewable energy technology at the Test Site.[52] And Harry Reid helped secure a $1.2-million DOE grant in September 1999 to establish a big-rig and specialty-truck drivers' training program at NTS. Operated by the Teamsters Union, the program is expected to turn out drivers who can readily find jobs in the booming construction industry around Las Vegas.[53]

State officials were likewise supportive of the DOE's conversion efforts. In addition to AB 528, the legislature passed two resolutions. In 1993, SJR 19 called on Congress to support the conversion of NTS and to develop contingency plans for its workers; and in 1997, AJR 16 expressed support for the Kistler Aerospace program being pursued by the NTSDC. Both Governors Bob Miller and Kenny Guinn strongly endorsed these DOE initiatives to help save jobs and diversify the economy. Politicians at all levels, however, were extremely careful to separate DOE operations at the Test Site from those at the proposed Yucca Mountain high-level waste repository site, which the state has officially and vociferously protested since the mid-eighties.

Despite this concerted push for commercial development through privatization that characterized the NTS during the nineties, the Site's primary mission continued to be national defense, ensuring that the nation's nuclear weapons needs were met. Because this could no longer be achieved through critical testing, however, the DOE had not only to develop new non-weapons programs but was forced to restructure its defense-related activities as well. As a result, rather than being a place to test nuclear weapons, the NTS became an essential part of the "stockpile stewardship" program. This science-based approach allows the U.S. to conduct experiments to ensure the safety and reliability of existing nuclear weapons without setting off a chain reaction and thereby violating the testing moratorium. NTS objectives under this modified initiative (as stated in the 1998 strategic plan, *Preserving Our Traditions . . . Forging Our Future*) have shifted to include conducting subcritical weapons experiments that do not involve nuclear reactions, performing hydrological tests at the Big Explosives Experimental Facility (BEEF), and maintaining a two- to three-year readiness capability should the need for testing resume.[54]

Operating expenses to support this initiative have dropped since the moratorium went into effect in 1992, from $457.5 million to a requested $177.1 million for FY 2000. Eleven subcritical tests had been conducted by the end of spring 2000, culminating with Oboe IV on April 6. Critics have argued that these experiments help in the design of new weapons, which is inconsistent with the spirit of a moratorium; that they are unnecessary; and that they may look like nuclear tests if not monitored intrusively. Secretary of Energy Bill Richardson counters, "These experiments are a key part of our scientific program to provide new tools and data that assess age-related complications and maintain the reliability and safety of the nation's nuclear deterrent."[55]

The transitional decade of the 1990s drew to a close with an unexpected turn of events. In the waning days of the twentieth century, the Republican-controlled Senate, acting out of partisan spite, refused to ratify the Comprehensive Test Ban Treaty that President Clinton had been negotiating since 1994. In September 1996, the U.N. General Assembly had voted 158 to 3 to adopt the treaty; President Clinton signed it immediately and sent it to the Senate in September 1997. For two years, the Senate stalled as Jesse Helms (R–North Carolina), chair of the Foreign Relations Committee, refused to bring it up for a vote. By the time a vote was finally taken on October 13, 1999, 154 countries had signed the treaty and 51 had ratified it, including Britain and France. In an almost straight party-line vote, with only 4 moderate Republicans joining 44 Democrats in favor of the treaty, it failed to receive the two-thirds approval needed for ratification. Robert Byrd (D–West Virginia) voted "present" because he wanted more time to work on some of his reservations; but the Republicans, knowing they had the votes, brought the treaty up for consideration at the last minute. Despite having opposed the original 1992 moratorium, both Nevada senators voted in support of the treaty, clearly indicating that attitudes toward and dependency on testing in Nevada had changed over the last decade.

President Clinton called rejection of the treaty "reckless" and "partisan" and vowed that "the fight is far from over." Minority leader Tom Daschle agreed, "This is a terrible, terrible mistake. If politics don't stop at the water's edge, nothing does." Republicans denied that their rejection was based on party politics, and Helms countered that the only terrible thing was the treaty itself. Diplomats and arms experts warned, however, that the worldwide fallout could be severe, with the most immediate impact being a loss of the U.S.'s ability to persuade India and Pakistan, the newest members of the nuclear club, to stop testing. The longer-term effect could be to undermine the United States' ability to stop nuclear proliferation in places like Iran and North Korea and to persuade Russia and China to keep lids on their nuclear arsenals.[56]

The day after voting against the treaty, a number of Republican senators, including John Warner (Virginia), Chuck Hagel (Nebraska),

Pete Domenici (New Mexico), and John McCain (Arizona), told the press they did not want the United States to resume testing and thought some of the problems of the treaty could be worked out.[57] Whether the treaty will ultimately be ratified could hinge on the 2000 election; on the Democratic side, Vice President Al Gore supports the treaty, while the Republican nominee, George W. Bush, opposes it. In the meantime, President Clinton's moratorium remains in place, and the NTS moves into the new millennium with a cloud of uncertainty rather than a mushroom cloud on the horizon.

Throughout the nineties, with concerted effort, the NTS positioned itself as an indispensable resource, uniquely equipped to contribute to both our national security and the local economy, in ways that are far less controversial than in the past. During this transitional period, the Test Site has seen its victims compensated, has begun to clean up its environmental mess, has welcomed commercial ventures within its boundaries, has revamped its defense role, has opened up its records, and has forged new partnerships with the state. As Tim Carlson commented shortly after the new year, "Even if they start testing again, we can continue our work. We have developed a good relationship with the DOE and have at the same time helped open a window for this State to take some ownership of property that it has never even been allowed on before. Our challenge now is to convince people at all levels that we have a jewel here at NTS which we should protect, support, and take advantage of."[58]

Perhaps the most poignant symbol of this transition is the newly created NTS Historical Foundation. Established on April 15, 1998, the Foundation Board is chaired by Cold Warrior Troy Wade, longtime employee of the NTS and former Assistant Secretary for Defense Programs under President Reagan. Wade is joined on the board by a number of other former Test Site workers, the president of the Desert Research Institute, and ironically, this author, who was long considered at best a hostile critic of the DOE. The group's mission as a self-proclaimed "steward of history" is to "preserve and foster public access to the history of the NTS." Accordingly, it hopes to "promote cultural, educational, and scientific programs to encourage the development and public exchange of views regarding the NTS and its impact on the nation."[59]

Currently, the Foundation operates a small history center at the Bechtel Nevada complex where exhibits of artifacts and photographs are on display. A small gift shop also features tee-shirts, caps, mugs, and pens bearing the Foundation's mushroom cloud logo. Reproductions of old postcards from the fifties are a popular item. What was once revered as a symbol of awesome power and later seen as a dreadful sign of power run amuck has now become a piece of nostalgia.

A major goal of the Foundation was realized in April 1999, when the Nevada legislature passed SB 371, introduced by State Senator Dina Titus (D-Clark County). This bill allows the University and Community College System of Nevada to issue revenue bonds to build a facility on the Desert Research Institute campus and to enter into a twenty-year partnership with the DOE to establish a Nevada Test Site Research Center. The Center will house Test Site artifacts; atomic-age exhibits; storage and retrieval services for 350,000 atomic documents and records; public reading and research space; and a conference area. The facility was granted affiliate status by the Smithsonian Institution in spring 2000 and is scheduled to open in 2001 to coincide with the fiftieth anniversary of the first atomic test at the NTS. Calling the story of the Test Site "our Cold War legacy," Titus urged her colleagues to vote "to preserve it, so we can better understand it and perhaps prevent the need for such a facility in the future."[60]

Conclusion

For over five decades the United States government has been involved in the development of nuclear armaments. From the beginning, this endeavor has been carried out in utmost secrecy as priorities have been set and crucial decisions made by a military-oriented elite established by civil authorities, but exempt from the accountability of the ballot box.

The original atomic bomb project was established by necessity in 1942 as a top-secret military operation. After the war, the Manhattan Project was dismantled, but the military maintained its position of dominance in the field of atomic development and many of the precedents set during the ascendancy of General Groves went unchallenged. Although the 1946 Atomic Energy Act mandated the creation of an administration whose membership was to be civilian, it clearly stated that the commission's "paramount objective [was] assuring the common defense and security." In order to accomplish this goal, the Defense Department was granted special decision-making authority over classified material, and a number of former military officers merely assumed new titles while remaining in positions of power.

Following the Soviet detonation of Joe One in 1949, President Truman approved NSC-68 as a foreign policy doctrine and the arms race began. Dominated by promilitary interests, the AEC escalated its weapons development program, built a Super-bomb, and commenced testing within the continental United States. Backed by Congress and the public, it proceeded for the next twenty years virtually unchecked in its drive to build a nuclear arsenal.

The AEC's ability to command public support for atomic testing throughout the fifties and early sixties can be attributed to several factors. First, the national political climate during this period was shaped by the Cold War. Frightened by possible Communist aggression, the American people were receptive to almost any government action that they believed would preserve the democratic way of life. Even if that action involved potential risks such as radioactive fallout, they felt the risks were worth taking. Reflecting their constituencies' attitudes, Congress and the presidents serving during these years were also highly supportive of the AEC's efforts. Likewise, the press endorsed the weapons program by praising scientific achievements, describing spectacular events, and seldom questioning any potential for danger.

Second, the AEC did not simply leave the fate of the weapons development program to the political whim of the American people. Instead, the commission assiduously worked to maintain popular support for testing through a full-scale public-relations campaign conducted nationwide, but of special significance to Nevadans. In addition to playing on public fear of the Soviets and emphasizing the necessity of testing for national security reasons, the AEC stressed the contributions made by testing to the development of atomic energy for progress and peace. The safety of the program for those directly involved in its execution and those living in its shadow was also repeatedly emphasized. Official press releases, films, lectures, Civil Defense drills, and brochures consistently reinforced this benign image of the testing program.

A third factor which contributed to the AEC's power during the era of atmospheric testing was the relative lack of public knowledge about radioactivity. This deficiency was due in part to a general paucity of medical evidence on the long-term effects of ionizing radiation. Prior to the development of atomic weapons, only a few scientists had actually conducted research on radiation exposure and health. The generally supportive attitude of the press tended to inhibit the dissemination of information that questioned the validity of AEC claims, and the government's control over classified information had not been eroded by the Freedom of Information Acts. These obstacles to accurate information flow were compounded by AEC sponsorship and distribution of dozens of official reports which supported its own position about the safety of testing. Scientists who disagreed and suggested a possible link between fallout and cancer were either repressed or summarily dismissed as disgruntled or disloyal.

When testing moved underground in 1963, the familiar mushroom cloud disappeared from the horizon and most of its critics went with it. Fallout was no longer a potential problem. As a result, people's attention turned to the more immediate concerns of the Vietnam War and the civil rights movement. Accustomed to living with the bomb, the American public paid relatively little heed over the next decade to the government's continuing program of developing and testing bigger and more sophisticated weapons.

By the late seventies, the sustaining forces of the previous decades had begun to weaken and the government's atomic weapons program came under unprecedented scrutiny and attack. The critique of government policy did not come so much from a reevaluation of defense policy as it did from the emergence of new domestic issues. By 1976 the American people had become more politically cynical and the media more aggressively inquisitive. A burgeoning worldwide anti-nuclear movement and an accident at Three Mile Island nuclear power plant alerted people to the dangers of ionizing radiation. Other contributing factors were a Smoky veteran with cancer, an ambitious senator from Utah, and a group of natives who wanted to go home.

Out of this political cauldron came the bid by alleged victims for recognition and compensation. For over ten years they fought valiantly, in the courts and in the halls of Congress, to gain redress for the harm they had suffered as a result of their own government's atomic policies. Finally, as the Cold War sputtered to a close, the nuclear imperative became less critical and the need to atone became more acute. Consequently, Congress moved to compensate veterans first, then downwinders and uranium miners, Test Site workers, and Pacific islanders. This "compassionate pay" was the U.S. government's way of apologizing to the victims of the arms race.

At the same time this door was being closed on the nation's atomic past, new doors were being opened and new challenges confronted. With only a limited need for a nuclear arsenal, the government had to find jobs for thousands of workers, had to protect the local economy of communities hit hard by the downsizing, and had to channel nuclear resources into post–Cold War operations. But before they could do any of this, they had to clean up the contamination caused by years of nuclear weapons development—they had to pay their environmental mortgage. Privatization and commercial development seemed the key.

As the new millennium dawns, the future of the NTS remains uncertain. Barring the ratification of the Comprehensive Test Ban Treaty, testing could resume. Meanwhile, high-tech aerospace industries are attempting to locate on the complex. Can this new public-private partnership work? And can the DOE maintain good relations with the state of Nevada at the Test Site even as the fight over Yucca Mountain heats up? Will Congress add underground test site workers to those eligible for compensation? And what will be the public's reaction to developments at NTS? Over four thousand people a month move into southern Nevada, bringing with them values and beliefs very different from the political culture of independence, isolation, and individualism that characterized the state for so many years and fostered support or at least tolerance for "bombs in the backyard."

Notes

CHAPTER 1. FROM *ATOMOS* TO A-BOMB

1. For a more detailed history of the development of atomic science, see: Kenneth Jay, "A Glance at Prehistory," Introduction to Margaret Gowing, *Britain and Atomic Energy 1939–1945* (New York: St. Martins Press, 1964); Lancelot L. Whyte, *Essay on Atomism* (Middletown, Conn.: Wesleyan University Press, 1961); J. R. Partington, "The Origins of Atomic Theory," *Annals of Science* 4(1939): 245–82; Ray E. Hiebert and Roselyn Hiebert, *Atomic Pioneers* (Oakridge, Tenn.: United States Atomic Energy Commission, Division of Technical Information, 1970); William Moore, *The Atomic Pioneers, from Irish Castle to Manhattan Project* (New York: Putnam, 1970).

2. Sir Isaac Newton, *Opticks or a treatise of the reflections, refractions, inflections and colours of light* (New York: Dover Publications, Inc., 1952), 400. For other discussions of Newton's contribution to atomic science, see: S. I. Vavilov, "Newton and the Atomic Theory," essay in the Royal Society's Newton Tercentenary Celebration volume (Cambridge: Cambridge University Press, 1947) cited in Whyte's *Essay on Atomism,* 107; James Seymour English, ". . . *and all was light": The Life and Work of Sir Isaac Newton* (Lincoln, England: Lincolnshire Library Service, 1977); Adolph J. Snow, *Matter and Gravity in Newton's Physical Philosophy* (New York: Arno Press, 1975); Benjamin Harrow, ed., *From Newton to Einstein: Changing Conceptions of the Universe,* 2nd ed. (New York: Van Nostrand, 1920); and Frederick Aicken, *Newton: Architect of the Scientific Society* (London: English Universities Press, 1971).

3. William Cramp, *Michael Faraday and Some of His Contemporaries* (London: Sir I. Pitman and Sons, Ltd., 1931); R. A. R. Tricker, *The Contributions of Faraday and Maxwell to Electrical Science* (Oxford: Pergamon Press, 1966); Brian Bowers, *Michael Faraday and Electricity* (London: Priory Press, 1974); Frank Greenaway, *John Dalton and the Atom* (Ithaca: Cornell University Press, 1966); Elizabeth C. Patterson, *John Dalton and the Atomic Theory* (Garden City, N.Y.: Doubleday, 1970); and David L. Anderson, *The Discovery of the Electron* (Princeton: Van Nostrand, 1964).

4. An excellent source on this period, which contains a bibliography of 1,044 additional references, is Otto Glasser, *Wilhelm Conrad Röntgen and the Early History of the Roentgen Rays* (Springfield, Ill.: Charles C. Thomas, 1934). Other more recent sources include Birn Dibner, *Wilhelm Conrad Röntgen and the Discovery of X Rays* (New York: F. Watts, 1968), and

The New Rays of Professor Röntgen (Norwalk, Conn.: Burndy Library, 1963); Keith T. Claxton, *Wilhelm Röntgen* (London: Heron Books, 1970); and Robert W. Nitske, *The Life of Wilhelm Conrad Röntgen, Discoverer of the X-ray* (Tucson: University of Arizona Press, 1971).

5. Stephen Hilgartner, Richard C. Bell, and Rory O'Connor, *Nukespeak: The Selling of Nuclear Technology in America* (New York: Penguin Books, 1982), 2–4; and Percy Brown, *American Martyrs to Science Through the Roentgen Rays* (Springfield, Ill.: Charles C. Thomas, 1936).

6. Glasser, 44.

7. Lawrence Badash, "Chance Favors the Prepared Mind: Henri Becquerel and the Discovery of Radioactivity," *Archives Internationales d'Histoire des Sciences* 18(1965): 55–66, "Becquerel's 'Unexposed' Photographic Plates," *Isis* 57(1966): 1086–88, and "Radioactivity before the Curies," *American Journal of Physics* 33(1965): 128–35; and Henri Becquerel, "Sur les radiatious emises par phosphorescence," *Comptes Rendus Hebdomadaires des Séances de l'Académie des Sciences* 122(1896): 501–3.

8. Lawrence Badash, "The Discovery of Thorium's Radioactivity," *Journal of Chemical Education* 43 (1966): 219–70; Eve Curie, *Marie Curie* (Garden City, N.Y.: Doubleday Doran, 1938); Robert Reid, *Marie Curie* (New York: Dutton, 1974); and Marie Curie, "Rayons emis par les composes de l'uranium et du thorium," *Comptes Rendus Hebdomadaires des Séances de l'Académie des Sciences* 126(1898): 1101–3.

9. Lawrence Badash, *Radioactivity in America: Growth and Decay of a Science* (Baltimore: The Johns Hopkins University Press, 1979), 17–32, and "Radium, Radioactivity, and the Popularity of Scientific Discovery," *Proceedings of the American Philosophical Society* 122(1978): 145–54; Harold Swanberg, *Radiologic Maxims* (Quincy, Ill.: Radiologic Review Publishing Co., 1932); H. C. Bolton, "New Sources of Light," *Popular Science Monthly* 57(1900): 318–22; William J. Hammer, "Radium and Other Radioactive Substances," *Scientific American Supplement* 55(1903): 22904–7; and Hilgartner, Bell, and O'Connor, 4–9.

10. Ernest Rutherford, "Uranium Radiation and the Electrical Conduction Produced by It," *Philosophical Magazine* 47(1899): 109–63; and Paul Villard, "Sur la reflexion en la refracion des rayons cathodiques en des rayons deviables du radion," *Comptes Rendus Hebdomadaires des Séances de l'Académie des Sciences* 130(1900): 1010–12.

11. Robert Oppenheimer, quoted in Robert Jungk, *Brighter Than a Thousand Suns* (New York: Harcourt, Brace and Company, 1958), 8.

12. Jungk, 6.

13. Ibid.

14. Niels Bohr and John Archibald Wheeler, "The Mechanism of Nuclear Fission," *Physical Review* 56(1939): 426–50.

15. Laura Fermi, *Atoms in the Family* (Chicago: University of Chicago Press, 1954); and Herbert L. Anderson, "Early Days of the Chain Reaction," *Science and Public Affairs* 29(1973): 8–12, and "The Legacy of Fermi and Szilard," *Bulletin of the Atomic Scientists* 30(1974): 56–62.

16. Dozens of books have been written which chronicle the development of the atomic bomb. Some excellent examples include: Henry DeWolf Smyth, *Atomic Energy for Military Purposes: The Official Report on the Development of the Atomic Bomb under the Auspices of the United States Government, 1940–1945* (Princeton: Princeton University Press, 1946); Arthur Holly Compton, *Atomic Quest: A Personal Narrative* (New York: Oxford University Press, 1956); William L. Laurence, *Men and Atoms* (New York: Simon and Schuster, 1946), and *Dawn Over Zero* (New York: Alfred A. Knopf, 1946); Daniel Lang, *Early Tales of the Atomic Age* (Garden City, N.Y.: Doubleday, 1948); Richard G. Hewlett and Oscar E. Anderson, Jr., *The New World 1939–46: A History of the United States Atomic Energy Commission* (University Park: Pennsylvania State University Press, 1962), vol. 1; Lansing Lamont, *Day of Trinity* (New York: Atheneum, 1965); Leslie R. Groves, *Now It Can Be Told: The Story of the Manhattan Project* (New York: Harper and Row, 1962); John Purcell, *The Best Kept Secret* (New York: Vanguard Press, 1963); Peter Pringle and James Spigelman, *The Nuclear Barons* (New York: Avon Books, 1983), 3–106; Martin J. Sherwin, *A World Destroyed: The Atomic Bomb and the Grand Alliance* (New York: Vintage Books, 1977), 14–63; James Phinney Baxter, III, *Scientists Against Time* (Boston: Little, Brown and Company, 1946); Gowing, *Britain and Atomic Energy;* and Jungk, *Brighter Than a Thousand Suns*. Collections which are also essential include the Office of Scientific Research and Development, Section 1 files, the Manhattan Engineer District files, and the AEC files in Record Group 326, all deposited at the National Archives in Washington, D.C. Assorted archival material is also available at the Department of Energy's Coordination and Information Center in Las Vegas, Nevada.

17. Compton, 25–26; and Jungk, 78.

18. Spencer R. Weart and Gertrude Weiss Szilard, eds., *Leo Szilard: His Vision of the Facts* (Cambridge, Mass.: The MIT Press, 1972); Bernard Feld, "Einstein and the Politics of Nuclear Weapons," *Bulletin of the Atomic Scientists* 35(1979): 5–16; Nicholas Halasz and Robert Halasz, "Leo Szilard, the Reluctant Father of the Atom Bomb," *New Hungarian Quarterly* 15(1974): 163–73; and Alice Kimball Smith, "The Elusive Dr. Szilard," *Harper's* (July 1960): 77–86.

19. Hewlett and Anderson, 17.

20. Lamont, 25–29; Jungk, 109–12; Compton, 28–64; Smyth, 75–78; and Hewlett and Anderson, 9–52.

21. Compton, 67–105; Smyth, 78–83; and Hewlett and Anderson, 53–71.

22. Groves, 3–11; Smyth, 83–87; Compton, 105–14; and Hewlett and Anderson, 71–115.

23. J. H. Manley, "Assembling the War Time Labs," *Bulletin of the Atomic Scientists* 30(1974): 42–47; Groves, 68–124; and Hewlett and Anderson, 116–254.

24. Jungk, 115. For detailed descriptions of life at Los Alamos, see: Lawrence Badash, Joseph Q. Hirschfelder, and Herbert P. Broida, *Reminiscences of*

Los Alamos (Boston: D. Reidel Publishing Company, 1980); David Hawkins, *Manhattan District History, Project Y, the Los Alamos Project* (Los Alamos, N. Mex.: University of California and United States Atomic Energy Commission, 1945), vol. 1; Eleanor Jette, *Inside Box 1663* (Los Alamos, N. Mex.: Los Alamos Historical Society, 1967); Barb Mulkin, "Los Alamos—P.O. Box 1663," *Westways* 69(1977): 31–34, 72; Boyce McDaniel, "A Physicist at Los Alamos," *Bulletin of the Atomic Scientists* 30(1974): 39–43; Robert R. Wilson, "A Recruit for Los Alamos," *Bulletin of the Atomic Scientists* 31(1975): 41–47; Lamont, 43–71; and Groves, 60–67, 149–69.

25. In a letter to the editor of the Book Review Section of the *New York Times*, Dan Kurzman wrote that his recent book, *Day of the Bomb: Countdown to Hiroshima*, reveals new evidence that, contrary to Truman's own assertions, Truman knew about the project before he became president. See *New York Times*, January 26, 1986, sec. 7, p. 42.

26. Klaus Fuchs was arrested in England in February 1950 and his subsequent trial lasted eighty-seven minutes. Because he had given information to a wartime ally and not an enemy, he was sentenced to fourteen years in prison rather than executed. Upon his early release in 1959, he moved to East Germany where he became the Director of the Central Institute for Nuclear Physics in Dresden. Lamont, 281–83, 309. See Chapter 6 for further details on the Rosenberg case.

27. This connection was later used against Oppenheimer by the Atomic Energy Commission. In 1953, after he publicly opposed the development of the hydrogen bomb, he was charged with maintaining Communist associations and acting in a way designed to promote the interest of the Russians. His security clearance was cancelled and his long-term government service was ended. See Chapter 6 for further discussion.

28. Peter Goodchild, *J. Robert Oppenheimer: Shatterer of Worlds* (Boston: Houghton Mifflin Company, 1981); Richard Rhodes, "I Am Become Death . . . The Agony of J. Robert Oppenheimer," *American Heritage* 28(1977): 70–83; Alice Kimball Smith and Charles Weiner, "Robert Oppenheimer: Letters and Recollections," *Bulletin of the Atomic Scientists* 36(1980): 19–27, and "Robert Oppenheimer: The Los Alamos Years," *Bulletin of the Atomic Scientists* 36(1980): 11–17; and N. P. Davis, *Lawrence and Oppenheimer* (New York: Simon and Schuster, 1968).

29. Groves, 63.

30. Arthur Steiner, "Baptism of the Atomic Scientists," *Bulletin of the Atomic Scientists* 31(1975): 21–28; Brian L. Villa, "A Confusion of Signals: James Franck, The Chicago Scientists and Early Efforts to Stop the Bomb," *Bulletin of the Atomic Scientists* 31(1975): 36–42; Herbert F. York, "Sounders of the Alarm," *Bulletin of the Atomic Scientists* 31(1975): 43–45; Farrington Daniels and Arthur H. Compton, "A Poll of Scientists at Chicago," *Bulletin of the Atomic Scientists* 4(1948): 44; and Compton, 219–47.

31. Examinations of the decision to use the atomic bomb against Japan can be found in: H. W. Baldwin, *Mistakes of the War* (New York: Harper and

Brothers, 1950); Herbert Feis, *The Atomic Bomb and the End of World War II* (Princeton: Princeton University Press, 1966); Barton J. Bernstein, "Hiroshima Reconsidered: Thirty Years Later," *Foreign Service Journal* 52(1975): 8–13, 32–33; "Roosevelt, Truman, and the Atomic Bomb, 1941–1945: A Reinterpretation," *Political Science Quarterly* 90(1975): 23–69; and "The Uneasy Alliance: Roosevelt, Churchill, and the Atomic Bomb, 1940–1945," *Western Political Quarterly* 29(1976): 202–30. Gar Alperovitz, *Atomic Diplomacy—Hiroshima and Potsdam* (New York: Simon and Schuster, 1965); Edward S. Shapiro, "The Military Options to Hiroshima: A Critical Examination of Gar Alperovitz's *Atomic Diplomacy,*" *Amerika Studien* 23(1978): 60–72; Henry L. Stimson, "The Decision to Use the Atomic Bomb," *Harper's* (February 1947): 101–2; Jonathon Harris, *Hiroshima: A Study in Science, Politics and the Ethics of War* (Menlo Park, Calif.: Addison-Wesley Publishing Company, 1970); Len Giovannitti and Fred Freed, *The Decision to Drop the Bomb* (New York: Coward-McCann, 1965); Leon V. Sigal, "Bureaucratic Politics and Tactical Uses of Committees: The Interim Committee and the Decision to Drop the Atomic Bomb," *Polity* 10(1978): 326–64; Alice Kimball Smith, "Behind the Decision to Use the Atomic Bomb, Chicago 1944–45," *Bulletin of the Atomic Scientists* 14(1958): 351–52; Hewlett and Anderson, 361–72; and Sherwin, 193–238.

32. Jungk, 171; and Groves, 221.
33. Gordon Thomas and Max M. Wetts, *Enola Gay* (New York: Simon and Schuster, 1977); Merle Miller and Abe Spitzer, *We Dropped the A-Bomb* (New York: Thomas Crowell Company, 1946); Anonymous, "Training Camp for the Atomic Age: Wendover Field," *Aerospace Historian* 20(1973): 137–39; and Otis Cary, "Atomic Bomb Targeting: Myths and Realities," *Japan Quarterly* 26(1979): 506–16, "The Sparing of Kyoto," *Japan Quarterly* 22(1975): 337–47, and *Mr. Stimson's "Pet City": The Sparing of Kyoto 1945* (Kyoto: Amherst House, Doshiska University, 1975); and Groves, 253–76.
34. John Savage and Barbara Storms, *Reach to the Unknown* (Los Alamos, N. Mex.: University of California and United States Atomic Energy Commission, 1965), 2–3.

CHAPTER 2. AN AWESOME DAWN

1. Several excellent accounts of the Trinity test have been published. See: Robert Cahn, "Behind the First Atomic Bomb," *Saturday Evening Post* (July 16, 1960): 17, 72–75; Val L. Fitch, "The View from the Bottom," *Bulletin of the Atomic Scientists* 31(1975): 43–46; "War Department Release on New Mexico Test July 16, 1945," reprinted as Appendix 6 in Smyth, 247–54; Lamont; Savage and Storms; Groves, 288–304; and Laurence.
2. Savage and Storms, 5.

3. Ibid., 6.
4. Ibid.
5. Jungk, 197.
6. Hilgartner, Bell, and O'Connor, 31.
7. Lamont, 180.
8. Savage and Storms, 18.
9. Lamont, 129; and Groves, 296–97.
10. A typical film of this genre is "The Day the Earth Caught Fire" (1962) produced by Val Guest. When the United States and the Soviet Union detonate simultaneous nuclear devices at the North and South Poles, the earth is thrown off balance and its tilt toward the sun is changed, causing everything to go up in flames. See Chapter 7 for further examination of popular culture during the cold war years.
11. Savage and Storms, 2.
12. Lamont, 175.
13. Savage and Storms, 19.
14. Lamont, 4–8.
15. Several informal impromptu experiments were conducted but produced no findings on the subject. Frank Oppenheimer scattered some building material scraps which represented portions of Japanese houses around the site, but all traces of the samples disappeared during the blast. And Stafford Warren strung some white mice up by their tails from signal wires to use as live guinea pigs, but they died of thirst before the shot. Lamont, 189.
16. Ibid., 158.
17. Ibid., 187–88.
18. Groves, 295–96.
19. Lamont, 158.
20. Ibid., 187.
21. Savage and Storms, 19–20.
22. Henry L. Stimson and McGeorge Bundy, *On Active Service in Peace and War* (New York: Harper and Brothers, 1948), 617–33; Winston Churchill, *Triumph and Tragedy* (Boston: Houghton Mifflin Company, 1953), 630–45; Harry S. Truman, *Year of Decisions* (Garden City, N.Y.: Doubleday, 1955), 415–16; Barton J. Bernstein, "Roosevelt, Truman, and the Atomic Bomb: A Reinterpretation"; Edward Mark, "Today Has Been a Historical One: Harry S. Truman's Diary of the Potsdam Conference," *Diplomatic History* 4(1980): 317–26; James F. Byrnes, *Speaking Frankly* (New York: Harper and Brothers, 1947), 257–64; United States Department of State, *Foreign Relations of the United States, Diplomatic Papers: The Conference of Berlin (Potsdam) 1945* (Washington, D.C.: U.S. Government Printing Office, 1960); Groves, 292–93; and Hewlett and Anderson, 80–401.
23. Groves, 293.
24. Ibid., 291.
25. Savage and Storms, 23.

26. Lamont, 235–36.
27. Hewlett and Anderson, 379.
28. Savage and Storms, 27.
29. Lamont, 235.
30. Savage and Storms, 28.
31. Later the N10,000 center was evacuated when instruments there showed an increase in radioactivity. This proved to be a false alarm—film badges worn by the personnel at the center indicated that no radioactivity had reached the shelter. Ibid., 29.
32. Ibid.
33. Lamont, 251–53.
34. Louis H. Hempelmann to Carroll L. Tyler, June 7, 1948, DBM Files, Box 3361, Folder 19MR+A Alamogordo, 1945–1950, United States Department of Energy Archives, Washington, D.C.
35. C. L. Comer, "The Fall-Out Problem," University of Tennessee and United States Atomic Energy Commission Agricultural Research Program, 1952; University of Tennessee and United States Atomic Energy Commission, "Mission Product Retention and Pathology of Alamogordo Cattle," 1952; and J. M. Bird, *The Effects of Irradiation from Atomic Bomb Fall-Out Upon a Group of Hereford Cattle* (Master's Thesis, University of Tennessee, 1952).
36. Many of the locals also capitalized on the theatrical aspects of the test. Arnie Gilworth charged people to see his atomic calf, a frost-colored creature born shortly after the detonation whose mother was said to have been scared by the blast. And Hugh McSmith changed the name of his black cat to "Atomic" when it developed a rash of spots; he later sold the cat for fifty dollars to a West Coast entrepreneur to put in a freak show. Lamont, 270.
37. Hempelmann to Tyler, June 7, 1948.
38. Groves, 301.
39. Howard L. Rosenberg, *Atomic Soldiers: American Victims of Nuclear Experiments* (Boston: Beacon Press, 1980), 71. The same approach, justified by the government on the grounds of national security, continues today. In fact, on January 30, 1984, President Reagan announced that nuclear tests conducted at the Nevada Test Site will no longer be publicized unless they are considered "significant"; this action presumably is designed to prevent the Soviets from determining the accuracy of their own detection devices. *Las Vegas Review-Journal*, January 30, 1984.
40. Lamont, 255.
41. Hewlett and Anderson, 395.
42. Ibid., 396.
43. Joseph Laurance Marx, *Seven Hours to Zero* (New York: Putnam, 1967); ibid., 396–401; Groves, 305–32; and Thomas and Wetts, 265–309.
44. Joseph Laurance Marx, *Nagasaki: The Necessary Bomb?* (New York: MacMillan, 1971); Groves, 341–55; and Lamont, 266.

45. Robert J. C. Butow, *Japan's Decision to Surrender* (Stanford: Stanford University Press, 1954); Herbert Feis, *Japan Subdued* (Princeton: Princeton University Press, 1961); and William Craig, *The Fall of Japan* (New York: Dial Press, 1967).
46. Hewlett and Anderson, 400.
47. Groves, 350.
48. See Chapter 6 for a discussion of various Atomic Energy Commission public-relations activities carried out during the fifties and early sixties.
49. Smyth, 236.
50. Naval Medical Research Institute, "Measurement of the Residual Radiation Intensity at the Hiroshima and Nagasaki Atomic Bomb Sites," NMRI–160A (Bethesda National Naval Medical Center, 1946); Senate Committee on Veteran's Affairs *Hearings*, 96th Cong., 1st sess., 1979, 196–214; Henry I. Shaw, Jr., *The United States Marines in the Occupation of Japan*, Marine Corps Historical Reference Pamphlet, United States Marine Corps, Washington, D.C., 1969; E. T. Arakawa, *Residual Radiation in Hiroshima and Nagasaki*, Technical Report 02–62, Atomic Bomb Casualty Commission, 1962; and United States Department of Defense, *Hiroshima and Nagasaki Occupation Forces* (Washington, D.C.: Defense Nuclear Agency, 1980).
51. Harvey Wasserman and Norman Solomon, *Killing Our Own: The Disaster of America's Experience with Atomic Radiation* (New York: Dell Publishing Company, 1982), 3–30; and Norman Solomon, "Nagasaki's Other Victims," *The Progressive* (July 1979): 21–27.
52. In 1946 President Truman ordered the National Academy of Sciences to form the Atomic Bomb Casualty Commission to care for and study the 100,000 severely affected survivors of the bomb. In 1975, the joint United States-Japanese Radiation Effects Research Foundation took over from the commission. See: Shields Warren, "Hiroshima and Nagasaki Thirty Years After," *Proceedings of the American Philosophical Society* 121(1977): 97–99; and Samuel Gladstone, ed., *The Effects of Nuclear Explosions* (Washington, D.C.: United States Atomic Energy Commission, 1962).
53. Although the government maintains that radiation was below the hazardous level when American troops moved into Japan (United States Department of Defense, *Radiation Dose Reconstruction: U.S. Occupation Forces in Hiroshima and Nagasaki, Japan, 1945–1946*), the *Washington Post* recently reported in an article published April 13, 1980, that research teams surveying the outskirts of Nagasaki two months after the atomic bombing found radiation that was "twice the level now considered safe for nuclear workers and over ten times the radiation safety standard for the general population." See Chapter 9 for discussion of current efforts by these veterans to obtain compensation from the United States government.
54. Lamont, 267–74.

CHAPTER 3. POLITICS OF CONTROL

1. Hewlett and Anderson, 415.
2. Stimson memo to President Truman, April 25, 1945, published in *Harper's* (February 1947): 99–100. Also see Leon V. Sigal, "Bureaucratic Politics and Tactical Uses of Committees," *Polity* (1978).
3. Hewlett and Anderson, 411–18.
4. As General Groves wrote, "Along with the Secretary of War, General Marshall, and everyone else who held a responsible position in the project, I was most anxious to have legislation passed promptly, for now that the MED had done the job for which it had been brought into being it was important to have a reasonably clear-cut national policy laid down for our future guidance." Groves, 389.
5. *Congressional Record,* 79th Cong., 1st sess., 1945, 8364–79.
6. Ibid., 9322–23.
7. See Hewlett and Anderson, 531–619, for a detailed account of Bernard Baruch's efforts, as the United States Representative on the United Nations Atomic Energy Commission, to secure an acceptable arrangement for international control of atomic power.
8. *Congressional Record,* 1945, 9396–406.
9. Two excellent examinations of the atomic scientists' movement are: Donald A. Strickland, *Scientists in Politics: The Atomic Scientists Movement, 1945–46* (Purdue: Purdue University Press, 1968); and Alice Kimball Smith, *A Peril and A Hope: The Scientists' Movement in America, 1945–47* (Chicago: University of Chicago Press, 1965).
10. Hewlett and Anderson, 435.
11. On September 6, 1945, Senator Vandenberg introduced a concurrent resolution establishing a joint committee of six Senators and six Representatives to make a complete study and report to Congress on matters related to the atomic bomb. The resolution was favorably reported by the Senate Foreign Relations Committee on September 26, and was passed by the chamber the following day. The House took no action on the resolution introduced there by Congressman Oren Harris (D-Arkansas). When Vandenberg's resolution stalled in the House, Senator Brien McMahon (D-Connecticut) introduced a new resolution (S. Res. 179) to create a special committee in the Senate to deal with atomic policy. The resolution was approved in mid-October and McMahon was appointed chairman of the new committee.
12. President Truman's letter, released to the press on February 1, 1946, endorsing the McMahon bill is reprinted in Volume 2 of his memoirs, *Years of Trial and Hope* (Garden City, N.Y.: Doubleday and Company, 1956), 4–5. Headlines in the *Washington Post* on February 3 read "Truman Asks Atom Rule by Civilians."
13. *Congressional Record,* 1945, 12406.
14. The only mention of safeguards was made in reference to the AEC's

distribution of fissionable material to licensees. In Sections 5a(4) and 7b of the proposed statute, the commission was given the authority to refuse to distribute any materials and to deny a license to any applicant "who is not equipped or who fails to observe such safety standards to protect health and to minimize danger from explosion as may be established by the Commission."

15. Hewlett and Anderson, 491–513.
16. Byron S. Miller, "A Law is Passed: The Atomic Energy Act of 1946," *University of Chicago Law Review* 15(1948): 809–13; *Congressional Record,* 79th Cong., 2nd sess., 1946, 6076–98; United States Atomic Energy Commission, *Legislative History of the Atomic Energy Act of 1946,* P.L. 585, 79th Congress (Washington, D.C.: United States Atomic Energy Commission, Division of Technical Information, 1965); and Alice L. Buck, *A History of the Atomic Energy Commission* (Washington, D.C.: United States Department of Energy, History Division, 1982).
17. *Congressional Record,* 79th Cong., 2nd sess., 1946, 9545–63; Miller, 813–17; and Hewlett and Anderson, 516–28.
18. The conference committee was composed of Brien McMahon, Richard Russell (D-Georgia), Edwin Johnson, Arthur Vandenberg, and Eugene Millikin (R-Colorado) from the Senate, and Andrew May, R. Ewing Thomason (D-Texas), Carl Durham (D-North Carolina), Charles Clason (R-Massachusetts), and J. Parnell Thomas (R-New Jersey) from the House. See *Congressional Record,* 1946, 10167, 10189–99, 10329, 10411.
19. Public Law 585, 79th Cong., 2nd sess., 1946, 60 Stat., 755–75; 42 U.S.C., 1801–19.
20. Remarks by Atomic Energy Commissioner Sumner T. Pike at Bowdoin College, Brunswick, Maine, on July 22, 1949, Washington, D.C., National Archives, Atomic Energy Commission files, R.G. 326, 2. (Hereafter referred to as NA/RG 326.)
21. As Groves wrote, "The only guidance that I could obtain was that I should continue to operate the project as I thought best." Groves, 390.
22. Ibid., 373.
23. Ibid., 373–88.
24. Groves also wrote in his memoirs, "In spite of the record, since the very start of the postwar period there has been a continuous stream of propaganda calculated to lead the American people and the people of the world to believe that the War Department—and General Groves in particular—was determined to retain close control of atomic energy. The effect of this propaganda has been truly remarkable, despite the fact that it was entirely false, and was known to be false by those who first originated it and by many of those who constantly repeated it." Groves, 391.
25. Public Law 585, Section 1(a).
26. Remarks by Captain James S. Russell, United States Navy, before American Legion, Yankton, South Dakota, on June 14, 1949, NA/RG 326, 101.

27. Public Law 585, Section 2(a) 4(b).
28. United States Atomic Energy Commission press release, "20 years of Nuclear Progress," November 15, 1962, NA/RG 326, 10. Appendix VI in Buck, 25, further indicates that from June 1940 through January 18, 1975, expenditures for the military development of atomic energy totaled $2,218.8 million compared to $14.6 million spent by the Office of Scientific Research and Development. Current outlays are examined later in this chapter.
29. Public Law 585, Section 2(a).
30. Groves, 395.
31. The other four original members of the AEC included Chairman David E. Lilienthal, Sumner T. Pike, William Waywack, and Dr. Robert F. Bacher. Corbin Alardice and Edward R. Trapnell, *The Atomic Energy Commission* (New York: Praejer Publishers, 1974), 33–34.
32. Public Law 585, Section 2(b).
33. Ibid., Section 15(b).
34. The JCAE continued as a unique body in Congress until it was abolished on September 20, 1977, with the enactment of Public Law 95–110 (95th Cong., 1st sess., 91 Stat., 884–85, 42 U.S.C., 2011). A thorough analysis of the JCAE during its years of operation is found in Harold P. Green and Alan Rosenthal, *Government of the Atom: The Integration of Powers* (New York: Atherton Press, 1963).
35. Sumner T. Pike, July 22, 1949, NA/RG 326, 3.
36. Public Law 585, Section 2(c). This was changed by amendment on October 11, 1949 (Public Law 347). The revised committee was to consist of an equal number of representatives from the Departments of the Army, Navy, and Air Force, selected by their respective secretaries, and a chairman chosen by the President with Senate confirmation.
37. Sumner T. Pike, July 22, 1949, NA/RG 326, 4.
38. Public Law 585, Section 2(c). The Armed Forces Special Weapons Project was initially directed by General Groves. Serving on both committees, Groves was able to prod the AEC on producing fissionable materials and weapons needed by the military in case of an emergency. Richard Hewlett and Francis Duncan, *Atomic Shield, 1947–1952: A History of the United States Atomic Energy Commission,* (University Park: Pennsylvania State University Press, 1969) vol. 2, 131–32; and Groves, 398–400.
39. Hewlett and Anderson, 512.
40. Public Law 585, Section 10(b)(1); and Allardice and Trapnell, 32.
41. David Lilienthal, *Journals: The Atomic Energy Years, 1945–50* (New York: Harper and Row, 1966), 582.
42. Remarks by Atomic Energy Commissioner Lewis Strauss before New York City Chamber of Commerce, New York, New York, on October 6, 1949, NA/RG 326.
43. Pringle and Spigelman, 86–103.
44. Herbert York, *The Advisors: Oppenheimer, Teller, and the Superbomb* (San

Francisco: W. H. Freeman and Sons, 1976); and Gregg Herken, *The Winning Weapon: The Atomic Bomb in the Cold War, 1945–1950* (New York: Vintage Books, 1982), 305–29.

45. Harry S. Truman, quoted in Herken, 329. For further discussion of the origins of the cold war, see: Walter LaFeber, *America, Russia and the Cold War* (New York: Random House, 1967); Thomas G. Paterson, *Soviet-American Confrontation: Postwar Reconstruction and the Origins of the Cold War* (Baltimore: Johns Hopkins University Press, 1973), and *On Every Front: The Making of the Cold War* (New York: Norton, 1979); Daniel Yergin, *Shattered Peace: The Origins of the Cold War and the National Security State* (Boston: Houghton Mifflin, 1977); John Gaddis, *The United States and the Origins of the Cold War, 1941–1947* (New York: Columbia University Press, 1972), and *Strategies of Containment: A Critical Appraisal of Postwar American National Security Policy* (New York: Oxford, 1982); and Samuel F. Wells, Jr., "Sounding the Tocsin: NSC68 and the Soviet Threat," *International Security* IV (1979): 116–38.

46. Pringle and Spigelman, 102.

47. Public Law 703, 83rd Cong., 2nd sess., 1954, 68 Stat., 919–61; 42 U.S.C., 1801.

48. Elizabeth S. Rolph, *Nuclear Power and the Public Safety: A Study in Regulation* (Lexington, Mass.: D.C. Heath and Co., 1979), 27–33; and Allardice and Trapnell, 41–47.

49. Public Law 703, Section 1.

50. Ibid., Sections 123–24.

51. Ibid., Section 3.

52. Ibid., Section 144.

53. Ibid., Section 123(a).

54. Ibid., Section 25(a).

55. Ibid., Section 143.

56. Public Law 585, Section 2(c).

57. Public Law 703, Section 27.

58. Ibid., Section 10.

59. Ibid., Section 103(b).

60. Ibid., Section 167.

61. Ibid.

62. Public Law 601, 79th Cong., 2nd sess., 1946, 60 Stat., 812, Section 403.

63. Public Law 93–438, 93rd Cong., 2nd sess., 1974, 88 Stat., 1233–54; 42 U.S.C., 5801.

64. Ibid., Section 2(b).

65. Ibid., Title II.

66. "President Signs Energy Reorganization Bill," *Congressional Quarterly Weekly Report* (October 19, 1974): 2926.

67. Public Law 95–91, 95th Cong., 1st sess., 1977, 91 Stat., 565–613; 42 U.S.C., 7101.

68. Ibid., Sections 203 and 309(b).

69. The United States Budget for Fiscal Year 1985, (8.78–8.82, indicates that 72 percent of the expected expenditures for the Department of Energy in 1985 will go for defense-related activities.

CHAPTER 4. VICTIMS OF PROLIFERATION

1. Michael Uhl and Tod Ensign, *GI Guinea Pigs: How the Pentagon Exposed Our Troops to Dangers More Deadly Than War* (New York: Wideview Books, 1980), 31–32; William A. Shurcliff, *Bombs at Bikini: The Official Report of Operation Crossroads* (New York: W. H. Wise Publishers, 1947), 9–15; and Hewlett and Anderson, 580–82.
2. Joint Task Force One, Office of the Historian, *Operation Crossroads, The Official Pictorial Record* (New York: W. H. Wise Publishers, 1946).
3. Jonathan M. Weisgall, "The Nuclear Nomads of Bikini," *Foreign Policy* 39(1980): 77.
4. Douglas McDonald described the *Nevada* as a proud and valiant ship which deserved the adjective "unsinkable." On July 1, 1946, the *Nevada* was only sixty yards from ground zero. She lost her funnel during that blast and much of her decking was torn away. Three weeks later during the Baker shot, she was moored one thousand yards from the underwater bomb, but suffered nothing more than a few minor leaks. However, she was now too radioactive to save, so she was sunk with a torpedo on July 31, 1948. Douglas McDonald, "Two Good Ships Bore Name 'Nevada'," *The Nevadan* (April 24, 1983): 6L. The other ships present for the first Bikini tests are described in *Operation Crossroads, The Official Pictorial Record*, 18.
5. Uhl and Ensign, 36.
6. Wasserman and Solomon, 38.
7. *U.S. News & World Report* (February 1, 1946): 27.
8. *Newsweek* (July 1, 1946): 21.
9. *Science News Letter* (May 11, 1946): 294.
10. *Newsweek* (April 1, 1946): 21–22; Hewlett and Anderson, 581–82; and Jungk, 245–46.
11. Uhl and Ensign, 37.
12. David Bradley, *No Place to Hide* (Boston: Little, Brown and Company, 1948), 58.
13. *New York Times*, August 4, 1946, p. 3.
14. *Time* (July 8, 1946): 20–21.
15. *Newsweek* (July 8, 1946): 19.
16. Hewlett and Anderson, 581.
17. Bradley, 62.
18. Ibid., 87–88.
19. Ibid., 100.

20. Ibid., 145.
21. Wasserman and Solomon, 42–46; and Studs Terkel, "The Good War," *The Atlantic* (July 1984): 72–75.
22. Joint Task Force One, 219, 171; and Uhl and Ensign, 43–44.
23. Bradley, 105.
24. Ibid., 103.
25. Ibid., 104.
26. Ibid., 116–17.
27. Ibid., 121.
28. Ibid., 131.
29. Ibid., 22–23.
30. *Las Vegas Review-Journal,* May 24, 1983.
31. Statement by Dr. Donald Kerr, Assistant Secretary for Defense Programs at the United States Department of Energy, cited in Uhl and Ensign, 43.
32. Bradley, 113.
33. Although President Truman had ordered the bombing of Japan and would continue to support the military development of atomic power, he was adamant in his position on civilian control. He would later give custody of weapons themselves to the AEC rather than to the military. See note 35.
34. Hewlett and Duncan, 129.
35. President Truman resolved the custody question on July 21, 1948, when he announced to AEC Chairman Lilienthal, "I regard the continued control of all aspects of the atomic energy program, including research, development, and the custody of atomic weapons as the proper functions of the civil authorities. Ibid., 170.
36. Ibid., 32. It should be noted that the committee later opposed the actual building of a hydrogen bomb. It did not oppose the expansion of weapons, however, but instead of the H-bomb recommended the development of smaller, tactical nuclear arms which could be used on the battlefield. Pringle and Spigelman, 96–97; and Hewlett and Duncan, 378–85.
37. Hewlett and Duncan, 64.
38. United States Atomic Energy Commission press release, April 19, 1948, NA/RG 326.
39. Hewlett and Anderson, 597–606.
40. Hewlett and Duncan, 84–85.
41. Hewlett and Duncan, 140–41.
42. Also spelled Enewetak.
43. *Scholastic* (January 5, 1948): 6.
44. *Operation Sandstone—1948* (Washington, D.C.: United States Defense Nuclear Agency, 1983), 18–20.
45. Hewlett and Duncan, 161–64.
46. Captain James S. Russell, June 14, 1949, NA/RG 326, 10.

47. United States Atomic Energy Commission press release, April 19, 1948, NA/RG 326.

48. Uhl and Ensign, 48.

49. United States Atomic Energy Commission press release, April 19, 1948, NA/RG 326.

50. Operation Sandstone—1948, 1.

51. Thomas H. Saffer and Orville E. Kelly, Countdown Zero (New York: G. P. Putnam's Sons, 1982), 95–111; Uhl and Ensign, 46–53; and Wasserman and Solomon, 49–51, 82–85.

52. Hewlett and Duncan, 163–64.

53. York, 19–20.

54. Sumner T. Pike, July 22, 1949, NA/RG 326, 11.

55. The Soviets actually exploded their first atomic bomb on August 29, 1949, in Siberia. An American weather reconnaisance plane of the Air Force's Long Range Detection System, flying at eighteen thousand feet over the North Pacific east of the Kamchatka Peninsula, detected the radiation almost immediately. President Truman, however, did not publicly announce the detonation until September 23, 1949. York, 33–35; Pringle and Spigelman, 86–87; and Hewlett and Duncan, 362–69.

56. See David Rees, Korea: The Limited War (Baltimore: Penguin Books Inc., 1970): Appendix E, 493–500.

57. Pringle and Spigelman, 100.

58. On January 31, 1950, President Truman announced that he was authorizing a feasibility study for the development of an H-bomb. He hoped that United States would never have to use these weapons but concluded that Russian behavior had left no choice but to make them. Hewlett and Duncan, 373–409. Newsweek responded, ". . . it was the only answer he could give," (February 13, 1950): 20.

59. President Truman approved the opening of the Nevada Test Site on December 18, 1950. See Chapter 5 for details.

60. Operation Greenhouse—1951 (Washington, D.C.: United States Defense Nuclear Agency, 1983); and remarks by General E. R. Quesada, June 13, 1951, NA/RG 326.

61. United States Department of Energy, The Meaning of Radiation at Bikini Atoll (Washington, D.C.: U.S. Government Printing Office, 1980), 1; The Enewetak Atoll Today, 1; and Announced United States Nuclear Tests, July 1945 Through December 1982 (Washington, D.C.: United States Department of Energy, Office of Public Affairs, 1983).

62. Newsweek (May 7, 1962): 26–30; and Announced United States Nuclear Tests.

63. Operation Castle—1954 (Washington, D.C.: United States Defense Nuclear Agency, 1982).

64. The actual number of islanders varies slightly depending upon the source. AEC Chairman Strauss mentions 236 in his March 31 press release (note

77); Wasserman and Solomon report 86 on Rongelap and 157 on Utirik 85–86; and Johnson says simply "more than 200," Giff Johnson, "Paradise Lost," *Bulletin of the Atomic Scientists* 36(1980): 27.

65. Edward Teller and Albert Latter, *Our Nuclear Future* (New York: Criterion Books, 1958), 87–94.

66. Statement by Atomic Energy Commission Chairman Lewis L. Strauss to the press on March 31, 1954, NA/RG 326.

67. The basic unit of radiation dosage is the rad, which is equal to 0.01 joule per kilogram deposited in any material by radiation. The U.S. Department of Energy defines a rem as the quantity of any type of radiation dose which causes the same biological effect as a rad of X-ray or gamma radiation. The rem, therefore, is a unit of radiation equivalence. The rem is obtained by multiplying the dose in rads by a quality factor, distribution factor, and any other necessary modifying factors. A roentgen—R— is a unit of radiation exposure and is limited to measurements in air of X-ray and gamma radiation. The number of rads produced in tissue or other matter depends upon the energy and the quantity of the X-ray or gamma photons that arrive at a particular point, and the length of the exposure at that point. *Radiation Protection at the Nevada Test Site* (Las Vegas: Reynolds Electrical and Engineering, 1979); *Radiological Health Handbook,* rev. ed. (Washington, D.C.: U.S. Department of Health, Education, and Welfare, 1970); and thanks to Dr. Hiram Hunt, Department of Radiological Sciences, University of Nevada, Las Vegas.

68. Johnson, "Paradise Lost," 27–28, and "Micronesia: America's 'Strategic' Trust," *Bulletin of the Atomic Scientists* 35(1979): 11–12; and Weisgall, 84–85.

69. Cited in Johnson, "Micronesia," 10.

70. Public Law 88–485, 88th Cong., 2nd sess., 1964, 78 Stat., 598.

71. Public Law 95–134, 95th Cong., 1st sess., 1977, 91 Stat., 1159–65; 48 U.S.C. 1681.

72. Public Law 88–485, Section 4; and ibid., Section 104(c).

73. Ralph E. Lapp, *The Voyage of the Lucky Dragon* (New York: Harper and Brothers, 1957); Stephen Salaff, "The Lucky Dragon," *Bulletin of the Atomic Scientists* 34(1978): 21–23; Ben Shahn and Richard Hudson, *Kuboyama and the Saga of the Lucky Dragon* (New York: Thomas Yoseloff, 1965); and Wasserman and Solomon, 87–89.

74. Lewis L. Strauss, AEC press release, March 31, 1954, NA/RG 326.

75. Lapp, 114.

76. Memorandum by Dr. John G. Bugher, director of the AEC's Division of Biology and Medicine, April 6, 1955. Cited in Salaff, 23.

77. Lapp, 178.

78. Lewis L. Strauss, AEC press release, March 31, 1954, NA/RG 326.

79. Lapp, 126.

80. Ibid., 129.
81. Ibid., 127.
82. Ibid., 132.
83. Atomic Energy Commission press release issued March 24, 1954, following a presidential press conference. Cited in Lapp, 126–27.
84. In a letter dated January 4, 1955, United States Ambassador John M. Allison made these provisions clear to the Japanese government, and allotted the funds accordingly. See Lapp, 182–84.
85. Richard Story, *A History of Modern Japan* (London: Penguin Books, 1960), 261.
86. Salaff, 22–23.
87. Robert C. Kiste, *The Bikinians: A Study of Forced Migration* (Menlo Park, Calif.: Cummings Publishing Co., 1974); Salaff, 78–83.
88. United States Department of Energy, *The Meaning of Radiation at Bikini Atoll;* Johnson, "Micronesia," 14–15; and Weisgall, 85–90.
89. Public Law 94–34, 94th Cong., 1st sess., 1975, 89 Stat., 212; and Public Law 95–348, 95th Cong., 2nd sess., 1978, 92 Stat., 488, Section 2(a).
90. *Newsweek* (June 11, 1984): 12–13D; *U.S. News & World Report* (October 18, 1982): 48–50; *New York Times,* May 2, 1984; *New York Times,* May 17, 1984; and *New York Times,* March 14, 1985.
91. Johnson, "Paradise Lost," 24–25; *Enewetak Atoll: Cleaning Up Nuclear Contamination* (Washington, D.C.: United States General Accounting Office, 1979), 1–2, 12–13; *Environmental Impact Statement: Cleanup, Rehabilitation, and Resettlement of Enewetak Atoll* (Washington, D.C.: United States Defense Nuclear Agency, 1975); *The Enewetok Atoll Today* (Washington, D.C.: United States Department of Energy, 1979); and Uhl and Ensign, 46–53.
92. *Enewetak Atoll: Cleaning Up,* 4–6, provides a detailed comparison between Bikini and Eniwetok.
93. Defense Nuclear Agency, "Fact-Sheet—Enewetak Operation," Washington, D.C., 1980; "Story of Eniwetok Clean-Up," *Atomic Veterans Newsletter* 2 (November/December 1979): 14; and Johnson, "Paradise Lost," 24.
94. *The Enewetak Atoll Today.*
95. In early 1978, American scientists concluded that the Bikinians' high levels of internal radiation were caused by their consumption of locally grown foods. The people were prohibited from eating these products, but when the outside food supply system failed to operate efficiently due to lack of shops and resources, the natives returned to their own crops for nourishment. Weisgall, 89.
96. Johnson, "Paradise Lost," 24–25.
97. Ibid., 24.
98. Ibid.

CHAPTER 5. BOMBS IN THE BACKYARD

1. "Project 'Nutmeg' " (United States Department of Defense, 1949), 42; and Frederick Reines, "Discussion of Radiological Hazards Associated with a Continental Test Site for Atomic Bombs," meeting notes, August 1, 1950, at Los Alamos Scientific Laboratory, Los Alamos, New Mexico.
2. Hewlett and Duncan, 535.
3. Truman, *Years of Trial and Hope*, 417–28.
4. Ibid., 312–15.
5. Rosenberg, 30; and Colonel K. E. Fields, "Selection of a Continental Test Site" (United States Atomic Energy Commission, Division of Military Application, December, 1950).
6. *Operation Ranger—1951* (Washington, D.C.: United States Defense Nuclear Agency, 1982), 21.
7. "The Nevada Test Site" (Nevada Legislative Counsel Bureau, Research Division, 1983), 2.
8. Rosenberg, 30–32.
9. Albin J. Dahl, *Nevada's Southern Economy* (Carson City: University of Nevada Press, 1969), 20; ibid., 33.
10. Frederick C. Worman, "Anatomy of the Nevada Test Site" (Los Alamos: Los Alamos Scientific Laboratory and University of California, 1965), 6.
11. Edwin B. Eckel, "Development of Geologic Knowledge at Nevada Test Site," *Nevada Test Site,* Proceedings of the Rocky Mountain Section of the Geological Society of America, Las Vegas, Nevada, 1968, 5–7.
12. E. B. Ekren, "Geological Setting of Nevada Test Site and Nellis Air Force Range," *Nevada Test Site,* 11–19; F. N. Houser, "Application of Geology to Underground Nuclear Testing, Nevada Test Site," *Nevada Test Site,* 21–33; Eckel, 5–10; and Worman, 2–4.
13. On December 18, 1970, a venting resulted from the "Baneberry" underground shot. Some nine hundred men working in Area 12 at the test site had to be evacuated and the facility was closed down until after the Christmas holiday. See Chapter 8 for further discussion. On February 15, 1984, a cave-in occurred which killed one test site worker and injured eleven others. *Las Vegas Sun*, February 16, 1984; and *Las Vegas Review-Journal*, February 16, 1984.
14. Truman, *Years of Trial and Hope*, 312–15.
15. Hewlett and Duncan, 535.
16. United States Atomic Energy Commission press release, January 11, 1951, NA/RG 326.
17. *Operation Ranger—1951*, 20.
18. *Operation Ranger—1951*.
19. "Operation Ranger: Operational Program Reports" (Los Alamos, New Mex.: Los Alamos Scientific Laboratory and University of California, January–February 1951).

20. Rosenberg, 34–35.
21. Ibid., 37–39.
22. Ibid., 38–39.
23. *Exercise Desert Rock Information and Guide* (United States Army, 1951).
24. Uhl and Ensign, 58; and Rosenberg, 43, 51.
25. Uhl and Ensign, 64–65; and Rosenberg, 40–52. Reports submitted by these two groups included: Human Resources Research Office, *Desert Rock I: A Psychological Study of Troop Reactions to an Atomic Explosion* (Washington, D.C.: George Washington University, February 1953); and *Desert Rock IV: Reactions of an Armored Infantry Battalion to an Atomic Bomb Maneuver* (Washington, D.C.: George Washington University, August 1953); and Operations Research Office, *Reactions of Troops in Atomic Maneuvers: Exercise Desert Rock IV* (Baltimore: Johns Hopkins University, July 1953).
26. *Operation Buster-Jangle—1951* (Washington, D.C.: United States Defense Nuclear Agency, 1982).
27. Rosenberg, 46.
28. Ibid., 47–48.
29. Ibid., 48–50.
30. Ibid., 57, 59–60.
31. Ibid., 61.
32. "Operation Upshot-Knothole Project 8.5: Thermal Radiation Protection Afforded Test Animals by Fabric Assemblies" (Albuquerque: Armed Forces Special Weapons Project, Sandia Base, 1953); and ibid., 61–63.
33. Public Law 920, 82nd Cong., 1st sess., 1951, 64 Stat., 1245–57; 50 U.S.C., 2251.
34. A graphic report of one of these Doom Town operations appeared on page 1 of the *Las Vegas Review-Journal,* May 6, 1955.
35. Samuel W. Mathews, "Nevada Learns to Live with the Atom," *National Geographic* (June 1953): 842–48; and Ensign and Uhl, 76–85.
36. *Las Vegas Review-Journal,* January 22, 1956; and *Las Vegas Sun,* January 19, 1956.
37. *Las Vegas Review-Journal,* June 8, 1963; and *Las Vegas Sun,* June 8, 1963.
38. John G. Fuller, *The Day We Bombed Utah: America's Most Lethal Secret* (New York: New American Library, 1984).
39. *Washington County News,* May 21, 1953.
40. Rosenberg, 64.
41. House Committee on Interstate and Foreign Commerce, "The Forgotten Guinea Pigs," 96th Cong., 2nd sess., 1980, 3–13; Fuller; and Wasserman and Solomon, 70–79.
42. For example, the AEC paid several hundred dollars for some horses that suffered beta radiation burns in 1953, but did not acknowledge sheep deaths which occurred during the same period. *Deseret News,* February 15, 1979.
43. United States Atomic Energy Commission press release, January 12, 1954, NA/RG 326.

44. James Hubert McBride, *The Test Ban Treaty: Military, Technological, and Political Implications* (Chicago: Henry Regnery Company, 1967). See Chapter 6 for further discussion.

45. "DOE's Nevada Operations Office: What It Does and Why" (United States Department of Energy, 1982), 1.

46. Ibid., 3; and Dahl, 30–32.

47. The expanded highway was completed in 1965. It was a $10-million project, to which both NASA and the AEC contributed $4.5 million each, and the state of Nevada $1 million.

48. Ibid., 1; and Dahl, 23–30.

49. "DOE's Nevada Operations Office," 2–3; Dahl, 32–33; and "NTS, Nevada Test Site" (United States Atomic Energy Commission, 1973), 20–21.

50. Dahl, 32.

51. "NTS, Nevada Test Site," 22.

52. "DOE's Nevada Operations Office," 3.

53. Ibid., 2; "Nevada Test Site," issued by United States Atomic Energy Commission, Public Office of Information, and published in *Nevada, The Silver State* (Carson City: Western States Historical Publishers, Inc., 1970) vol. 2, 719–22; and "NTS, Nevada Test Site," 6, 15.

54. "The Nevada Test Site," 8.

55. *Announced United States Nuclear Tests,* 1.

CHAPTER 6. SELLING THE BOMB

1. Truman, *Years of Trial and Hope,* 312–15.

2. These events are well documented in such works as: Morton Kaplan, *The Life and Death of the Cold War* (Chicago: Nelson Hale, 1976); Hans L. Trefousse, ed., *The Cold War: A Book of Documents* (New York: Putnam's, 1965), 73–166; John Lukacs, *A New History of the Cold War* (Garden City, N.Y.: Doubleday, 1966), 3–103; and Andrew Werth, *Russia: The Post War Years* (New York: Taplinger Publishers, 1971). See also Chapter 3, note 45.

3. William F. Buckley, ed., *The Committee and it. Critics* (New York: Putnam, 1962); Robert K. Carr, *The House Committee on Un-American Activities, 1945–1950* (Ithaca: Cornell University Press, 1952); Lawrence S. Wittner, *Cold War America: From Hiroshima to Watergate* (New York: Praeger, 1974), 86–109; William Manchester, *The Glory and the Dream: A Narrative History of America 1932–1972* (New York: Bantam Books, 1974), 473–517; Earl Latham, *The Communist Controversy in Washington from the New Deal to McCarthy* (Cambridge: Harvard University Press, 1966), 186–94; Walter Goodman, *The Committee: The Extraordinary Career of the House Committee on Un-American Activities* (New York:

Farrar, Straus, and Giroux, 1968); and Eric Bentley, ed., *Thirty Years of Treason: Excerpts from Hearings before House Committee on Un-American Activities 1938–1968* (New York: Viking, 1971).

4. Carr, 55–78; Larry Ceplair, *The Inquisition in Hollywood: Politics in the Film Community, 1930–60* (Garden City, N.Y.: Doubleday, 1980); Victor S. Navasky, *Naming Names* (New York: Viking Press, 1980); House Committee on Un-American Activities, "Communist Infiltration of the Motion Picture Industry," 80th Cong., 1st sess., 1947; Robert Vaughn, *Only Victims: A Study of Show Business Blacklisting* (New York: Putnam 1972); and John Cogley, *Report on Blacklisting: Movies* (New York: Meridian Books, 1956).

5. Carr, 88–131; Buckley, 143–75; Manchester, 502–12; Alistair Cooke, *A Generation on Trial* (New York: Knopf, 1951); Whittaker Chambers, *Witness* (New York: Random House, 1952); Alger Hiss, *In the Court of Public Opinion* (New York: Knopf, 1957); Nathan Glazer, *Twentieth Century Causes Celebres: Sacco-Vanzetti, Alger Hiss, the Rosenbergs* (Lake Bluff, Ill.: Regnery-Gateway, 1985); John C. Smith, *Alger Hiss: The True Story* (New York: Holt, Rinehart, and Winston, 1976); and Allen Weinstein, *Perjury: The Hiss-Chambers Case* (New York: Knopf, 1978).

6. Manchester, 512–30; 700–718; Wittner, 93–102; Latham, 319–55; Robert Griffith, *The Politics of Fear: Joseph R. McCarthy and the Senate* (Lexington: University of Kentucky Press, 1970); Richard M. Fried, *Men Against McCarthy* (New York: Columbia University Press, 1976); Jack Anderson and R. W. May, *McCarthy* (Boston: Beacon Press, 1952); Richard Rovere, *Senator Joe McCarthy* (Toronto: Longmans, 1959); Fred J. Cook, *The Nightmare Decade* (New York: Random House, 1971); Thomas C. Reeves, *The Life and Times of Joe McCarthy: A Biography* (New York: Stein and Day, 1982); "McCarthyism: Interpretations Since Hofstadter," *Wisconsin Magazine of History* 60 (1976): 42–54; and "The Search for Joe McCarthy," *Wisconsin Magazine of History* 60 (1977): 185–96.

7. *Smith Act*, June 28, 1940, Public Law 670, Chap. 439, 76th Cong., 2nd sess., 54 Stat., 670; 18 U.S.C., 2385.

8. *McCarran Act*, June 27, 1952, Public Law 414, Chap. 477, 82nd Cong., 2nd sess., 66 Stat., 163; 8 U.S.C., 1101–1503.

9. *Communist Control Act*, August 24, 1954, Public Law 637, Chap. 886, 83rd Cong., 2nd sess., 68 Stat., 775; 50 U.S.C., 841.

10. See *Dennis v. United States*, 341 U.S. 494 (1951); Edward C. Smith, *The Constitution of the United States*, 11th ed. (New York: Barnes and Noble, 1979), 103–5; *Scales v. United States*, 367 U.S. 703 (1961); *Yates v. United States*, 354 U.S. 298 (1957); and *Communist Party v. Subversive Activities Control Board*, 367 U.S. 1(1961).

11. Solomon A. Fineberg, *The Rosenberg Case* (New York: Oceana Publication, 1953); Louis Nizer, *The Implosion Conspiracy* (Garden City, N.Y.: Doubleday, 1973); Jonathan Root, *The Betrayers: The Rosenberg Case—A Reappraisal of an American Crisis* (New York: Coward-McCann, 1963);

Alvin H. Goldstein, *The Unquiet Death of Julius and Ethel Rosenberg* (Westport, Conn.: Lawrence Hill, 1975); Ronald Radosh and Joyce Milton, *The Rosenberg File: A Search for the Truth* (New York: Holt, Rinehart and Winston, 1983); and Glazer.

12. Manchester, 493–96; Truman, *Years of Trial and Hope,* 269–93; Wittner, 36–39; Eleanor Bontecou, *The Federal Loyalty-Security Program* (Cornell University Press, 1953); Richard Freeland, *The Truman Doctrine and the Origins of McCarthyism* (New York: Knopf, 1972), 115–34; Athan G. Theoraris, *Seeds of Repression: Harry S. Truman and the Origins of Mc-Carthyism* (Chicago: Quadrangle Books, 1971), 98–114; and David Caute, *The Great Fear: The Anti-Communist Purge Under Truman and Eisenhower* (New York: Simon and Schuster, 1978), 267–72, 274–93.

13. Manchester, 671–72; Wittner, 176–78; and Caute, 273–93.

14. Public Law 920, 82nd Cong., 1st sess., 1951.

15. Warren Cheney, "You and Your Atomic Future," *Film News* XI (1951): 4–7, 27.

16. A. Costandina Titus, "Back to Ground Zero: Old Footage Through New Lenses," *Journal of Popular Film and Television* 11(1983): 2–11; United States Office of Civil Defense Mobilization, *Motion Pictures on Civil Defense* (Washington, D.C., 1958); and United States Civil Defense Preparedness Agency, *Motion Picture Catalog* (Washington, D.C., 1975).

17. Rosenberg, 43, 51; and Uhl and Ensign, 58.

18. Statement by Chairman Lewis L. Strauss, United States Atomic Energy Commission before the Joint Committee on Atomic Energy, April 15, 1955, NA/RG 326, 9. For a better understanding of Strauss's position, see his own book, *Men and Decisions* (New York: Doubleday, 1962); and Richard Pfau, *No Sacrifice Too Great: The Life of Lewis Strauss* (Charlottesville: University Press of Virginia, 1984).

19. Dr. W. F. Libby, Commissioner of the AEC, to Dr. Albert Schweitzer on April 25, 1957, NA/RG 326.

20. Teller and Latter, 144.

21. United States Atomic Energy report issued on June 29, 1954, NA/RG 326, 1–2.

22. Phillip M. Stern, *The Oppenheimer Case: Security on Trial* (New York: Harper and Row, 1969); Goodchild, 191–269; Harold Green, "The Oppenheimer Case: A Study in the Abuse of the Law," *Bulletin of the Atomic Scientists* 33(1977): 12–16, 56–61; and John Major, *The Oppenheimer Hearing* (London: Batsford, 1971).

23. Lewis L. Strauss, April 15, 1955, NA/RG 326, 9.

24. Pringle and Spigelman, 103.

25. *Las Vegas Review-Journal,* January 28, 1984.

26. Ibid., February 24, 1984.

27. Captain James S. Russell, June 14, 1949, NA/RG 326.

28. Lewis L. Strauss, April 15, 1955, NA/RG 326, 10.

29. Ibid., March 31, 1954, NA/RG 326, 4.

30. Ibid., April 15, 1955, NA/RG 326, 9.
31. Lewis L. Strauss to Carl T. Durham, Chairman of the Joint Committee on Atomic Energy, May 4, 1958, NA/RG 326, 2.
32. United States Atomic Energy Commission press release, May 29, 1957, NA/RG 326.
33. United States Atomic Energy Commission press release, December 22, 1947, NA/RG 326.
34. Statement by Major General Percy W. Clarkson, Joint Task Force 132, released by Atomic Energy Commission, November 16, 1952, NA/RG 326.
35. Pringle and Spigelman, 121–24; and Allardice and Trapnell, 200–201.
36. Pringle and Spigelman, 123. Other informational films about peaceful uses of atomic power which were distributed by the AEC during this era included "The Magic of the Atom" (1954), "Dawn's Early Light" (1955), "The Peaceful Atom" (1957), "Industrial Applications of Nuclear Explosions" (1958), "Atoms on the Farm" (1959), and "Atomic Weathermen" (1961). Titus, "Back to Ground Zero."
37. *Congressional Record,* 84th Cong., 1st sess., 1955, 608, 8794, 8886.
38. Hilgartner, Bell, and O'Connor, 44, 48.
39. Quoted in Pringle and Spigelman, 124.
40. Green and Rosenthal, 124; and United States Congress, H. R. Doc. No. 328, "Message from the President of the United States Transmitting Recommendations Relative to the Atomic Energy Act of 1946," 83rd Cong., 2nd sess., 1954.
41. Allardice and Trapnell, 201–3.
42. United States Atomic Energy Commission press release, December 31, 1956, NA/RG 326, 6–7.
43. Pringle and Spigelman, 201–16.
44. David B. Brooks and John V. Krutilla, *Peaceful Use of Nuclear Explosives: Some Economic Aspects* (Baltimore: Johns Hopkins Press, 1969); Allardice and Trapnell, 81–82; "DOE's Nevada Operations Office: What It Does and Why," 1, and United States Atomic Energy Commission press release, June 9, 1958, NA/RG 326.
45. Lewis L. Strauss, April 15, 1955, NA/RG 326, 5–6.
46. United States Atomic Energy Commission press release, August 28, 1951, NA/RG 326.
47. Ibid., May 13, 1957, NA/RG 326, 1.
48. Ibid., May 1, 1958, NA/RG 326.
49. United States Atomic Energy Commission, *Atomic Tests in Nevada* (Washington, 1957), 3–6.
50. Dahl, 21.
51. "DOE's Nevada Operations Office," 2.
52. *Atomic Tests in Nevada.*
53. Defense Civil Preparedness Agency, *Motion Picture Catalog,* 9. The film described is entitled "About Fallout" (1964) and is still being shown

today. The quote from Jones is cited in Robert Scheer, *With Enough Shovels: Reagan, Bush, and Nuclear War* (New York: Random House, 1982), 18, 21.

54. Statement by Lewis L. Strauss, February 15, 1955, NA/RG 326, 6.
55. Lewis L. Strauss, April 15, 1955, NA/RG 326, 6–7.
56. Dr. W. F. Libby to Dr. Albert Schweitzer, April 25, 1957, NA/RG 326.
57. Letter from General Advisory Committee to the United States Atomic Energy Commission, May 4, 1959, NA/RG 326, 2.
58. *Fallout from Nuclear Tests at the Nevada Test Site* (Washington, D.C.: United States Atomic Energy Commission, 1959), 21.
59. *Las Vegas Sun*, June 8, 1963.
60. *Las Vegas Review-Journal*, December 20, 1970.
61. Ibid., October 26, 1984.
62. Defense Nuclear Agency, *Compilation of Local Fallout Data from Test Detonations, 1945–1962*, Report No. DNA1251-1-EX (May 1979); and United States Department of Energy Dose Assessment Advisory Group, *Reports*, (1980–1984), vols. 1–10.
63. *Las Vegas Sun*, May 15, 1986.
64. Raymond E. Brim and Patricia Condon, "Another A-Bomb Cover-Up," *Washington Monthly* (January 1981): 48.
65. Statement by Strauss, April 15, 1955, NA/RG 326, 4.
66. *U.S. News & World Report* (March 25, 1955): 21–26.
67. Austin Brues, "Critique of the Linear Theory of Carcinogenesis," *Science* (September 26, 1958): 693–99.
68. Wasserman and Solomon, 93–94.
69. House Committee on Interstate and Foreign Commerce, Subcommittee on Oversight and Investigations, *Hearings on Low-Level Radiation Effects on Health*, 96th Cong., 1st sess., 1979, 38.
70. *Salt Lake Tribune*, May 11, 1984.
71. *Las Vegas Review-Journal*, June 25, 1985.
72. George T. Mazuzan and J. Samuel Walker, *Controlling the Atom: The Beginnings of Nuclear Regulation 1946–1962* (Berkeley: University of California Press, 1984), 57.

CHAPTER 7. LIVING UNDER THE MUSHROOM CLOUD

1. George Gallup, *The Gallup Poll, Public Opinion, 1935–1971* (New York: Random House, 1972), vol. 2, 895, 907, 1460, 1744.
2. Ibid., 888, 895.
3. Ibid., 1229, 1452, 1552, 1759.
4. Ibid., 1488, 1553, 1745.
5. Wasserman and Solomon, 113.
6. Richard Scammon, ed., *America Votes, A Handbook of Contemporary Election Statistics, 1956–57* (New York: MacMillan, 1958), 2.

7. *Political History of Nevada,* 4th ed. (Carson City, State Printing Office, 1960), 226.

8. Scammon, 410.

9. Ibid.

10. Ibid., 241.

11. Ibid.; and Clark County, Nevada, Registrar of Voters, January 29, 1985.

12. *Guide to the Congress of the United States: Origins, History and Procedure* (Washington, D.C.: Congressional Quarterly Service, 1971), 5a, 83a, 104a.

13. Kevin Rafferty, Jayne Loader, and Pierce Rafferty, *The Atomic Cafe: The Book of the Film* (New York: Bantam Books, 1982), 38, 103; Heinz Haber, *The Walt Disney Story of Our Friend the Atom* (New York: Simon and Schuster, 1956).

14. Boy Scouts of America, *Atomic Energy* (Irving, Tex.: Boy Scouts of America, 1965); and Hilgartner, Bell, and O'Connor, 74.

15. Hilgartner, Bell, and O'Connor, 74.

16. Rafferty, Loader, and Rafferty, 36.

17. Ibid., 65.

18. Ibid., 42.

19. Ibid., 104.

20. See Joe Kane, "Nuclear Films," *Take One* 6 (1969): 9–11; Jack G. Shaheen, ed., *Nuclear War Films* (Carbondale: Southern Illinois University Press, 1978); and A. Costandina Titus, "Selling the Bomb: Hollywood and the Government Join Forces at Ground Zero," *Halcyon* 7 (1985): 17–30.

21. Metro Goldwyn Mayer, *Facts About the Making of "The Beginning or the End?"* (Hollywood, 1947); and Michael J. Yavenditti, "Atomic Scientists and Hollywood: 'The Beginning or the End?,' " *Film and History* 8 (1978): 73–88.

22. John Baxter, *Science Fiction in the Cinema* (New York: A. S. Barnes, 1970); Denis Gifford, *Science Fiction Film* (New York: Dutton, 1971); Brian Murphy, "Monster Movies: They Came from Beneath the Fifties," *Journal of Popular Film* 1 (1972): 31–44; Dennis Saleh, *Science Fiction Gold: Film Classics of the Fifties* (New York: McGraw-Hill, 1979); and M. Wood, "Kiss Tomorrow Hello," *American Film* II (1977): 14–17.

23. A typical film of this type is "The World, the Flesh, and the Devil," (1959) starring Inger Stevens, Mel Ferrer, and Harry Belafonte as the only three people left on earth after an atomic war. This love triangle is further complicated by the fact that one of the members is black. Other examples include "Five" (1951), "The Incredible Shrinking Man" (1956), and "The Last Woman on Earth" (1960).

24. One sci-fi film appeared during this period, Stanley Kramer's "On the Beach" (1959), which did not follow the pattern of Hollywood's other atomic movies. Set in Australia in the year 1964, the film featured a small group of people, including Gregory Peck, Ava Gardner, Fred Astaire,

and Anthony Perkins, awaiting death as a fallout cloud approached. The movie was praised by Dr. Linus Pauling as being the film that could save the world. Its message was clearly that life is beautiful and man must do all he can to save it from annihilation while there is still time. Despite Pauling's optimistic assessment, however, the public impact of the film at the time of its first release was less than spectacular; it evoked a much greater response from later showings on television and in certain small cult theatres. The general public was just not ready to accept this message in 1959; consequently, several years passed before Hollywood attempted any further productions along these lines.

25. For reviews of the movies discussed in this chapter, see *The New York Times Film Reviews* (New York: Arno Press, 1970), vols. 4, 5.

26. *Las Vegas Review-Journal,* October 18, 1955.

27. Daniel Lang, "Our Far-Flung Correspondents: Blackjack and Flashes," *New Yorker* 8 (September 20, 1952): 97; Georgia Lewis, " 'Atomized' Las Vegas Danced 'Atomic Boogie,' " *The Nevadan,* January 23, 1983, 7L, A. Costandina Titus, "A-Bombs in the Backyard: Southern Nevada Adapts to the Nuclear Age, 1951–1963," *Nevada Historical Society Quarterly* 26 (Winter 1983): 250–51.

28. Lang, 95–96; and Lewis, 7L.

29. *Las Vegas Review-Journal,* April 2, 1946.

30. Ibid., November 6, 1945.

31. Pictures available from the Las Vegas News Bureau, Las Vegas, Nevada.

32. Rosenberg, 82.

33. Lang, 90.

34. *Las Vegas Review-Journal,* March 13, 1953.

35. Hilgartner, Bell, and O'Connor, 90.

36. Uhl and Ensign, 77.

37. Lang, 91.

38. An excellent example of this seal can be found on the cover of the 1958–1959 annual statistical report issued by the Clark County Planning Department. The seal was changed by the Clark County Commissioners on March 20, 1962, and the mushroom cloud was replaced with a sketch of the convention center.

39. Las Vegas High School, *Wildcat Echo* (1953).

40. For example, see Southern Nevada Telephone Directory for August 1955 and July 1956.

41. The card was distributed by the "C.T. Photochrom" Post Card Company in Chicago. Other cards featuring shots of giant mushroom clouds were also available.

42. "Operation 'Doom Town,' " *Nevada Highways and Parks* 13 (June–December 1952): 1–17.

43. Lang, 90–99.

44. Samuel W. Matthews, "Nevada Learns to Live with the Atom," *National Geographic* 103 (June 1953): 839–50.

45. *Life*, November 12, 1951, p. 37.
46. *New York Times*, February 13, 1955.
47. Uhl and Ensign, 76–77, 83.
48. *Las Vegas Sun*, March 13, 1955.
49. *Las Vegas Review-Journal*, March 11, 1955.
50. Ibid., March 22, 1955.
51. *Las Vegas Sun*, May 1, 1958.
52. Ibid., April 6, 1958.
53. Ibid., March 13, 1958.
54. *Las Vegas Review-Journal*, April 12, 1953.
55. Ibid., May 6, 1955.
56. Ibid., March 17, 1953.
57. Ibid., January 15, 1951.
58. *Las Vegas Sun*, January 30, 1951.
59. Lang, 97–98.
60. *Las Vegas Review-Journal*, May 24, 1953.
61. *Las Vegas Sun*, February 18, 1955.
62. *Las Vegas Review-Journal*, February 18, 1955.
63. Nevada Senate Joint Resolution 7 introduced on February 17, 1955, by Nevada State Senator Leutzinger.
64. Nevada Assembly Bill 13 (Ch. 202) introduced on January 19, 1955, by Nevada Assemblyman Donald Leighton.
65. Nevada Senate Joint Resolution 3 (File No. 14) introduced on January 30, 1957, by Senator Leutzinger, the same gentleman who previously introduced a measure in 1955 calling for the AEC to stop atomic testing in Nevada.
66. Nevada Senate Joint Resolution 15 (File No. 28) introduced on March 1, 1957, by Senators Leutzinger and Farrell Seevers.
67. Lang, 97.
68. Jerome Edwards, *Pat McCarran: Political Boss of Nevada* (Reno: University of Nevada Press, 1982).
69. Sister Margaret P. McCarran, "Patrick Anthony McCarran: 1876–1954," *Nevada Historical Society Quarterly* 12 (Spring 1969): 50; and *Las Vegas Review-Journal*, May 26, 1953.
70. House Committee on Interstate and Foreign Commerce, *Hearings*, 96th Cong., 1st sess., 1979, 31.
71. Wasserman and Solomon, 94–96.
72. Douglas T. Miller and Marion Nowak, *The Fifties: The Way We Really Were* (New York: Doubleday, 1977), 413.
73. Ibid., 63.
74. Ibid., 80; and *Las Vegas Sun*, May 11, 1958, and June 2, 1958.
75. *Las Vegas Sun*, May 14, 1958.
76. Fuller, 5–12, 50–51.
77. House Committee on Interstate and Foreign Commerce, 39.

78. Donald L. Bartlett and James B. Steele, *Empire: The Life, Legend, and Madness of Howard Hughes* (New York: Norton, 1979), 340–47.
79. Edgerton, Germeshausen, and Green, Inc., *The Nevada Test Site and Southern Nevada*, Report No. L–512 (March 15, 1961), 12.
80. *Las Vegas Review-Journal*, August 25, 1963.
81. The Clark County Commissioners kept the question off the ballot with a vote of 4 to 1.
82. *Las Vegas Review-Journal*, January 28, 1984.
83. Ibid., March 3, 1984.
84. *Las Vegas Sun*, June 29, 1984.
85. On January 7, 1983, Congress passed P.L. 97–425, the Nuclear Waste Policy Act (96 Stat., 2201; 42 U.S.C., 10101), which called for the development of repositories for the disposal of high-level radioactive waste. The list of potential sites has been narrowed to three with Yucca Mountain at the Nevada Test Site tentatively classified as first on the list. The final decision will be made by 1991. The governor of Nevada, Democrat Richard Bryan, and the city government of Las Vegas opposed having the repository located at the NTS. See U.S. Department of Energy, *Draft Environmental Assessment Overview* (December, 1984); *Las Vegas Sun*, five-part series on nuclear waste, January 2–6, 1985; and Carl Behrens, "Nuclear Waste Management," Issue Brief No. IB83010, (Washington, D.C.: Congressional Research Service, January 17, 1983).

CHAPTER 8. POLITICAL FALLOUT FROM ABOVE-GROUND
TESTS

1. Paul Boyer, "From Activism to Apathy: The American People and Nuclear Weapons, 1963–1980," *Journal of American History* 70(1984): 821–44.
2. Linus Pauling, *No More War* (New York: Dodd, Mead and Co., 1958), and *Science and Peace, The Nobel Peace Prize Lecture* (New York: Center for the Study of Democratic Institutions, 1964).
3. *Congressional Record*, 88th Cong., 1st sess., 1963, 9415, 9483–90.
4. Senate Committee on Foreign Relations, *Hearings on the Nuclear Test Ban Treaty*, 88th Cong., 1st sess., 1963, 622.
5. Senate Committee on Armed Services, Preparedness Investigating Sub-committee, *Hearings on Military Aspects and Implications of Nuclear Test Ban Proposals and Related Matters*, 88th Cong., 1st sess., 1963, 470.
6. Senate Committee on Foreign Relations, 455.
7. "Text of President Kennedy's Treaty Message to the Senate," *Congressional Quarterly Weekly Report* (August 16, 1963): 1457.
8. Senate Committee on Armed Services, 721.

9. Ibid., 187.

10. Ibid., 970.

11. See McBride, *The Test Ban Treaty,* 76–119, for a discussion of the military advantages and disadvantages of the treaty.

12. "Senate Ratifies Test Ban Treaty by Substantial Margin," *Congressional Quarterly Weekly Report* (September 27, 1963): 1677–79; and "Nuclear Test Ban Treaty Ratified," *Congressional Quarterly Almanac,* XIX, 1963, 248–54, 686.

13. *Congressional Quarterly Weekly Report* (September 27, 1963): 1692.

14. Chalmers M. Roberts, *The Nuclear Years: The Arms Race and Arms Control, 1945–70* (New York: Praeger, 1970); Walter C. Clemens, Jr., *The Superpowers and Arms Control: From Cold War to Interdependence* (Lexington, Mass.: D. C. Heath, 1973).

15. Theodore Sorensen, *Kennedy* (New York: Harper and Row, 1965), 828.

16. House Committee on Interstate and Foreign Commerce, 1979, 301–6.

17. Ibid., 1980, 19.

18. Memorandum from Nathan H. Woodruff to A. R. Luedecke, January 11, 1963, cited in House Committee on Interstate and Foreign Commerce, 1980, 19.

19. Edward S. Weiss, "Leukemia Mortality Studies in Southwestern Utah," a proposed article (September 14, 1965); cited in House Committee on Interstate and Foreign Commerce, 1980, 15.

20. Ibid.

21. Memorandum from Dwight Ink to AEC Chairman Seaborg, September 9, 1965; ibid.

22. Edward Weiss, Richard Olsen, Carlyle Thompson, and Alfonse Masi, "Surgically Treated Thyroid Disease Among Young People in Utah, 1948–1962," *American Journal of Public Health* 15 (1967): 1807–14.

23. House Committee on Interstate and Foreign Commerce, 1980, 16.

24. Ibid.

25. See Joseph Lyon, et al., "Childhood Leukemias Associated with Fallout from Nuclear Testing," *New England Journal of Medicine* 300 (1979): 397–402.

26. Paul Duckworth, *Baneberry, A Nuclear Disaster* (Las Vegas: Harris Printers, 1976), 3–4.

27. Ibid., 4–6.

28. *Las Vegas Review-Journal,* December 19, 1970; and *Las Vegas Sun,* December 19, 1970.

29. Duckworth, 6.

30. Weisgall, 78–83.

31. Uhl and Ensign, 89–92; and Saffer and Kelly, 149–56.

32. Glyn Caldwell, Delle Kelley, and Clark Heath, Jr., "Leukemia Among Participants in Military Maneuvers at a Nuclear Bomb Test," *Journal of the American Medical Association* 244 (1980): 1575–78.

33. *Washington Post,* February 25, 1978.

34. Saffer and Kelly, 155, 157–58.
35. House Committee on Public Health and the Environment, *Hearings,* 95th Cong., 2nd sess., 1978.
36. Freedom of Information Act, Public Law 93–502, 93rd Cong., 2nd sess., 1974, 80 Stat., 383; 5 U.S.C., 552. See "Freedom of Information Veto Overridden," *Congressional Quarterly Almanac* XXX, 1974, 648–54; and "Congress Clears Freedom of Information Bill," *Congressional Quarterly Weekly Report* (October 12, 1974): 2882.
37. *Report of the Interagency Task Force on the Health Effects of Ionizing Radiation* (Washington, D.C.: U.S. Department of Health, Education and Welfare, 1979), iii–x.
38. Ibid., 103.
39. Ibid., 28.
40. *Report of the Interagency Task Force on Compensation for Radiation-Related Illnesses* (Washington, D.C.: U.S. Department of Justice, 1980), 30.
41. Ibid., 25.
42. Ibid., 37.
43. Ibid., 37–57.
44. Public Law 95–622, 95th Cong., 2nd sess., 1978, 92 Stat., 3412; 42 U.S.C., 2689.
45. *Allen et al. v. U.S., 527 F. Supp.* 476, (1981), filed August 30, 1979, in Federal District Court in Salt Lake City.
46. Saffer and Kelly, 133–200.
47. The normal rate of leukemia among a comparable number of American males, as established by the CDC's Smoky participants study (see note 32), would be less than four.
48. Wasserman and Solomon, 118–21.
49. National Association of Radiation Survivors, information brochure (Sacramento, Calif., 1983).
50. *Newsweek* (April 9, 1979): 26.
51. Ibid, 24–42; *Time* (April 9, 1979): 8–20; Carl Behrens, "Nuclear Power: Cleaning Up Three Mile Island," U.S. Library of Congress, Congressional Research Service, Issue Brief Number IB81176, 1981, 1–4; and Warren Donnelly, *Congressional Response to the Nuclear Accident at Three Mile Island, March Through September 1979: A 6-Month Status Report,* Report no. 79–225 ENR (U.S. Library of Congress, Congressional Research Service, 1979), 1–3.

CHAPTER 9. MORE LIKELY THAN NOT

1. Sir William Blackstone, *Commentaries on the Laws of England* (Philadelphia: Robert Bell Union Library, 1771), 237–48.
2. *Cohens v. Virginia,* 19 U.S. 264 (1821), 411–12.

3. *Gibbons v. United States,* 75 U.S. 269 (1869), 274.
4. Irvin M. Gottlieb, "Federal Legislation—Tort Claims Against the United States," *Georgetown Law Journal* 30 (1942): 464.
5. "According to the President's Message on January 14, 1942, House Doc. No. 562 of the 77th Congress, 2nd session, more than 2,000 private claim bills [were] introduced in each Congress and a substantial percentage of these [were] for property damage or personal injury," ibid., 464–65.
6. Federal Tort Claims Act, 1946, Public Law 601, 79th Cong., 2nd sess., 60 Stat., 842; 28 U.S.C., 921–46. Hereafter referred to as FTCA.
7. The legislative history of the FTCA is summarized in "Report of the Joint Committee on the Organization of Congress to Accompany S. 2177," Sen. Rep. No. 1400, 79th Cong., 2nd sess. (1946). See also "The Federal Tort Claims Act," *Yale Law Journal* 56 (1947): 534–36.
8. For general discussion of the principles of the FTCA see: Ibid., 534–61; Gottlieb, "Federal Legislation," 462–72, and "The Federal Tort Claims Act—A Statutory Interpretation," *Georgetown Law Journal* 35 (1947): 1–67; Lester Jayson, *Handling Federal Tort Claims: Administrative and Judicial Remedies* (Albany, New York: M. Bender, 1964); Sidney H. Willig, "The Breadth of the Tort Perspective: Judicial Review for Tortuous Conduct of Government Agencies and Agents," *Missouri Law Review* 45 (1980): 621–38; and "Symposium on Federal Tort Claims Act," *Federal Bar Journal* 26 (1966): 1–81.
9. FTCA, Section 410a.
10. Ibid., Section 421.
11. Ibid., Section 421a.
12. See Debra Sholl, "The Nevada Proving Grounds: An Asylum for Sovereign Immunity," *Southwestern University Law Review* 4 (1980): 633–43; Howard Ball, "The Nevada Test Site Nuclear Testing Litigation: The Role of the Federal Courts in Negligence Suits Brought by 'Downwind' Civilians Under the Federal Tort Claims Act" (Paper presented at the Western Political Science Association meeting, Seattle, Washington, March 24, 1983), 13–22, and *Justice Downwind: America's Nuclear Testing Program in the Fifties* (New York: Oxford, 1986); Osborne M. Reynolds, "The Discretionary Function Exception of the Federal Tort Claims Act," *Georgetown Law Journal* 57 (1968): 81–132; and Bruce Jenkins, "Memorandum Opinion," Civil No. C79–0515 J, United States District Court for the District of Utah Central Division, *Irene Allen, et al. v. United States,* 13–59.
13. *Dalehite v. United States,* 346 U.S. 15 (1953).
14. Ibid., 30–36.
15. *Indian Towing Co. v. United States,* 350 U.S. 61 (1955).
16. Ibid., 319–21.
17. *United Airlines v. Weiner,* 335 F. 2d. 379 (1964).
18. *Doe v. McMillan,* 412 U.S. 306 (1973).
19. Ball, 21.

20. *Bulloch v. United States,* 145 F. Supp. 824 (1956).
21. Ibid., 826–27.
22. *Bartholomae v. United States,* 253 F. 2d. 716 (1957).
23. Despite its ruling against the claimant, however, the court did add that there is a duty to act with "due care" in the implementation of any policy, ibid., 718.
24. *Blaber v. United States,* 332 F. 2d. 629 (1964).
25. Ibid., 631.
26. *Kuhne v. United States,* 267 F. Supp. 649 (1967).
27. Ibid., 658.
28. Roger Foley, "Findings of Fact and Conclusions of Law," Civil LV 1766 RDF, United States District Court—District of Nevada, *Dorothy Roberts, et al. v. United States,* and *Louise Nunamaker v. United States,* 104–7.
29. Bruce Jenkins, 148–51.
30. Ibid., 152.
31. Ibid., 152–57.
32. 28 U.S.C. 2401(b). See: Adolpho A. Franco, "*Wollman v. Gross:* Statute of Limitations and the FTCA," *Creighton Law Review* 15 (1981): 1073–79; and "The Application of the Statute of Limitations to Actions for Tortuous Radiation Exposure," *Alabama Law Review* 31 (1980): 502–21.
33. Jenkins, 160.
34. *United States v. Kubrick,* 444 U.S. 111 (1979).
35. Jenkins, 160–61.
36. Ibid., 161–62.
37. Ibid., 162.
38. Samuel D. Estep and Edward H. Forgotson, "Legal Liability for Genetic Injuries from Radiation," *Louisiana Law Review* 24 (1963): 1–53; W. Noel Keyes and John L. Howarth, "Approaches to Liability for Remote Causes: The Low Level Radiation Example," *Iowa Law Review* 56 (1971): 531–75; Diane C. Maleson, "Historical Roots of the Legal System's Response to Nuclear Power," *Southern California Law Review* 55 (1982): 597–640; Thomas J. O'Toole, "Radiation, Causation, and Compensation," *Georgetown Law Journal* 54 (1966): 751–76; E. Blythe Stason, "Tort Liability for Radiation Injuries," *Vanderbilt Law Review* 12 (1958): 93–114; Richard Delgado, "Beyond *Sindell:* Relaxation of Cause-in-Fact Rules for Indeterminate Plaintiffs," *California Law Review* 70 (1982): 881–908; and Charles L. Moore, "Radiation and Preconception Injuries: Some Interesting Problems in Tort Law," *Southwestern Law Journal* 28 (1974): 414–36.
39. Testimony by Dr. Chase Peterson, House Committee on Interstate and Foreign Commerce, 1979, 363.
40. Samuel S. Epstein, *The Politics of Cancer* (San Francisco: Sierra Club Books, 1978), 38–53; Abraham M. Lilienfeld, *Foundations of Epidemiology* (Oxford University Press, 1976); Brian MacMahon and Thomas F. Pugh, *Epidemiology: Principles and Methods* (Boston: Little, Brown, 1970); John W. Gofman, *Radiation and Human Health* (San Francisco: Sierra Club

Books, 1981), 162–233; *Las Vegas Sun,* January 6, 1985; Charles E. Land, "The Hazards of Fallout or of Epidemiological Research," *New England Journal of Medicine* 300 (1979): 431–32; and Alice Stewart, *An Epidemiologist Takes a Look at Radiation Risks* (Washington, D.C.: United States Public Health Service, 1973), 1–10.

41. *Bulloch v. United States,* 826.
42. Ibid., 826–28.
43. *Las Vegas Review-Journal,* September 24, 1982, and August 4, 1983; and Ball, 27–28.
44. *Las Vegas Review-Journal,* November 24, 1983.
45. Ibid., April 4, 1984; comments from office of Dan Bushnell, attorney for Bulloch, Salt Lake City, March 21, 1985, and July 31, 1985; and *Las Vegas Sun,* March 20, 1986.
46. Foley, 112–13.
47. Ibid., 114.
48. Interview with Judge Roger Foley, March 7, 1985. Originally twelve other plaintiffs who were exposed to radiation during the Baneberry venting filed suit with Roberts. Because they could show no illness at the time, however, the government sought the dismissal of their cases arguing that if there was no evident damage, there were no grounds for suit. Recognizing the latency period for radiation illness, Judge Foley did not dismiss the cases but "put them on the back burner" pending further developments. As of 1985, thirteen years after the incident, the twelve plaintiffs remain in good health, and therefore it is likely that their claims will be dismissed.
49. Jenkins, 319.
50. Ibid., 323.
51. *Bolger v. Chris Anderson Roofing Co.,* 112 N. J. Super. 383 (1970).
52. *Smith v. Humboldt Dye Works, Inc.,* 34 App. Div. 2d. 1041 (1970).
53. *Besner v. Walter Kidde Nuclear Labs,* 24 App. Div. 2d. 1045 (1965).
54. *Krumback v. Dow Chemical Co.,* 676 P. 2d. 1215 (Colo. App. 1983).
55. Jenkins, 339.
56. Ibid., 415–16; *Los Angeles Times,* May 11, 1984; *Las Vegas Review-Journal,* May 10, 1984; and *Las Vegas Sun,* May 13, 1984.
57. Jenkins, 418.
58. In the past, claims by radiation workers have met with little success under existing Workmen's Compensation statutes because, like the FTCA, they also require proof of causation. This problem is exacerbated by the general inadequacy of such statutes in providing coverage for industrial diseases, especially slowly developing diseases as compared to industrial accidents. See: "Workers' Compensation: Redefinition of Occupational Disease and the Applicable Compensation Statute," *Wake Forest Law Review* 16 (1980): 288–313; "Workers' Compensation and Occupational Disease," *Montana Law Review* 43 (1982): 75–107; David J. Cochrane, "Occupational Disease and Accident Compensation," *New Zealand Law*

Journal 5 (1978): 25–31; Harry W. Dahl, "Trends in Occupational Disease Compensation," *Forum* 14 (1979): 467–72; Fred H. Kumpf, "Occupational Disease Claims under the Workers' Compensation Reforms," *Seton Hall Law Review* 12 (1982): 470–83; Albert Kutchins, "Most Exclusive Remedy is no Remedy at all: Workers' Compensation Coverage for Occupational Disease," *Labor Law Journal* 32 (1981): 212–28; Charles N. Miller, "Workers' Compensation: Preparing the Occupational Disease Claim," *Trial* 16 (1980): 26–30; Mark E. Solomons, "Workers' Compensation for Occupational Disease Victims: Federal Statutes and Threshold Problems," *Albany Law Review* 41 (1977): 198–249; S. R. Wilson, "Occupational Disease: The Problems of a Comprehensive System of Coverage," *Industrial Law Journal* 11 (1982): 141–55.

59. *Prescott v. United States*, 523 F. Supp. 918 (1981); *Annotations to Nevada Revised Statutes*, vol. 6, 1981, NRS617.190 and NRS617.200; *Las Vegas Sun*, April 26, 1984; and interview with Judge Roger Foley, March 7, 1985.

60. *Las Vegas Review-Journal*, April 26, 1984.

61. "Military Personnel and the Federal Tort Claims Act," *Yale Law Journal* 58 (1949): 615–27; "In Support of the *Feres* Doctrine and a Better Definition of 'incident to service'," *St. Johns Law Review* 56 (1982): 485–514; "Effect of the *Feres* Doctrine on Tort Actions Against the U.S. by Family Members of Servicemen," *Fordham Law Review* 50 (1982): 1241–67; "Federal Tort Claims Act: A Cause of Action for Servicemen," *Valparaiso University Law Review* 14 (1980): 527–76; "From *Feres* to *Stencel*: Should Military Personnel Have Access to F.T.C.A. Recovery?" *Michigan Law Review* 77 (1979): 1099–1126; Caria DeDominicis, "Atomic Vets Take Their Case to Court," *California Law Review* 2 (1982): 28–31; Allan Favish, "Radiation Injury and the Atomic Veteran: Shifting the Burden of Proof on Factual Causation," *Hastings Law Journal* 32 (1981): 933–74; Jamie Kalnen, "The Legal Quandary," *Bulletin of the Atomic Scientists* 39 (1983): 27; and Lorna Hislop-Brumfield, "Judicial Recovery for the Post-Service Tort: A Veteran's Last Battle," *Pacific Law Journal* 14 (1983): 333–55.

62. *Feres v. United States*, 340 U.S. 135 (1950), 146.

63. Ibid.

64. *Jefferson v. United States*, 178 F. 2d. 518 (1949).

65. *Griggs v. United States*, 178 F. 2d. 1 (1949).

66. "Military Personnel and the Federal Tort Claims Act," 618–22.

67. In *Stencel v. United States*, 431 U.S. 666 (1977), the court prohibited a third-party claim for the faulty design of an ejection system which caused permanent injuries to a serviceman.

68. *Jaffee v. United States*, 663 F. 2d. 1226 (3rd Cir. 1981); Cert denied, 102 S. Ct. 2234 (1982).

69. Ibid., 1231–33.

70. Favish, 861–62.

71. Hislop-Brumfield, 340–46.
72. *Brown v. United States,* 348 U.S. 110 (1954).
73. Ibid., 112–13.
74. *Thornwell v. United States,* 471 F. Supp. 344 (D.D.C. 1979).
75. Ibid., 352–53.
76. *Lombard v. United States,* 530 F. Supp. 918 (D.D.C. 1981).
77. *Lasswell v. Brown,* 524 F. Supp. 847 (1981); affrmd 683 F. 2d. 261 (1982).
78. *Kelley v. United States,* 512 F. Supp. 356 (1981).
79. *Everette v. United States,* 492 F. Supp. 318 (1980).
80. Ibid., 326.
81. *Broudy v. United States,* 661 F. 2d. 125 (9th Cir. 1981).
82. Ibid., 129.
83. Mary Ann Galante, " 'Atomic Vets' Win Major Round," *National Law Journal* (May 26, 1986): 3, 37.
84. *Los Angeles Herald Examiner,* March 11, 1979, cited in Wasserman and Solomon, 121.

CHAPTER 10. TIME TO BUILD A MONUMENT

1. House Committee on Public Health and the Environment, 1978.
2. House Committee on Interstate and Foreign Commerce, 1979.
3. Ibid., 1980, 21–22.
4. Caldwell, Kelley, and Heath.
5. Lyon, et al.
6. House Committee on Interstate and Foreign Commerce, 1980, 13–22.
7. Ibid., 3–13.
8. Ibid., 31–36.
9. Senate Committee on Veteran's Affairs, *Hearings,* 96th Cong., 1st sess., 1979.
10. Public Law 88–485, 88th Cong., 2nd sess., 1964, 78 Stat., 598; see Chapter 4 for further details.
11. "Black Lung Benefits," *Congressional Quarterly Almanac,* XXXIV (1978): 266–67.
12. "Toxic Substances," *Congressional Quarterly Almanac,* XXXIII (1977): 676–77.
13. Public Law 85–256, 85th Cong., 1st sess., 1957, 71 Stat., 576; 42 U.S.C., 2012, 1973, 42 U.S.C. 210–2222.
14. Ibid., sections 2210(a), 2210(b), and 2210(c); and *Las Vegas Review-Journal,* February 27, 1986.
15. Ibid., 2210(i).
16. Keyes and Howarth, 547.
17. For further discussion on the Price-Anderson Act, see: "Price-Anderson Act: A Constitutional Dilemma," *Environmental Affairs* 6 (1978): 565–96;

"Limited Liability for Nuclear Accidents," *Ecology Law Quarterly* 8 (1979): 163–85; Berndt I. Bauer, "Price-Anderson Act: A Constitutional Milestone of Tort Liability," *Hastings Constitutional Law Quarterly* 8 (1981): 371–96; Joel R. Burcat, "Uncompensated Victims of Low Level Radiation: Unnecessary Hostages of the Price-Anderson Act," *Forum* 15 (1980): 847–59; Robert Lowenstein, "Price-Anderson Act: An Imaginative Approach to Public Liability Concerns," *Forum* 12 (1977): 594–604; Jeffrey Trauberman, "Compensating Victims of Toxic Substances Pollution: An Analysis of Existing Federal Statutes," *Harvard Environmental Law Review* 5 (1981): 14–17; and Richard Wilson, "Nuclear Liability and the Price-Anderson Act," *Forum* 12 (1977): 617–21.

18. "Victims of Radiation, Other Environment-Related Illness Seeking Help from Congress," *Congressional Quarterly Weekly Report* (February 23, 1980): 549–56.

19. "Compromise Superfund Proposition Cleared," *Congressional Quarterly Weekly Report* (December 6, 1980): 3509.

20. Public Law 97–72, 97th Cong., 1st sess., 1981, 95 Stat., 1047; 38 U.S.C., 610.

21. H.R. 4766, 96th Cong., 1st sess., 1979.

22. S. 1865, 96th Cong., 1st sess., 1979; and *Congressional Record*, 96th Cong., 1st sess., 1979, 27467–471.

23. H.R. 8278, 96th Cong., 2nd sess., 1980.

24. H.R. 1733, February 5, 1981, 97th Cong., 1st sess.

25. H.R. 872 was introduced by Henry Gonzales, D-Texas, on January 16, 1981; H.R. 2229 by Tony Coelho, D-California on March 2, 1981; and H.R. 4012 by Robert Davis, R-Michigan on June 25, 1981. There were no corresponding bills dealing specifically with veterans in the Senate.

26. Public Law 97–72; and *Congressional Record*, 97th Cong., 1st sess., 1981, 56194–95, 6259.

27. Cited in *Atomic Veterans Newsletter*, November–December 1981, 7.

28. In a letter dated April 8, 1982, John P. Murphy, General Counsel for the VA, explained to Senator Hatch that there had been only twelve cases in which the VA had "recognized a relationship between exposure to ionizing radiation in service and the post-service development of cancer. More recently it was noted before Congress that of 4,474 medical claims filed by atomic veterans, only 14 have been allowed by the VA. *Las Vegas Review-Journal*, March 24, 1955.

29. S. 1483, 97th Cong., 1st sess., 1981.

30. News release, "From the Office of Orrin Hatch," July 15, 1981.

31. "Senate Committee Reports Measure to Help Radiation Victims Win Damage Suits," *Congressional Quarterly Weekly Report* (April 24, 1982): 954.

32. Senate Committee on Labor and Human Resources, *Hearings*, 97th Cong., 1st sess., 1981, 1982; and *Washington Post*, March 13, 1982.

33. "Senate Committee Reports Measure to Help Radiation Victims Win Damage suits," 954.
34. H.R. 6052, 97th Cong., 2nd sess., 1982; and *Congressional Record,* 97th Cong., 2nd sess., 1982, H1407.
35. *Congressional Record,* 97th Cong., 1st sess., 1981, 57632–33.
36. Public Law 97-414, 98th Cong., 1st sess., 1983, 96 Stat., 2049, 21 U.S.C., 301; and "Orphan Drug Bill Cleared, May Face Veto," *Congressional Quarterly Weekly Report* (December 25, 1982) 3131–32.
37. Interview with Mr. Ron Preston, Legislative Aide to Senator Orrin Hatch, June 16, 1983.
38. S. 921, March 24, 1983, 98th Cong., 1st sess.
39. H.R. 5167, authorization bill for Department of Defense, June 21, 1984, 98th Cong., 2nd sess., Sec. 330, 570–71; and *Congressional Record,* 1984, H10310–12. The House bill eventually became Public Law 980-525.
40. *Las Vegas Review-Journal,* November 12, 1984.
41. Ibid.
42. Interview with Judge Roger Foley.
43. *Congressional Record,* 1984, S13398, S13425.
44. Ibid., 1984, H11635–38.
45. *Las Vegas Review-Journal,* October 31, 1984.
46. Interview with Ron Preston.
47. *Congressional Quarterly Weekly Report* (October 24, 1984): 1529.
48. 38 C.F.R. 3.311b, now designated 3.311.
49. *Combee v. Brown,* 34 F. 3d 1039.
50. Department of Veterans Affairs, Testimony before U.S. Senate Committee on Veterans Affairs (March 21, 1998): 2.
51. *Las Vegas Sun,* March 2, 1985.
52. S.707, 99th Cong., 1st sess., 1985; and *Las Vegas Review-Journal,* March 24, 1985.
53. *Las Vegas Review-Journal,* May 14, 1986.

CHAPTER 11. TRANSITIONS OF THE 1990s

1. *Proliferation and the Former Soviet Union* (Washington, D.C.: Office of Technology Assessment, Congress of the U.S., 1994); Wayne LeBaron, *America's Nuclear Legacy* (Commack, N.Y.: Nova Science Publishers, Inc., 1998), 245–78.
2. *Congressional Quarterly Weekly Report* (October 31, 1992): 3486; Stephen Schwartz (ed.), *Atomic Audit* (Washington, D.C.: Brookings Institution Press, 1998), 335–36, 495–96.
3. *Las Vegas Review Journal,* June 17, 1992, October 18 and 19, 1999, November 5 and 6, 1999; *Congressional Quarterly Weekly Report* (November 2, 1996): 3158; *Las Vegas Sun,* April 14, 2000.

4. *Las Vegas Sun,* March 31, 1992; *Las Vegas Review Journal,* July 24, 1992, October 3, 1992; *Congressional Quarterly Weekly Report* (August 8, 1992): 2404.
5. *Las Vegas Review Journal,* August 5, 1993; Matthew Coolidge, *The Nevada Test Site: A Guide to America's Nuclear Proving Ground* (Los Angeles: Center for Land Use Interpretation, 1996), 25.
6. Jonathan Medalia, "Nuclear Testing and Comprehensive Test Ban: Chronology Starting September 1992," *CRS Report for Congress* (October 19, 1999).
7. *Las Vegas Review Journal,* September 28, 1990.
8. The original law covered only thirteen cancers. Two additional illnesses, cancer of the urinary tract and of the salivary glands, were added in 1992 via an amendment introduced by Representative Evans (H.D. 3236). See *Congressional Quarterly Weekly Report* (October 10, 1992): 3176.
9. Ibid. (April 16, 1988): 1030, 1176, 1186, 1246; Nancy Hogan, "Shielded from Liability," *ABA Journal* (May 1994): 56–61.
10. Department of Veterans Affairs, Testimony before U.S. Senate Committee on Veterans Affairs (April 21, 1998).
11. *Las Vegas Sun,* October 31, 1994; *Atomic Veterans Newsletter,* a quarterly publication that invariably addresses this topic. Special thanks to Mrs. Lee Iddings for providing me with the files from her late husband's unsuccessful attempts to receive compensation for cancer that he believed he contracted as an atomic veteran at the NTS.
12. "News" from Congressman Lane Evans (March 26, 1999); Department of Veterans Affairs, Testimony; William Brady, Testimony before U.S. Senate Committee on Veterans Affairs (April 21, 1998).
13. *Las Vegas Review Journal,* October 16, 1990, May 23, 1993; Stephen Redhead, "Memo on Radiation Exposure Compensation Programs," Congressional Research Service, December 1999; "What Is the Radiation Exposure Compensation Act?" @http://www.frontier.net/dawesr/radiate/htm.
14. *Las Vegas Review Journal,* October 27, 1990; *Las Vegas Sun,* October 27, 1990.
15. *Las Vegas Review Journal,* May 23, 1993; *Las Vegas Sun,* August 3, 1990.
16. Orrin Hatch, Statement before the U.S. Senate (August 5, 1999); Jonathan Samet, Statement before the U.S. Senate Committee on the Judiciary (October 7, 1998); *Las Vegas Review Journal,* November 3, 1999; *Las Vegas Review Journal,* June 28, 2000.
17. Bobbie A. Mason, "Fallout: Paducah's Secret Nuclear Disaster," *New Yorker* (January 10, 2000): 30–36; *DOE News,* Media Advisory (April 12, 2000); *Las Vegas Sun* (April 12 and 13, 2000); *Las Vegas Review Journal* (April 13 and 17, 2000).
18. *Las Vegas Review Journal* (May 11, 2000); *Las Vegas Sun* (June 1, 2000).
19. *Las Vegas Sun* (May 19, 2000); *Las Vegas Review Journal* (June 9, 2000).
20. Jonathan M. Weisgall, *Operation Crossroads: The Atomic Tests at Bikini Atoll* (Annapolis: Naval Institute Press, 1994); Oscar Debrum, Statement be-

fore the Committee on Resources, U.S. House of Representatives (May 11, 1999); *Congressional Quarterly Weekly Report* (November 30, 1985): 2507–2508.

21. For a detailed look at the uranium miners' story, see James Baker, "Keeping a Deadly Secret," *Newsweek* (June 18, 1990): 20; *Las Vegas Review Journal*, August 8, 1993; Peter Eichstaedt, *If You Poison Us: Uranium and Native Americans* (Santa Fe: Red Crane Books, 1994); Stewart Udall, *The Myths of August: A Personal Exploration of Our Tragic Cold War Affair with the Atom* (New York: Pantheon Books, 1994).

22. *Begay v. United States,* 768 F. 2d. 1059 (9th Cir. 1985); cert denied 485 U.S. 935.

23. *Allen v. United States,* 816 F. 2d. 1417 (10th Cir. 1987); cert denied 484 U.S. 1004.

24. *Congressional Quarterly Weekly Report* (August 6, 1988): 2209.

25. *Las Vegas Review Journal,* July 21, 1994; *Las Vegas Sun,* May 20, 1996.

26. Author's interview with attorney Larry Johns, January 6, 2000.

27. Author's interview with attorney Alan Johns, January 6, 2000.

28. *Las Vegas Sun,* May 21, 1996.

29. John Fuller, *The Day We Bombed Utah*; Howard Rosenberg, *Atomic Soldiers*; Thomas Saffer and Orville Kelly, *Countdown Zero*; Richard Miller, *Under the Cloud* (New York: Free Press, 1986); Richard Wyden, *Day One: Before Hiroshima and After* (New York: Warner Books, 1984); Paul Loeb, *Nuclear Culture* (Philadelphia: New Society Publishers, 1986); Philip L. Fradkin, *Fallout: An American Nuclear Tragedy* (Tucson: University of Arizona Press, 1989).

30. Jonathan Weisgall, *Operation Crossroads*; Howard Ball, *Justice Downwind*; Peter Schwenger, *Letter Bomb: Nuclear Holocaust and the Exploding Word* (Baltimore: Johns Hopkins, 1992); Spencer R. Weart, *Nuclear Fear: A History of Images* (Cambridge: Harvard University Press, 1988); Lawrence Wittner, *Resisting the Bomb, 1954–1970* (Stanford: Stanford University Press, 1997); Frances McCrea and Gerald Markle, *Minutes to Midnight* (Newbury Park: Sage Publications, 1989); Paul Boyer, *By the Bomb's Early Light: American Thought and the Dawn of the Atomic Age* (New York: Pantheon Books, 1985); Michele S. Gerber, *On the Homefront: The Cold War Legacy of the Hanford Nuclear Site* (Lincoln: University of Nebraska Press, 1992); Barton Hacker, *The Dragon's Tail: Radiation Safety in the Manhattan Project 1942–1946* (Berkeley: University of California Press, 1987); William Lawren, *The General and the Bomb: A Biography of General Leslie R. Groves* (New York: Dodd, Mead and Co., Inc., 1988); Michael D'Antonio, *Atomic Harvest* (New York: Crown Publishers, 1994).

31. Bruce Havly and John M. Findlay (eds.), *The Atomic West* (Seattle: University of Washington Press, 1998); Stephen Tchudi (ed.), *Science, Values, and the American West* (Reno: Nevada Humanities Committee, 1997).

32. Martin Cruz Smith, *Stallion Gate* (New York: Random House, 1986); Joseph Kanon, *Los Alamos* (New York: Doubleday, 1997); Robert Olen

Butler, *Countrymen of Bones* (New York: Henry Holt and Co., 1983); Carolyn See, *Golden Days* (New York: Random House, 1987); Umberto Eco and Eugenio Carmi, *The Bomb and the General* (New York: Harcourt Brace Jovanovich, 1989).

33. Peter Goin, *Nuclear Landscapes* (Baltimore: Johns Hopkins University Press, 1991); Carole Gallagher, *American Ground Zero: The Secret Nuclear War* (Lunenburg, Vermont: Stinehour Press, 1993); Katrina Mason, *Children of Los Alamos: An Oral History of the Town Where the Atomic Age Began* (New York: Twain Publishers, 1995); Peter Bacon Hales, *Atomic Spaces: Living on the Manhattan Project* (Urbana: University of Illinois Press, 1997); Rachel Fermi and Esther Sumra, *Picturing the Bomb: Photographs from the Secret World of the Manhattan Project* (New York: Harry Abrams, 1995).

34. A. Costandina Titus and Jerry L. Simich, "From 'Atomic Bomb Baby' to 'Nuclear Funeral': Atomic Music Comes of Age, 1945–1990," *Popular Music and Society* 14 (1990): 11–37.

35. James Lull, "The Social Uses of Popular Music" (unpublished paper presented to the International Communication Association, May 24–28, 1984): 41.

36. Jonathan Schell, "The Unfinished Twentieth Century: What We Have Forgotten About Nuclear Weapons," *Harper's* (January 2000): 41–56.

37. Russell Watson, "America's Nuclear Secrets," *Newsweek* (December 27, 1993): 14–18; Bruce Frankel, "Revolt of the Innocents," *People* (May 18, 1998): 113–16; *Las Vegas Review Journal,* January 16, 1994; *Las Vegas Sun,* August 18, 1995; Advisory Committee on Human Radiation Experiments, *Final Report* (New York: Oxford University Press, 1996); Merril Eisenbud, "Radiation Report in Retrospect," *Forum for Applied Research and Public Policy* (Fall 1997): 122–27; A. Makhijani, "Energy Enters Guilty Plea," *Bulletin of Atomic Scientists* (March/April, 1994): 18–29.

38. "Special Report: Nuclear Waste," *Nuclear Energy* (2nd Quarter 1994); National Safety Council, "Frequently Asked Questions: Yucca Mountain," *(http://www.nsc.org/ehc.htm)*; James Flynn et al., *One Hundred Centuries of Solitude* (Boulder: Westview Press, 1995); League of Women Voters, *The Nuclear Waste Primer* (New York: Nick Lyons Books, 1985); Mark Holt, "Civilian Nuclear Waste Disposal," *CRS Issue Brief* (September 30, 1999); Dina Titus, "The NIMBY Syndrome: Dealing with Nuclear Waste," in *Battle Born,* ed. A. C. Titus (Dubuque: Kendall/Hunt Publishing Company, 1989), 162–80.

39. Richard Bryan, Statement before Nevada Senate Committee on Commerce and Labor, May 4, 1993.

40. David Bearden, "Defense Cleanup and Environmental Programs: Authorization and Appropriations for FY 2000," *CRS Report for Congress* (October 15, 1999); General Accounting Office, "Environmental Cleanup: Defense Funding Allocation Process and Reported Funding Impacts," GAO/NSIAD 99-34 (November 1998); *Congressional Quarterly Weekly Report* (April 25, 1992): 1066–73.

41. *Las Vegas Review Journal,* September 25, 1999; *CAB News,* monthly newsletter published by DOE/Community Advisory Board; U.S. Department of Energy/Nevada Operations, "Environmental Restoration and Waste Management," fact sheets. See also *http://www.doe.nv.gov; EM Update* (newsletter); U.S. Department of Energy/Nevada Operations, "Accelerating Cleanup: Paths to Closure" (June 1998).

42. *Las Vegas Sun,* June 13, 1994; Stephen Budiansky, "The Dim Glow of History," *U.S. News and World Report* (April 18, 1994): 74–75; "Cold War Museum in Hot Nevada Desert," *DRI News* (2nd Quarter 1993): 4–8; Colleen Beck and William Johnson, "Nevada Test Site Historic Structure Survey," *DRI Report* (1994); Hugh Jackson, "The Economics of Our Atomics," *Nevada Business Press* (February 1, 1999): 4.

43. *Congressional Quarterly Weekly Report* (September 22, 1990): 3026–29.

44. U.S. Department of Energy, "Draft Policy and Planning Guidance for Community Transition Activities" (May 1999); U.S. General Accounting Office, "Energy Downsizing: Criteria for Community Assistance Needed" (December 1995); *Congressional Quarterly Weekly Report* (April 25, 1992): 1066–73, (March 7, 1992): 542–45.

45. Women Legislators' Lobby, White Paper, "Defense Reinvestment and Conversion" (March 11, 1993).

46. Las Vegas *Construction Connection* (September 1999); author's interview with Tim Carlson, President, Nevada Test Site Development Operations, January 4, 2000; NTSDC, brochure, timeline, and *http://www.ntsdev.com.*

47. NTS Development Corporation, press release, June 3, 1996.

48. NTS Development Corporation, "Client and Project Update," monthly reports.

49. Paul Proctor, "Kistler Foresees RLV Flight in 2000," *Aviation Week and Space Technology* (March 8, 1999): 38; Jeffrey Kincaid, "The Reusable Playing Field," *Launchspace* (July/August/September 1999): 28–50; *Las Vegas Sun,* September 10 and 13, 1999; *Las Vegas Review Journal,* July 28, 1999.

50. *Las Vegas Sun,* September 6, 1999.

51. Matthew Coolidge, *The Nevada Test Site;* DOE Privatization Working Groups, "Harnessing the Market: The Opportunities and Challenges of Privatization" (January 1997); U.S. DOE Nevada Operations Office, *Strategic Plan* (1999 addendum); NTS Contractors Association, "Nevada Test Site Mission Statement" (April 13, 1992); *http://www.nv.doe.gov; Images of the Nevada Test Site,* quarterly magazine published by DOE/NV and Bechtel Nevada.

52. *Las Vegas Review Journal,* December 20, 1992; *solarrenew@aol.com;* CSTRR, "Interim Report" (July 1999).

53. *Las Vegas Sun,* September 13, 1999; DOE Office of Worker and Community Transition, "Program Update" (July–September 1999): 5; *Las Vegas Review Journal,* September 11, 1999.

54. Office of Defense Programs, "Stockpile Stewardship Plan: Second Annual Update" (April 1998); *http://www.dp.doe.gov.*

55. Jonathan Medalia, "Nuclear Weapons Production Issues: Implication for the Comprehensive Test Ban Treaty," *CRS Report for Congress* (August 19, 1999); "Nuclear Weapons: Comprehensive Test Ban Treaty," ibid. (November 2, 1999): 9–11.

56. Medalia, "Nuclear Weapons Production Issues"; Jonathan Medalia, "Comprehensive Test Ban Treaty: Pro and Con," *CRS Report for Congress* (October 19, 1999); Medalia, "Nuclear Testing and Comprehensive Test Ban: Chronology"; *Washington Post,* October 14, 1999.

57. *Washington Post,* October 15, 1999.

58. Author's interview with Tim Carlson.

59. *Las Vegas Review Journal,* October 1, 1993; Nevada Test Site Historical Foundation, *Annual Report* (October 1999); *News Nob* (NTSHF newsletter), *www.ivrj.com/communitylink/NTShistorical.*

60. Nevada Legislature, *Senate Daily Journal* (April 1, 1999): 20.

Bibliography

Books

Aicken, Frederick. *Newton: Architect of the Scientific Society*. London: English Universities Press, 1971.

Alardice, Corbin, and Edward R. Trapnell. *The Atomic Energy Commission*. New York: Praeger, 1974.

Alperovitz, Gar. *Atomic Diplomacy—Hiroshima and Potsdam*. New York: Simon and Schuster, 1965.

Anderson, David L. *The Discovery of the Electron*. Princeton: Van Nostrand, 1964.

Anderson, Jack, and R. W. May. *McCarthy*. Boston: Beacon, 1952.

Badash, Lawrence. *Radioactivity in America: Growth and Decay of a Science*. Baltimore: Johns Hopkins, 1979.

Badash, Lawrence, Joseph Q. Hirschfelder, and Herbert P. Broida. *Reminiscences of Los Alamos*. Boston: Reidel, 1980.

Baldwin, H. W. *Mistakes of the War*. New York: Harper, 1950.

Ball, Howard. *Justice Downwind: America's Nuclear Testing Program in the Fifties*. New York: Oxford, 1986.

Bartlett, Donald L., and James B. Steele. *Empire: The Life, Legend, and Madness of Howard Hughes*. New York: Norton, 1979.

Baxter, James Phinney. *Scientists Against Time*. Boston: Little, Brown, 1946.

Baxter, John. *Science Fiction in the Cinema*. New York: Barnes, 1970.

Bentley, Eric, ed. *Thirty Years of Treason: Excerpts from Hearings before House Committee on Un-American Activities 1938–1968*. New York: Viking, 1971.

Bird, J. M. *The Effects of Irradiation from Atomic Bomb Fall-Out Upon a Group of Hereford Cattle*. Knoxville, Tenn.: University of Tennessee, 1952.

Blackstone, Sir William. *Commentaries on the Laws of England*. Philadelphia: Robert Bell Union Library, 1771.

Bontecou, Eleanor. *The Federal Loyalty-Security Program*. Ithaca: Cornell, 1953.

Bowers, Brian. *Michael Faraday and Electricity*. London: Priory, 1974.

Boy Scouts of America. *Atomic Energy*. Irving, Tex.: Boy Scouts of America, 1965.

Bradley, David. *No Place to Hide*. Boston: Little, Brown, 1948.

Brooks, David B., and John V. Krutilla. *Peaceful Use of Nuclear Explosives: Some Economic Aspects*. Baltimore: Johns Hopkins, 1969.

Brown, Percy. *American Martyrs to Science Through the Roentgen Rays*. Springfield, Ill.: Thomas, 1936.

Buck, Alice. *A History of the Atomic Energy Commission*. Washington, D.C.: United States Department of Energy, 1982.

Buckley, William F., ed. *The Committee and its Critics*. New York: Putnam, 1962.

Butow, Robert J. C. *Japan's Decision to Surrender*. Stanford, Calif.: Stanford University, 1954.

Byrnes, James F. *Speaking Frankly*. New York: Harper, 1947.

Carr, Robert K. *The House Committee on Un-American Activities, 1945–1950*. Ithaca: Cornell, 1952.

Cary, Otis. *Mr. Stimson's "Pet City": The Sparing of Kyoto 1945*. Kyoto, Japan: Doshiska University, 1975.

Caute, David. *The Great Fear: The Anti-Communist Purge Under Truman and Eisenhower*. New York: Simon and Schuster, 1978.

Ceplair, Larry. *The Inquisition in Hollywood: Politics in the Film Community, 1930–60*. Garden City, N.Y.: Doubleday, 1980.

Chambers, Whitaker. *Witness*. New York: Random, 1952.

Churchill, Winston. *Triumph and Tragedy*. Boston: Houghton Mifflin, 1953.

Claxton, Keith T. *Wilhelm Röntgen,* London: Heron, 1970.

Comer, C. L. *The Fallout Problem*. Oakridge, Tenn.: United States Energy Commission, 1952.

Compton, Arthur H. *Atomic Quest: A Personal Narrative*. New York: Oxford, 1956.

Cook, Fred J. *The Nightmare Decade*. New York: Random, 1971.

Cooke, Alistair. *A Generation on Trial*. New York: Knopf, 1951.

Cozley, John. *Report on Blacklisting: Movies*. New York: Meridian, 1956.

Craig, William. *The Fall of Japan*. New York: Dial, 1967.

Cramp, William. *Michael Faraday and Some of His Contemporaries*. London: Pitman, 1931.

Curie, Eve. *Marie Curie*. Garden City, N.Y.: Doubleday, 1938.

Dahl, Albin J. *Nevada's Southern Economy*. Carson City, Nev.: University of Nevada, 1969.

Davis, N. P. *Lawrence and Oppenheimer*. New York: Simon and Schuster, 1968.

Dibner, Birn. *The New Rays of Professor Röntgen*. Norwalk, Conn.: Burndy, 1963.

———. *Wilhelm Conrad Röntgen and the Discovery of X rays*. New York: Watts, 1968.

Duckworth, Paul. *Baneberry, A Nuclear Disaster*. Las Vegas: Harris Printers, 1976.

Edwards, Jerome. *Pat McCarran: Political Boss of Nevada*. Reno: University of Nevada, 1982.

English, James S. *". . . and all was light": The Life and Work of Sir Issac Newton*. Lincoln, England: Lincolnshire Library, 1977.

Epstein, Samuel S. *The Politics of Cancer*. San Francisco: Sierra Club, 1978.

Feis, Herbert. *Japan Subdued*. Princeton: Princeton University, 1961.

———. *The Atomic Bomb and the End of World War II*. Princeton: Princeton University, 1966.

Fermi, Laura. *Atoms in the Family.* Chicago: University of Chicago, 1954.

Fineberg, Solomon. *The Rosenberg Case.* New York: Oceana, 1953.

Freeland, Richard. *The Truman Doctrine and the Origins of McCarthyism.* New York: Knopf, 1972.

Fried, Richard M. *Men Against McCarthy.* New York: Columbia, 1976.

Fuller, John G. *The Day We Bombed Utah: America's Most Lethal Secret.* New York: New American Library, 1984.

Gaddis, John. *Strategies of Containment: A Critical Appraisal of Postwar American National Security Policy.* New York: Oxford, 1982.

————. *The United States and the Origins of the Cold War, 1941–1947.* New York, 1972.

Gallup, George. *The Gallup Poll: Public Opinion, 1935–1971.* New York: Random House, 1972.

Gifford, Denis. *Science Fiction Film.* New York: Dalton, 1971.

Giovannitti, Len, and Fred Freed. *The Decision to Drop the Bomb.* New York: Coward-McCann, 1965.

Gladstone, Samuel, ed. *The Effects of Nuclear Explosions.* Washington, D.C.: United States Atomic Energy Commission, 1962.

Glass, Mary Ellen. *Nevada's Turbulent 50s.* Reno: University of Nevada Press, 1981.

Glasser, Otto. *Wilhelm Conrad Röntgen and the Early History of the Roentgen Rays.* Springfield, Ill.: Thomas, 1934.

Glazer, Nathan. *Twentieth Century Causes Celebres: Sacco-Vanzetti, Alger Hiss, and the Rosenbergs.* Lake Bluff, Ill.: Regnery-Gateway, 1985.

Gofman, John W. *Radiation and Human Health.* San Francisco: Sierra Club, 1981.

Goldstein, Alvin H. *The Unquiet Death of Julius and Ethel Rosenberg.* Westport, Conn.: Lawrence Hill, 1975.

Goodchild, Peter. *J. Robert Oppenheimer: Shatterer of Worlds.* Boston: Houghton Mifflin, 1981.

Goodman, Walter. *The Committee: The Extraordinary Career of the House Committee on Un-American Activities.* New York: Farrar, Straus and Giroux, 1968.

Gowing, Margaret. *Britain and Atomic Energy 1939–1945.* New York: St. Martins, 1964.

Green, Harold P., and Alan Rosenthal. *Government of the Atom: The Integration of Powers.* New York: Atherton, 1963.

Greenaway, Frank. *John Dalton and the Atom.* Ithaca: Cornell, 1966.

Griffith, Robert. *The Politics of Fear: Joseph R. McCarthy and the Senate.* Lexington: University of Kentucky, 1970.

Groves, Leslie R. *Now It Can Be Told: The Story of the Manhattan Project.* New York: Harper and Row, 1962.

Haber, Heinz. *The Walt Disney Story of Our Friend the Atom.* New York: Simon and Schuster, 1956.

Harris, Jonathan. *Hiroshima: A Study in Science, Politics and the Ethics of War.* Menlo Park, Calif.: Addison-Wesley, 1970.

Harrow, Benjamin, ed. *From Newton to Einstein: Changing Conceptions of the Universe.* 2nd ed. New York: Van Nostrand, 1920.

Hawkins, David. *Manhattan District History, Project Y, the Los Alamos Project.* Vol. 1. Los Alamos, N.M.: United States Atomic Energy Commission, 1945.

Herken, Gregg. *The Winning Weapon: The Atomic Bomb in the Cold War, 1945–1950.* New York, 1982.

Hewlett, Richard G., and Francis Duncan. *Atomic Shield, 1947–1952: A History of the United States Atomic Energy Commission.* Vol. 2. University Park: Penn State University, 1969.

Hewlett, Richard G., and Oscar E. Anderson, Jr. *The New World 1939–46: A History of the United States Atomic Energy Commission,* Vol. 1. University Park: Penn State University, 1962.

Hiebert, Ray E., and Roselyn Hiebert. *Atomic Pioneers.* Oakridge, Tenn.: United States Atomic Energy Commission, 1970.

Hilgartner, Stephen, Richard C. Bell, and Rory O'Connor. *Nukespeak: The Selling of Nuclear Technology in America.* New York: Penguin, 1982.

Hiss, Alger. *In the Court of Public Opinion.* New York: Knopf, 1957.

Jayson, Lester. *Handling Federal Tort Claims: Administrative and Judicial Remedies.* Albany, N.Y.: Bender, 1964.

Jette, Eleanor. *Inside Box 1663.* Los Alamos, N.M.: Los Alamos Historical Society, 1967.

Jungk, Robert. *Brighter Than a Thousand Suns.* New York: Harcourt Brace, 1958.

Kaplan, Morton. *The Life and Death of the Cold War.* Chicago: Nelson Hall, 1976.

Kiste, Robert C. *The Bikinians: A Study of Forced Migration.* Menlo Park, Calif.: Cummings, 1974.

Kurzman, Dan. *Day of the Bomb: Countdown to Hiroshima.* New York: McGraw-Hill, 1986.

La Feber, Walter. *America, Russia and the Cold War.* New York: Wiley, 1967.

Lamont, Lansing. *Day of Trinity.* New York: Atheneum, 1965.

Lang, Daniel. *Early Tales of the Atomic Age.* Garden City, N.Y.: Doubleday, 1948.

Lapp, Ralph E. *The Voyage of the Lucky Dragon.* New York: Harper, 1957.

Latham, Earl. *The Communist Controversy in Washington From the New Deal to McCarthy.* Cambridge: Harvard, 1966.

Laurence, William L. *Dawn Over Zero.* New York: Knopf, 1946.

———. *Men and Atoms.* New York: Simon and Schuster, 1946.

Lilienfeld, Abraham M. *Foundations of Epidemiology.* Oxford: Oxford University Press, 1976.

Lilienthal, David. *Journals: The Atomic Energy Years, 1945–50.* New York: Harper and Row, 1966.

Lukas, John. *A New History of the Cold War.* Garden City, N.Y.: Doubleday, 1966.

MacMahon, Brian, and Thomas F. Pugh. *Epidemiology: Principles and Methods.* Boston: Little, Brown, 1970.

Major, John. *The Oppenheimer Hearing.* London: Batsford, 1971.

Manchester, William. *The Glory and the Dream: A Narrative History of America 1932–1972.* New York: Bantam, 1974.

Marx, Joseph L. *Nagasaki: The Necessary Bomb.* New York: MacMillan, 1971.

———. *Seven Hours to Zero.* New York: Putnam, 1967.

Mazuzan, George T., and J. Samuel Walker. *Controlling the Atom: The Beginnings of Nuclear Regulation 1946–1962.* Berkeley: University of California, 1984.

McBride, James Hubert. *The Test Ban Treaty: Military, Technological, and Political Implications.* Chicago: Regnery, 1967.

Metro Golden Mayer. *Facts About the Making of "The Beginning or the End?"* Hollywood: MGM, 1947.

Miller, Douglas T., and Marion Nowak. *The Fifties: The Way We Really Were.* New York: Doubleday, 1977.

Miller, Merle, and Abe Spitzer. *We Dropped the A-Bomb.* New York: Crowell, 1946.

Moore, William. *The Atomic Pioneers, from Irish Castle to Manhattan Project.* New York: Putnam, 1970.

Navasky, Victor S. *Naming Names.* New York: Viking, 1980.

The Nevada Test Site and Southern Nevada. Las Vegas: Edgerton, Germeshausen, and Green, Inc., 1961.

Newton, Sir Isaac. *Opticks.* New York: Dover, 1952.

Nitske, Robert W. *The Life of Wilhelm Conrad Röntgen.* Tucson: University of Arizona, 1971.

Nizer, Louis. *The Implosion Controversy.* Garden City, N.Y.: Doubleday, 1973.

Paterson, Thomas G. *The Making of the Cold War.* New York, 1979.

———. *Soviet-American Confrontation: Post-War Reconstruction and the Origins of the Cold War.* Baltimore: Johns Hopkins, 1973.

Patterson, Elizabeth C. *John Dalton and the Atomic Theory.* Garden City, N.Y.: Doubleday, 1970.

Pauling, Linus. *The More War.* New York: Dodd, Mead, 1958.

———. *Science and Peace, The Nobel Peace Prize Lecture.* New York: Center for the Study of Democratic Institutions, 1969.

Pfau, Richard. *No Sacrifice Too Great: The Life of Lewis Strauss.* Charlottesville: University of Virginia, 1984.

Pringle, Peter, and James Spigelman. *The Nuclear Barons.* New York: Avon, 1983.

Purcell, John. *The Best Kept Secret.* New York: Vanguard, 1963.

Radosh, Ronald, and Joyce Milton. *The Rosenberg File: A Search for the Truth.* New York: Holt, Rinehart and Winston, 1983.

Rafferty, Kevin, Jayne Loader, and Pierce Rafferty. *The Atomic Cafe: The Book of the Film.* New York: Bantam, 1982.

Rees, David. *Korea: The Limited War.* Baltimore: Penguin, 1970.

Reeves, Thomas C. *The Life and Times of Joe McCarthy: A Biography.* New York: Stein and Day, 1982.

Reid, Robert. *Marie Curie.* New York: Sutton, 1974.

Roberts, Chalmers M. *The Nuclear Years: The Arms Race and Arms Control, 1945–70.* New York: Praeger, 1970.

Rolph, Elizabeth S. *Nuclear Power and the Public Safety: A Study in Regulation.* Lexington, Mass.: Heath, 1979.

Root, Jonathan. *The Betrayers: The Rosenberg Case—A Reappraisal of an American Crisis.* New York: Coward-McCann, 1963.

Rosenberg, Howard L. *Atomic Soldiers: American Victims of Nuclear Experiments.* Boston: Beacon, 1980.

Rovere, Richard. *Senator Joe McCarthy.* Toronto: Longmans, 1959.

Saffer, Thomas H., and Orville E. Kelly. *Countdown Zero.* New York: Putnam, 1982.

Saleh, Dennis. *Science Fiction Gold: Film Classics of the Fifties.* New York: McGraw-Hill, 1979.

Savage, John, and Barbara Storms. *Reach to the Unknown.* Los Alamos, N.M.: United States Atomic Energy Commission, 1965.

Scammon, Richard, ed. *America Votes, A Handbook of Contemporary Election Statistics, 1956–57.* New York: MacMillan, 1958.

Scheer, Robert. *With Enough Shovels: Reagan, Bush, and Nuclear War.* New York: Random, 1982.

Shaheen, Jack G., ed. *Nuclear War Films.* Carbondale: Southern Illinois University, 1978.

Shahn, Ben, and Richard Hudson. *Kuboyama and the Saga of the Lucky Dragon.* New York: Yoseloff, 1965.

Sherwin, Martin A. *A World Destroyed: The Atomic Bomb and the Grand Alliance.* New York: Vintage, 1977.

Shurcliff, William A. *Bombs at Bikini: The Official Report of Operation Crossroads.* New York: Wise, 1947.

Smith, Alice K. *A Peril and A Hope: The Scientists' Movement in America, 1945–47.* Chicago: University of Chicago, 1965.

Smith, Edward C. *The Constitution of the United States.* 11th ed. New York: Barnes and Noble, 1979.

Smith, Henry D. *Atomic Energy for Military Purposes: The Official Report on the Development of the Atomic Bomb under the Auspices of the United States Government, 1940–1945.* Princeton: Princeton University Press, 1946.

Smith, John C. *Alger Hiss: The True Story.* New York: Holt, Rinehart and Winston, 1976.

Snow, Adolph J. *Matter and Gravity in Newton's Physical Philosophy.* New York: Arno Press, 1975.

Sorensen, Theodore. *Kennedy.* New York: Harper and Row, 1965.

Stern, Phillip M. *The Oppenheimer Case: Security on Trial.* New York: Harper and Row, 1969.

Stewart, Alice. *An Epidemiologist Takes a Look at Radiation Risks.* Washington, D.C.: United States Public Health Service, 1973.

Stimson, Henry L., and McGeorge Bundy. *On Active Service in Peace and War.* New York: Harper, 1948.

Story, Richard. *A History of Modern Japan.* London: Penguin, 1960.

Strauss, Lewis. *Men and Decisions*. New York: Doubleday, 1962.

Strickland, Donald A. *Scientists in Politics: The Atomic Scientists Movement, 1945–46*. Purdue, Ind.: Purdue University, 1968.

Swanberg, Harold. *Radiologic Maxims*. Quincy, Ill.: Radiologic Review Publishing, 1932.

Teller, Edward, and Albert Latter. *Our Nuclear Future*. New York: Criterion, 1958.

Theoraris, Athan G. *Seeds of Repression: Harry S. Truman and the Origins of McCarthyism*. Chicago: Quadrangle, 1971.

Thomas, Gordon, and Max M. Wetts. *Enola Gay*. New York: Simon and Schuster, 1977.

Trefousse, Hans L., ed. *The Cold War: A Book of Documents*. New York: Putnam, 1965.

Tricker, R. A. R. *The Contributions of Faraday and Maxwell to Electrical Science*. Oxford: Pergamon, 1966.

Truman, Harry S. *Year of Decisions*. Garden City, N.Y.: Doubleday, 1955.

——. *Years of Trial and Hope*. Garden City, N.Y.: Doubleday, 1956.

Uhl, Michael, and Tod Ensign. *GI Guinea Pigs: How the Pentagon Exposed Our Troops to Dangers More Deadly Than War*. New York: Wideview, 1980.

Vaughn, Robert. *Only Victims: A Study of Show Business Blacklisting*. New York: Putnam, 1972.

Wasserman, Harvey, and Norman Solomon. *Killing Our Own: The Disaster of America's Experience with Atomic Radiation*. New York: Dell, 1982.

Weart, Spencer R., and Gertrude W. Szilard, eds. *Leo Szilard: His Vision of the Facts*. Cambridge, Mass.: MIT, 1972.

Weinstein, Allen. *Perjury: The Hiss-Chambers Case*. New York: Knopf, 1978.

Werth, Andrew. *Russia: The Post War Years*. New York: Taplinger, 1971.

Whyte, Lancelot L. *Essay on Atomism*. Middletown, Conn.: Wesleyan, 1961.

Wittner, Lawrence S. *Cold War America: From Hiroshima to Watergate*. New York: Praeger, 1974.

Worman, Frederick C. *Anatomy of the Nevada Test Site*. Los Alamos, N.M.: United States Atomic Energy Commission, 1965.

Yergin, Daniel. *Shattered Peace: The Origins of the Cold War and the National Security State*. Boston, Houghton Mifflin, 1977.

York, Herbert. *The Advisors: Oppenheimer, Teller, and the Superbomb*. San Francisco: Vintage, 1976.

Articles

Anderson, Herbert L. "Early Days of the Chain Reaction." *Science and Public Affairs* (1973): 8–12.

——. "The Legacy of Fermi and Szilard." *Bulletin of the Atomic Scientists* (1974): 56–62.

"The Application of the Statute of Limitations to Actions for Tortuous Radiation Exposure." *Alabama Law Review* (1980): 502–21.

Badash, Lawrence. "Becquerel's 'Unexposed' Photographic Plates." *Isis* (1966): 1086–88.

———. "Chance Favors the Prepared Mind: Henri Becquerel and the Discovery of Radioactivity." *Archives International d'Histoire des Sciences* (1965): 55–66.

———. "The Discovery of Thorium's Radioactivity." *Journal of Chemical Education* (1966): 219–70.

———. "Radioactivity before the Curies." *American Journal of Physics* (1965): 128–35.

———. "Radium, Radioactivity, and the Popularity of Scientific Discovery." *Proceedings of the American Philosophical Society* (1978): 145–54.

Bauer, Berndt I. "Price-Anderson Act: A Constitutional Milestone of Tort Liability." *Hastings Constitutional Law Quarterly* (1981): 371–96.

Becquerel, Henri. "Sur les radiations émises par phosphorescence." *Comptes Rendus Hebdomadaires des Séances de l'Académie des Sciences* (1896): 501–3.

Bernstein, Barton J. "Hiroshima Reconsidered: Thirty Years Later." *Foreign Service Journal* (1975): 8–13.

———. "Roosevelt, Truman, and the Atomic Bomb, 1941–1945: A Reinterpretation." *Political Science Quarterly* (1975): 27–69.

———. "The Uneasy Alliance: Roosevelt, Churchill, and the Atomic Bomb, 1940–1945." *Western Political Quarterly* (1976): 202–30.

Bohr, Niels, and John A. Wheeler. "The Mechanism of Nuclear Fission." *Physical Review* (1939): 426–50.

Bolton, H. C. "New Sources of Light." *Popular Science Monthly* (1900): 318–22.

Boyer, Paul. "From Activism to Apathy: The American People and Nuclear Weapons, 1963–1980." *Journal of American History* (1984): 821–44.

Brim, Raymond E., and Patricia Condon. "Another A-Bomb Cover-Up." *Washington Monthly* (January 1981): 48.

Brues, Austin. "Critique of the Linear Theory of Carcinogenesis." *Science* (September 1958): 693–99.

Burcat, Joll R. "Uncompensated Victims of Low Level Radiation: Unnecessary Hostages of the Price-Anderson Act." *Forum* (1980): 847–59.

Cahn, Robert. "Behind the First Atomic Bomb." *Saturday Evening Post* (July 16, 1960): 17, 72–75.

Caldwell, Glyn, Delle Kelley, and Clark Heath, Jr. "Leukemia Among Participants in Military Maneuvers at a Nuclear Bomb Test." *Journal of the American Medical Association* (1980): 1975–78.

Cary, Otis. "Atomic Bomb Targeting: Myths and Realities." *Japan Quarterly* (1979): 506–16.

———. "The Sparing of Kyoto." *Japan Quarterly* (1975): 337–47.

Cheney, Warren. "You and Your Atomic Future." *Film News* (1951): 4–7, 27.

Cochrane, David J. "Occupational Disease and Accident Compensation." *New Zealand Law Journal* (1978): 25–31.

Curie, Marie. "Rayons émis par les composés de l'uranium et du thorium." *Comptes Rendus Hebdomadaires des Séances de l'Académie des Sciences* (1898): 1101–3.

Dahl, Harry W. "Trends in Occupational Disease Compensation." *Forum* (1979): 467–72.

Daniels, Farrington, and Arthur H. Compton. "A Poll of Scientists at Chicago." *Bulletin of the Atomic Scientists* (1948): 44.

DeDominicis, Caria. "Atomic Veterans Take Their Case to Court." *California Law Review* (1982): 28–31.

Delgado, Richard. "Beyond Sindell: Relaxation of Cause-in-Fact Rules for Indeterminate Plaintiffs." *California Law Review* (1982): 881–908.

Eckel, Edwin B. "Development of Geologic Knowledge at Nevada Test Site." *Nevada Test Site*, Proceedings of the Rocky Mountain Section of the Geological Society of America (1968): 5–10.

Ekren, E. B. "Geological Setting of Nevada Test Site and Nellis Air Force Range." *Nevada Test Site*, Proceedings of the Rocky Mountain Section of the Geological Society of America (1968): 11–19.

Estep, Samuel D., and Edward H. Forgotson. "Legal Liability for Genetic Injuries from Radiation." *Louisiana Law Review* (1963): 1–53.

Favish, Allan. "Radiation Injury and the Atomic Veteran: Shifting the Burden of Proof on Factual Causation." *Hastings Law Journal* (1981): 933–74.

"The Federal Tort Claims Act." *Yale Law Journal* (1947): 534–61.

"Federal Tort Claims Act: A Cause of Action for Servicemen." *Valparaiso University Law Review* (1980): 527–76.

Feld, Bernard. "Einstein and the Politics of Nuclear Weapons." *Bulletin of the Atomic Scientists* (1979): 5–16.

"From *Feres* to *Stencel:* Should Military Personnel Have Access to F.T.C.A. Recovery?" *Michigan Law Review* (1979): 1099–1126.

Fitch, Val L. "The View from the Bottom." *Bulletin of the Atomic Scientists* (1975): 43–46.

Franco, Adolpho A. "*Wollman v. Gross:* Statute of Limitations and the FTCA." *Creighton Law Review* (1981): 1073–79.

Gottlieb, Irvin M. "Federal Legislation—Tort Claims Against the United States." *Georgetown Law Journal* (1942): 462–65.

———. Federal Tort Claims Act—A Statutory Interpretation." *Georgetown Law Journal* (1947): 1–67.

Green, Harold. "The Oppenheimer Case: A Study in the Abuse of the Law." *Bulletin of the Atomic Scientists* (1977): 12–16.

Halasz, Nicholas, and Robert Halasz. "Leo Szilard, the Reluctant Father of the Atom Bomb." *New Hungarian Quarterly* (1974): 163–73.

Hammer, William J. "Radium and Other Radioactive Substances." *Scientific American Supplement* (1903): 22904–7.

Hislop-Brumfield, Lorna. "Judicial Recovery for the Post-Service Tort: A Veteran's Last Battle." *Pacific Law Journal* (1983): 333–55.

Houser, F. N. "Application of Geology to Underground Nuclear Testing,

Nevada Test Site." *Nevada Test Site,* Proceedings of the Rocky Mountain Section of the Geological Society of America (1968): 21–33.

Jay, Kenneth. "A Glance at Prehistory." In *Britain and Atomic Energy 1939– 1945,* edited by Margaret Gowing. New York, St. Martin's, 1964.

Johnson, Giff. "Micronesia: America's 'Strategic' Trust." *Bulletin of the Atomic Scientists* (1979): 10–15.

———. "Paradise Lost." *Bulletin of the Atomic Scientists* (1980): 24–29.

Kalmen, Jamie. "The Legal Quandary." *Bulletin of the Atomic Scientists* (1983): 27.

Kane, Joe. "Nuclear Films." *Take One* (1969): 9–11.

Keyes, W. Noel, and John L. Howarth. "Approaches to Liability for Remote Causes: The Low Level Radiation Example." *Iowa Law Review* (1971): 531–75.

Kumpf, Fred H. "Occupational Disease Claims and the Workers' Compensation Reforms." *Seton Hall Law Review* (1982): 470–83.

Kutchins, Albert. "Most Exclusive Remedy is No Remedy At All: Workers' Compensation Coverage for Occupational Disease." *Labor Law Journal* (1981): 212–28.

Land, Charles E. "The Hazards of Fallout or of Epidemiological Research." *New England Journal of Medicine* (1979): 431–32.

Lang, Daniel. "Our Far-flung Correspondents: Blackjack and Flashes." *New Yorker* (September 1952): 90–99.

Lewis, Georgia. " 'Atomized' Las Vegas Danced 'Atomic Boogie'." *The Nevadan* (January 23, 1983): 6–7, 12–13.

"Limited Liability for Nuclear Accidents." *Ecology Law Quarterly* (1979): 163–85.

Lowenstein, Robert. "Price-Anderson Act: An Imaginative Approach to Public Liability Concerns." *Forum* (1977): 594–604.

Lyon, Joseph, Melville Klauber, John Gardner, and King Udall. "Childhood Leukemias Associated with Fallout from Nuclear Testing." *New England Journal of Medicine* (1979): 397–402.

Maleson, Diane C. "Historical Roots of the Legal System's Response to Nuclear Power." *Southern California Law Review* (1982): 597–640.

Manley, J. H. "Assembling the War Time Labs." *Bulletin of the Atomic Scientists* (1974): 42–47.

Mark, Edward. " 'Today Has Been a Historical One': Harry S. Truman's Diary of the Potsdam Conference." *Diplomatic History* (1980): 317–26.

Mathews, Samuel W. "Nevada Learns to Live with the Atom." *National Geographic* (June 1953): 842–48.

McCarran, Sister Margaret P. "Patrick Anthony McCarran: 1876–1954. Part II." *Nevada Historical Society Quarterly* (1969): 3–75.

McDaniel, Boyce. "A Physicist at Los Alamos." *Bulletin of the Atomic Scientists* (1974): 39–43.

"Military Personnel and the Federal Tort Claims Act." *Yale Law Journal* (1949): 615–27.

Miller, Byron S. "A Law is Passed: The Atomic Energy Act of 1946." *University of Chicago Law Review* (1948): 809–13.

Miller, Charles N. "Workers' Compensation: Preparing the Occupational Disease Claim." *Trial* (1980): 26–30.

Moore, Charles L. "Radiation and Preconception Injuries: Some Interesting Problems in Tort Law." *Southwestern Law Journal* (1974): 414–36.

Mulkin, Barb. "Los Alamos—P.O. Box 1663." *Westways* (1977): 31–34.

Murphy, Brian. "Monster Movies: They Came from Beneath the Fifties." *Journal of Popular Film* (1972): 31–44.

"Operation 'Doom Town'." *Nevada Highways and Parks* (1952): 1–17.

O'Toole, Thomas J. "Radiation, Causation, and Compensation." *Georgetown Law Journal* (1966): 751–76.

Partington, J. R. "The Origins of Atomic Theory." *Annals of Science* (1939): 245–82.

"Price-Anderson Act: A Constitutional Dilemma." *Environmental Affairs* (1978): 565–96.

Reeves, Thomas C. "McCarthyism: Interpretation Since Hofstadter." *Wisconsin Magazine of History* (1976): 42–54.

———. "The Search for Joe McCarthy." *Wisconsin Magazine of History* (1977): 185–96.

Rhodes, Richard. "I Am Become Death . . . The Agony of J. Robert Oppenheimer." *American Heritage* (1977): 70–83.

Rutherford, Ernest. "Uranium Radiation and the Electrical Conduction Produced by It." *Philosophical Magazine* (1899): 109–63.

Salaff, Stephen. "The Lucky Dragon." *Bulletin of the Atomic Scientists* (1978): 21–23.

Shapiro, Edward S. "The Military Options to Hiroshima: A Critical Examination of Gar Alperovitz's *Atomic Diplomacy.*" *Americka Studien* (1978): 60–72.

Sholl, Debra. "The Nevada Proving Grounds: An Asylum for Sovereign Immunity." *Southwestern University Law Review* (1980): 633–43.

Sigal, Leon V. "Bureaucratic Politics and Tactical Uses of Committees: The Interim Committee and the Decision to Drop the Atomic Bomb." *Polity* (1978): 326–64.

Smith, Alice K. "Behind the Decision to Use the Atomic Bomb, Chicago 1944–45." *Bulletin of the Atomic Scientists* (1958): 351–52.

———. "The Elusive Dr. Szilard." *Harper's* (July 1960): 77–86.

Smith, Alice K., and Charles Weiner. "Robert Oppenheimer: Letters and Recollections." *Bulletin of the Atomic Scientists* (1980): 19–27.

———. "Robert Oppenheimer: The Los Alamos Years." *Bulletin of the Atomic Scientists* (1980): 11–17.

Solomon, Norman. "Nagasaki's Other Victims." *The Progressive* (July, 1979): 21–27.

Solomons, Mark E. "Workers' Compensation for Occupational Disease Victims: Federal Statutes and Threshold Problems." *Albany Law Review* (1977): 198–249.

Stason, E. Blythe. "Tort Liability for Radiation Injuries." *Vanderbilt Law Review* (1958): 93–114.

Steiner, Arthur. "Baptism of the Atomic Scientists." *Bulletin of the Atomic Scientists* (1975): 21–28.

Stimson, Henry L. "The Decision to Use the Atomic Bomb." *Harper's* (February, 1947): 101–2.

"In Support of the *Feres* Doctrine and a Better Definition of 'Incident to Service'." *St. Johns Law Review* (1982): 485–514.

"Symposium on Federal Tort Claims Act." *Federal Bar Journal* (1966): 1–81.

Terkel, Studs. "The Good War." *The Atlantic* (July 1984): 72–75.

Titus, A. Costandina. "A-Bombs in the Backyard: Southern Nevada Adapts to the Nuclear Age, 1951–1963." *Nevada Historical Society Quarterly* (1983): 235–54.

———. "Back to Ground Zero: Old Footage Through New Lenses." *Journal of Popular Film and Television* (1983): 2–11.

———. "Selling the Bomb: Hollywood and the Government Join Forces at Ground Zero." *Halcyon* (1985): 17–30.

"Training Camp for the Atomic Age: Wendover Field." *Aerospace Historian* (1973): 137–39.

Trauberman, Jeffrey. "Compensating Victims of Toxic Substances Pollution: An Analysis of Existing Federal Statutes." *Harvard Environmental Law Review* (1981): 1–29.

Vavilov, S. I. "Newton and the Atomic Theory." In *Royal Society's Newton Tercentenary Celebration* volume. Cambridge, England: 1947.

Villa, Brian L. "A Confusion of Signals: James Franck, The Chicago Scientists and Early Efforts to Stop the Bomb." *Bulletin of the Atomic Scientists* (1975): 36–42.

Villard, Paul. "Sur la reflexion en la refracion des rayons cathodiques en des rayons deviables du radion." *Comptes Rendus Hebdomadaires des Séances de l'Académie des Sciences* (1900): 1010–12.

Warren, Shields. "Hiroshima and Nagasaki Thirty Years After." *Proceedings of the American Philosophical Society* (1977): 97–99.

Weisgall, Jonathan M. "The Nuclear Nomads of Bikini." *Foreign Policy* (1980): 74–98.

Weiss, Edward, Richard Olsen, Carlyle Thompson, and Alfonse Masi. "Surgically Treated Thyroid Disease Among Young People in Utah, 1948–1962." *American Journal of Public Health* (1967): 1807–14.

Wellig, Sidney H. "The Breadth of the Tort Perspective: Judicial Review for Tortuous Conduct of Government Agencies and Agents." *Missouri Law Review* (1980): 621–38.

Wells, Samuel F., Jr. "Sounding the TOCSIN: NSC68 and the Soviet Threat." *International Security* (1979): 116–38.

Wilson, E. R. "Occupational Disease: The Problems of a Comprehensive System of Coverage." *Industrial Law Journal* (1982): 141–55.

Wilson, Richard. "Nuclear Liability and the Price-Anderson Act." *Forum* (1977): 617–21.

Wilson, Robert R. "A Recruit for Los Alamos." *Bulletin of the Atomic Scientists* (1975): 41–47.

Wood, M. "Kiss Tomorrow Hello." *American Film* (1977): 14–17.

"Workers' Compensation: Redefinition of Occupational Disease and the Applicable Compensation Statute." *Wake Forest Law Review* (1980): 288–313.

Yavenditti, Michael J. "Atomic Scientists and Hollywood: 'The Beginning or the End?' " *Film and History* (1978): 73–88.

York, Herbert F. "Sounders of the Alarm." *Bulletin of the Atomic Scientists* (1975): 43–45.

Newspapers and Periodicals—1942 to present

Atomic Veterans Newsletter
Congressional Quarterly Almanac
Congressional Quarterly Weekly Report
Deseret News
Las Vegas Review-Journal
Las Vegas Sun
Newsweek
New York Times
U.S. News & World Report
Washington County News (Utah)
Washington Post

Legal Cases

Allen v. United States
Bartholomae v. United States
Besner v. Walter Kidde Nuclear Labs
Blaber v. United States
Bolger v. Chris Anderson Roofing Co.
Broudy v. United States
Brown v. United States
Bulloch v. United States
Communist Party v. Subversive Activities Control Board
Dalehite v. United States
Dennis v. United States

Doe v. McMillan
Everette v. United States
Feres v. United States
Griggs v. United States
Indian Towing Co. v. United States
Jaffee v. United States
Jefferson v. United States
Kelley v. United States
Krumback v. Dow Chemical Co.
Kuhne v. United States
Lasswell v. Brown
Lombard v. United States
Prescott v. United States
Roberts, et al. v. United States
Scales v. United States
Smith v. Humboldt Dye Works, Inc.
Stencel v. United States
Thornwell v. United States
United Airlines v. Weiner
Yates v. United States

Government Documents

In addition to archival material, the following published sources have been consulted. Note that unless otherwise indicated, these were published in Washington, D.C., by the U.S. Government Printing Office.

Congressional Record. 1945–1985.
Nevada Legislative Counsel Bureau. *The Nevada Test Site.* Carson City, 1983.
Nevada. *Political History of Nevada.* 4th ed. Carson City: State Printing Office, 1960.
U.S. Armed Forces Special Weapons Project. *Operation Upshot-Knothole Project 8.5: Thermal Radiation Protection Afforded Test Animals by Fabric Assemblies.* 1953.
U.S. Army, Joint Task Force One. *Operation Crossroads, The Official Pictorial Record.* New York: W. H. Wise, 1946.
U.S. Army. *Exercise Desert Rock Information and Guide.* 1951.
U.S. Atomic Bomb Casualty Commission. *Residual Radiation in Hiroshima and Nagasaki.* 1962.
U.S. Atomic Energy Commission. *Atomic Tests in Nevada.* 1957.
———. *Fallout From Nuclear Tests at the Nevada Test Site.* 1959.

————. *Legislative History of the Atomic Energy Act of 1946,* P.L. 585, 79th Congress. 1965.

————. *Operation Ranger: Operational Program Reports.* Los Alamos, N. Mex., 1951.

U.S. Atomic Energy Commission, Human Resources Research Office. *Desert Rock I: A Psychological Study of Troop Reactions to an Atomic Explosion.* Washington, D.C.: George Washington University, 1953.

————. *Desert Rock IV: Reactions of an Armored Infantry Battalion to an Atomic Bomb Maneuver.* Washington, D.C.: George Washington University, 1953.

U.S. Atomic Energy Commission, Operations Research Office. *Reactions to Troops in Atomic Maneuvers—Exercise Desert Rock IV.* Baltimore: Johns Hopkins University, 1953.

U.S. Civil Defense Preparedness Agency. *Motion Picture Catalog.* 1975.

U.S. Congress. *Guide to the Congress of the United States.* 1971.

U.S. Congress, Congressional Research Service. *Congressional Response to the Nuclear Accident at Three Mile Island, March Through September 1979: A 6-Month Status Report.* 96th Cong., 1st sess., 1979.

————. *Nuclear Power: Cleaning Up Three Mile Island.* 97th Cong., 1st sess., 1981.

————. *Nuclear Waste Management.* 98th Cong., 1st sess., 1983.

U.S. Congress. House. Committee on Interstate and Foreign Commerce. Subcommittee on Oversight and Investigations. *The Forgotten Guinea Pigs.* 96th Cong., 2d sess., 1980.

————. *Hearings on Low Level Radiation Effects on Health.* 96th Cong., 1st sess., 1979.

U.S. Congress. House. Committee on Public Health and the Environment. *Hearings.* 95th Cong., 2d sess., 1978.

U.S. Congress. House. *Message from the President of the United States Transmitting Recommendations Relative to the Atomic Energy Act of 1946.* 83rd Cong., 2d sess., 1954. H. Doc. 328.

U.S. Congress. Senate. Committee on Armed Services. Subcommittee on Preparedness Investigation. *Hearings on Military Aspects and Implications of Nuclear Test Ban Proposals and Related Matters.* 88th Cong., 1st sess., 1963.

U.S. Congress. Senate. Committee on Foreign Relations. *Hearings on the Nuclear Test Ban Treaty.* 88th Cong., 1st sess., 1963.

U.S. Congress. Senate. Committee on Labor and Human Resources. *Hearings.* 97th Cong., 1st sess., 1981.

U.S. Congress. Senate. Committee on Veterans' Affairs. *Hearings.* 96th Cong., 1st sess., 1979.

U.S. Congress. Senate. *Report of the Joint Committee on the Organization of Congress to Accompany S. 2177.* 79th Cong., 2d sess., 1946. S. Rept. 1400.

U.S. Defense Nuclear Agency. *Compilation of Local Fallout Data from Test Detonations, 1945–1962.* Report DNA1251-1-EX. 1979.

————. *Environmental Impact Statement: Cleanup, Rehabilitation, and Resettlement of Enewetok Atoll.* 1975.

————. *Fact-Sheet—Enewetok Operation.* 1980.
————. *Operation Buster-Jangle—1951.* 1982.
————. *Operation Castle—1954.* 1982.
————. *Operation Greenhouse—1951.* 1983.
————. *Operation Ranger—1951.* 1982.
————. *Operation Sandstone—1948.* 1983.
U.S. Department of Defense. *Radiation Dose Reconstruction: U.S. Occupation Forces in Hiroshima and Nagasaki, Japan, 1945–1946.* 1980.
————. *Project "Nutmeg".* 1949.
U.S. Department of Energy. *DOE's Nevada Operations Office: What It Does and Why.* 1982.
————. *Announced United States Nuclear Tests, July 1945 Through December 1982.* 1983.
————. *Budget.* 1985.
————. *Draft Environmental Assessment Overview.* 1984.
————. *The Enewetok Atoll Today.* 1979.
————. *The Meaning of Radiation at Bikini Atoll.* 1980.
U.S. Department of Energy, Dose Assessment Group. *Reports.* Volumes 1–10. 1980–1984.
U.S. Department of Health, Education, and Welfare. *Report of the Interagency Task Force on the Health Effects of Ionizing Radiation.* 1979.
U.S. Department of Justice. *Report of the Interagency Task Force on Compensation for Radiation-Related Illnesses.* 1980.
U.S. Department of State. *Foreign Relations of the United States, Diplomatic Papers: The Conference of Berlin (Potsdam) 1945.* 1960.
U.S. General Accounting Office. *Enewetok Atoll: Cleaning Up Nuclear Contamination.* 1979.
U.S. Marine Corps. *The United States Marines in the Occupation of Japan.* Washington, D.C.: Marine Corps, Historical Branch, G-3 Division, 1969.
U.S. Naval Medical Research Institute. *Measurement of the Residual Radiation Intensity at the Hiroshima and Nagasaki Atomic Bomb Sites.* Bethesda, Maryland: National Naval Medical Center, 1946.
U.S. Office of Civil Defense Mobilization. *Motion Pictures on Civil Defense.* 1958.

Unpublished Material

Unpublished reports, press releases, letters, and memos are available primarily from two sources: the Atomic Energy Commission files, Record Group 326, at the National Archives in Washington, D.C.; and the Department of Energy's Coordination and Information Center in Las Vegas, Nevada.

Statutes cited can be found in the *United States Code* and the *Nevada Revised Statutes*. Three of the most significant include: Atomic Energy Act of 1946, 42 *U.S.C.* 1801; Federal Tort Claims Act of 1946, 28 *U.S.C.* 921; Price Anderson Act of 1957, 42 *U.S.C.* 2102.

Material on the Baneberry and Allen cases came from the respective judges' opinions: Roger Foley, Judge in the United States District Court for the District of Nevada. *Findings of Fact and Conclusions of Law*. Dorothy Roberts, et al., Plaintiffs vs. United States of America, Defendant (Civil LV 1766 RDF) and Louise Nunamaker, Plaintiff vs. United States of America, Defendant (Civil LV 76-259 RDF) June 14, 1984; Bruce Jenkins, Judge in the United States District Court for the District of Utah, Central District. *Memorandum Opinion*. Irene Allen, et al., Plaintiffs vs. United States of America, Defendant (Civil No. C79-0515-J) May 1, 1984.

Interviews

Bushnell, Dan. Interview with author. Salt Lake City, Utah, March 21, 1985, and July 31, 1985.

Foley, Roger. Interview with author. Las Vegas, Nevada, March 7, 1985.

Preston, Ron. Legislative Assistant to Utah Senator Orrin Hatch. Interview with author. Washington, D.C., June 16, 1983.

Index

Acheson, Dean, 30
Agent Orange, xi, 135, 136, 141, 142
Alamo, Nev., 57
Alamogordo Army Air Base, 12, 18, 19, 56
Alaska, atomic testing in, 68
Albuquerque, N.M., 19
Allen and Hanson, Las Vegas, 93
Allen et al. v. United States, 111, 119, 120, 124
Allison, John M., 50
Alvarez, Luis, 30
Amboy, Calif., 67
American Legion, 76
American Museum of Atomic Energy, 89
Ancho, N.M., 18
Anderson, Clinton, 19, 88
Anderson, George, 102
Anderson, Herbert L., 17
Anderson, Oscar E., Jr., 39
Angel's Peak, Nev., 94
Anticommunism: congressional investigations and, 71–72; played on to support nuclear weapons testing, 70–75, 91
Aomon, Marshall Is., 44, 45
Appalachian (ship), 37–38
Aristotle, 1
Arizona, radiation fallout from Nevada Test Site in, 105, 111
Arkansas (battleship), 37
Armed Forces Special Weapons Project, 28, 30, 62, 158n. 38
AT&T Technologies, Inc., 68
Atchison, Topeka, and Santa Fe Railroad, 66

Atomic bomb, 9, 20. *See also* Atomic testing; Hydrogen (Super) bomb; Manhattan Project
Atomic Bomb Casualty Commission, 115n. 52
Atomic energy: civilian control of, 25–26, 29, 31, 35, 43; Eisenhower policy on, 31–32, 77–79; health and safety concerns about, 25, 33; international cooperation and controls of, 24, 32, 38, 43, 77–79; military control of, 24–28, 31–35, 157n. 24, 158n. 28; national security concerns about, 57, 58; peaceful uses of, 22–25, 27, 31–32, 43, 47–48, 66, 76–79; postwar regulation of, 22–26; private industry use of, 31, 33; public interest in, 86–91; Truman policy on. *See* Truman, Harry S
Atomic Energy Act of 1946, 26–28, 43; amended 1954, 31–34, 78; amended 1957, 134
Atomic Energy Commission (AEC), xi–xiii, 15, 38; abolishment of, 34; concerns for questions of liability of, 15, 17, 22, 33–34, 105, 109; compensation to victims of atomic testing by, 36, 99, 101, 106; congressional directives to, 27–28, 32–34; control of industrial nuclear power by, 33; control of information on atomic matters by, 19–22, 26, 28–29, 32–33, 58, 101, 109, 130, 137, 146, 154n. 39; establishment of, 39, 43; involvement in Nevada Test Site of, 56–77 *passim;*

(AEC), *(cont.)*
    involvement in South Pacific
    testing of, 43, 46–50; minimizes
    effects of radiation exposure, 76,
    82–85, 95–96, 98, 102, 103–5,
    121, 132, 139; opposes atomic
    testing ban, 102; plays on anti-
    communism in public relations,
    71, 74–76, 86–87, 146; protests
    directed to, 98–100; standards
    and concerns for health and
    safety of, 33, 36, 58–77 *passim,*
    80–85, 104, 106, 118–20, 122,
    132; supported by Nevada offi-
    cials, 97–100
Atomic radiation. *See* Radiation
Atomic testing, 9–10, 36; atmo-
    spheric testing, 11, 57, 63, 65,
    70, 80, 81, 87, 101–2, 133; blast
    damage, 59, 118; criteria for test
    sites, 11, 12, 36–37, 55, 56–57;
    government promotion of, 70;
    public acceptance of, 86–88, 105,
    146; safety standards and prac-
    tices in, 11, 14, 17, 40–43, 45,
    70, 80–82, 120, 121, 129, 132;
    underground testing, 57, 65, 70,
    81, 83–88 *passim,* 101, 104, 105–
    6, 133, 146; underwater tests, 40.
    See also Bikini Atoll; Eniwetok
    Atoll; Nevada Test Site; Radio-
    active fallout; Trinity test
Atomic weapons, xii–xiii; arms
    control and, 79; as deterrent to
    war, 75–76; postwar proliferation
    of, 24, 27–31, 33, 45–46, 71, 75,
    79, 86–87, 103, 147; public inter-
    est in and support of, 86–91,
    146; public opposition to, 98. *See
    also* Atomic bomb; Hydrogen
    (Super) bomb; Trinity test
Atoms: early history of understand-
    ing, 1–4; first considered for
    military use, 5–6; nuclear fission
    and, 4–6
Avalon, Frankie, 92

Bainbridge, Kenneth Q., 11, 15
Ball, S. H., 57
Balos, Henschi, 52
Baneberry accident, 83, 105–6. *See
    also Nunamaker v. United States*
Bartholomae v. United States, 118
Baruch, Bernard, 38
Beadle, George, 85
Beatty, Nev., 57
Becquerel, Henry, 2–3
Bennett, Wallace, 103
Bible, Alan, 103
Bijire, Marshall Is., 44
Bikini Atoll, Marshall Is., 26, 36;
    atomic tests at, described, 37–41;
    attempt to decontaminate, 53–54;
    Operation Greenhouse and, 46;
    press coverage of tests at, 37–39;
    purpose of atomic tests at, 44,
    46; radiation damage at, 51–52,
    105–7, 164 n. 95; relocation of
    native people of, 37, 51–52, 53,
    54. *See also* Bravo atomic test
Bikini Compensation Act of 1964,
    140
Blaber v. United States, 118
Blanchard, Lowell, and the Valley
    Trio, 89
Blandy, W. H. P., 26, 36, 37
Bohr, Niels, 4
*Bolger v. Chris Anderson Roofing
    Co.,* 124
Booth, Robert, 102
Borden, William, 29
Born, Max, 4
Boy Scouts of America, 88–89
Bradbury, Norris, 26, 102
Bradley, David, on Bikini Atoll
    atomic tests, 38, 40–42
Bradley, Omar, 30
Bravo atomic test: compensation to
    fallout victims of, 48–50, 134,
    140; radiation fallout accident in,
    46–50, 140
*Bressner v. Walter Kiddle Nuclear
    Labs,* 125

Briggs, Lyman J., 6
Brim, Raymond, 84
Bristol Mountains, Calif., 67
Broudy v. United States, 129
Brown, Harold, 95
Brown v. United States, 128
Brues, Austin, 84
Bryan, Richard, 175 n. 85
Bullock v. United States, 117–18, 119, 121, 122–23
Burke, Arleigh, 102
Bush, Vannevar, 6, 7, 24

Cactus Springs, Nev., 56
Caldwell, Glyn, 108
Caliente, Nev., 57
California Division of Highways, 66–67
Calleia, Joseph, 90
Camp Desert Rock, Nev., military maneuvers during atomic tests at, 60–61, 63
Camp Lejune, N.C., 56
Camp Mercury, Nev., 56
Cannon, Howard, 88, 103, 139–40
Carlsbad, N.M., 66
Carrizozo, N.M., 12, 17–18
Carter, Jimmy, 110, 135
Carter, Tim Lee, 108–9, 131, 133, 136
Cavendish Laboratory, Cambridge, 3, 4
Cedar City, Nev., 64–65
Cellar, Emanuel, 127
Chadwick, James, 4
Charleston Range, Nev., 94
Chiang Kai-shek, 19
China, atomic weapons in, 103
Christensen, Sherman, 117–18, 119, 122
Christmas Island, 46
Chupadera Mesa, N.M., 18
Churchill, Winston, 13, 15, 19
Citizens' Protective League, 72
Civil defense. *See* Federal Civil Defense Administration

Clark, Thomas, 75, 84
Clark County, Nev., 86, 94, 97, 100
Clarkson, Percy, 76–77
Coe, Donald, 108–9
Cohens v. Virginia, 114
Cole, Sterling, 31
Colorado, atomic testing in, 66, 68
Committee of Atomic Bomb Survivors, 112
Committee of Survivors, 111
Communist Control Act, 72
Communist party, 8, 72. *See also* Anticommunism
Community Mental Health Centers Act, 111
Compania Hill, N.M., 14
Conant, James B., 7, 20
Considine, Bob, 95
Cooper, Paul, 107–8
Cosgriff, Thomas, 107
Coughlin, Charles Edward, 72
Coyote, N.M., 18
Cranston, Alan, 133, 136–37
Crawford, Meredith, 60
Cronkite, Walter, 95
Cronyn, Hume, 90
Cuba, N.M., 11
Curie, Marie, 3

DSM Project. *See* Manhattan Project
Dalehite v. United States, 116–17
Dalton, John, 1
Darvi, Bella, 90–91
Davies, Marion, 95
Dean, Gordon, 31, 59–60, 65, 98
Death Valley Junction, Nev., 57
Defense Atomic Support Agency, 102
Defense Nuclear Agency, xiii
Democratic National Convention, 1956, 87
Department of Energy Reorganization Act, 35
Desert Inn, Las Vegas, 93

Dies, Martin, 72
Disabled American Veterans, 107–8
Disney, Walt, 88
Dodd, Thomas, 102
Doe v. McMillan, 117
Doll, Jackie, and His Pickled Peppers, 89
Donlevy, Brian, 90
Dugway Proving Ground, Utah, 56
Dunning, Gordon, 83

Eckhardt, Bob, 131
Edgerton, Germeschausen and Grier, Inc., 68, 83, 100
Edison, Thomas, 2
Edwards, Blake, 91
Einstein, Albert, 5, 6, 26
Eisenhower, Dwight D., 99; "Atoms for Peace" program of, 31–32, 77–79; ends South Pacific atomic tests, 46; internal security program of, 73; pro-weapons platform of, 87
Elliott, William, 130
El Paso, Tex., 19
Energy Reorganization Act of 1974, 34
Energy Research and Development Administration, 34–35
Eniwetok Atoll, Marshall Is., xiii, 99; atomic tests at, 44–47; attempts to decontaminate, 53–54; relocation of native people of, 44, 52–54
Enjebi, Marshall Is., 45
Environmental Protection Agency, 67, 110, 133–35
Eureka, Nev., 56
Eureka County, Nev., 96, 97
Evans, Lane, 143
Everette v. United States, 129

Fallon, Nev., 56
Faraday, Michael, 1
Farrell, Thomas, 16, 17

Federal Bureau of Investigation, 90
Federal Civil Defense Administration, 63, 73–74, 82, 96
Federal Employee Loyalty Program, 73
Federal Tort Claims Act of 1946, 34, 65, 111; applicability to armed services personnel, 126–30; court interpretations of "discretionary function," 116–20; efforts to modify provisions of, 131, 133, 136; legislative background of, 114–15; "proof of causation" test in, 121–25, 136, 138; provisions of, 115–16; statute of limitations on, 120–21
Fenix & Scisson, Inc., 68
Feres v. United States, 126–29, 133, 142
Fermi, Enrico, 4–5, 6, 17, 90
Fields, K. E., 27, 62
Flamingo Hotel, Las Vegas, 93
Foley, Roger, 119, 123–24, 126, 142, 180 n. 48
Ford, Gerald R., 109
Forrestal, James, 24
Foster, John, 102
France, atomic testing by, 103
Francen, Victor, 91
Franck, James, 4
Frederick, Donald, 105
Fredonia, Ariz., 105
Freedom of Information Act, 109–10, 130
Frenchman Flat, Nev., 56, 58, 59
Friedel, Hymes, 15
Fuchs, Klaus, 8, 46, 151 n. 26
Fukuryu Maru (Lucky Dragon) (Japanese trawler), fallout effects on, 49–50

Gaillard, Slim, Quartet, 89
Galloway, Dave, 95
Gallup, N.M., 19
Gallup Poll, surveys of public on atomic matters by, 86–87

Garn, Jake, 139
General Public Utilities, 113
German-American Bund, 72
Gibbons v. United States, 114
Gilmore, Sandy, 107
Gilworth, Arnie, 154n. 36
Golden Rule (ketch), 99
Goudsmit, Samuel, 9
Grants, N.M., 11
Graves, Alvin C., 65
Great Sand Dunes National Monument, 11
Greenglass, David, 8
Groom Mine, Nev., 57, 99
Ground zero, 13
Groves, Leslie R., 75, 90, 156n. 4, 157n. 24; as director of military activities, Manhattan Project, 7–9, 14, 15, 17, 26, 28, 30, 151n. 21, 158n. 38; on Oppenheimer, 8–9
Guest, Val, 92

Hager, Jean, 92
Halda, Louis, 18
Hanford, Wash., 7
Harris, Oren, 156n. 11
Hart, Gary, 100
Hatch, Orrin, 137–39, 141–43
Hawthorne, Nev., 97
Hazardous waste disposal, xi. See also Nuclear waste disposal
Hempelmann, Louis H., 18, 154nn. 34, 37
Hewlett, Richard G., 39
Hilbert, David, 4
Hill, Gladwin, 95
Hiroshima, Japan, atomic bombing of, 20, 21, 51, 90
Hirschfelder, Joseph Oakland, 40, 42
Hiss, Alger, 72, 73
Holmes & Narner, 68
Hooper, S. C., 5
Hopper, Jerry, 90
Hughes, Howard, 99–100

Hughes (destroyer), 41
Hull, John E., 44
Human Resources Research Office, 60–61
Humphrey, Hubert, 72, 102
Hydrogen (Super) bomb: development of 30–31, 55, 161n. 36; fears for U.S.S.R. use of, 86–87, 162n. 58; first test of, 46–48; Oppenheimer opposed to, 75; protests against, 75, 98–99

Idaho National Laboratory, 83
Independence (aircraft carrier), 37
India, atomic weapons in, 103
Indian Springs, Nev., 56, 96
Indian Springs Air Force Base, Nev., 56
Indian Towing Co. v. United States, 116–17
Ink, Dwight, 105
International Atomic Energy Agency, 78, 79
International Congress on Peaceful Uses of Atomic Energy, 78
International School of Nuclear Science and Engineering, 78
Iron County, Utah, 18, 65
Israel, atomic weapons in, 103

Jackass Flat, Nev., 66
Jackson, C. D., 77–78
Jackson, Henry, 29, 88
Jaffee v. United States, 127–28
Japan: atomic bombing of, 20, 21, 67, 90, 155n. 53; effects of fallout on fishing industry in, 49–50; petition against nuclear weapons in, 51; postbomb cleanup operations in, 133; Tokyo Peace Park, 51; U.S. reparations to, 50–51, 140; World War II surrender of, 19–20
Japtan Is., Eniwetok Atoll, 111
Jefferson v. United States, 127
Jenkins, Bruce, 111, 119–20, 124–25

Johns, Larry, 106, 123
Johnson, Edwin C., 24
Johnson, Louis, 30
Johnson, Lyndon B., 99
Johnston Is., 46
Joint Committee on Atomic Energy (JCAE), 76, 80, 158n. 34; guides revisions to Atomic Energy Act, 31, 33; Atomic Energy Commission and, 19, 28; Lilienthal conflict with, 29–30; Strauss reports to, 76, 80, 82–83; weapons development urged by, 55, 74–75, 88; witnesses to Eniwetok Atoll atomic tests, 45
Jones, "Boob," 93
Jones, Ken, 100
Jones, Thomas K., 82
Jungk, Robert, 7

Kanab, Utah, 105
Karasti, Frank, 41
Kay, Jackson, 93
Kelley v. United States, 129
Kelly, Orville, 111–12
Kelly, Wanda, 112
Kennan, George, 30–31
Kennedy, Edward, 132, 135–36, 137, 138
Kennedy, John F., 46, 102–3
Kessibuki, Juda, 37
Khrushchev, Nikita, 86
Kili, Marshall Is., 51
Kistiakowsky, George, 13
Knapp, Harold, 104
Korean Conflict, 46, 55, 74
Krumback v. Dow Chemical Company, 125
Kuboyama, Aikichi, 49, 51
Kuhne v. United States, 119
Kwajalein Atoll, Marshall Is., 37, 44, 47, 48, 51

Lae, Marshall Is., 37
LaFalce, John, 135
Lang, Daniel, 94

Langan, Glenn, 92
Lasswell v. Brown, 129
Las Vegas, Nev., 56, 59, 99–100, 130; newspaper coverage of atomic tests in, 95–97, 100; popularity of atomic theme in, 93, 94–95; proximity to Nevada Test Site of, 57, 65
Las Vegas Chamber of Commerce, uses atomic tests to boost tourism, 93–94, 95
Las Vegas High School, 94
Las Vegas Review-Journal, on atomic testing, 96–97
Las Vegas Sun, on atomic testing, 96–97, 100
Las Vegas-Tonopah Bombing and Gunnery Range, 56, 58
Lathrop Wells, Nev., 57
Laurence, William L., at first atomic test, 14, 17, 38, 39
Lausche, Frank, 103
Lawrence, Ernest, 29
Lawrence Livermore National Laboratory, 66, 68, 102
Laxalt, Paul, 139
Leavitt, Jack, 41
Legislative Reorganization Act of 1946, 115
Le May, Curtis, 102
Leucippus, 1
Leutzinger, E. C., 96–97
Levy, Benny, 112
Lewis, B. E., 98
Libassi, Peter, 110
Libby, Willard, 74, 83, 84
Lilienthal, David: as first AEC chairman, 29–30, 31; opposes H-bomb development, 29–31
Limited Test Ban Treaty, 65
Little Caesar, 89
Lombard v. United States, 129
Long, Russell, 102
Los Alamos, N.M.: converted to national laboratory, 26, 31, 44, 45, 68, 102; Manhattan Proj-

ect site, 7, 8, 11–12, 18; museum, 89
Love Canal, N.Y., 135
Lovett, Robert, 58
Luedecke, A. R., 27, 62
Lyon, Joseph, 132

McCarran, Patrick, 56, 88, 97–98
McCarran International Security Act, 72
McCarthy, Joseph R., xiii, 71, 72
McClain, Joe, 96
McDonald Ranch, N.M., 14
McElroy, Neil H., 99
McKay, Gunn, 135
McMahon, Brien, 25, 29, 30, 36, 156 n. 11
McMahon Bill (S. 1717), 25, 28–29, 156 n. 14
McNish, George, 41
McSmith, Hugh, 154 n. 36
Maketani, Mitsu, 50
Malone, George W., 98
Manhattan Project, xii; creation and goals of, 7; demobilization of, 26; end of secrecy regarding, 20, 22; museum, 89; and security, 7–9, 46, 73, 75; Smyth report, 20, 21. *See also* Trinity test
Marbury, William L., 23
Marriott, Dan, 138
Marshall, George, 58
Marshall, John, 114
Marshall Islands, atomic bomb testing in, 36, 46, 98–99. *See also* Bikini Atoll; Eniwetok Atoll
Martell, Edward, 54
Matthews, Samuel, 94
May, Andrew Jackson, 24, 25
May-Johnson bill (H.R. 4280), 24–25, 26
Mercury, Nev., 56, 66
Milland, Ray, 92
Miller, Dave, 75
Mineta, Norman, 136
Mississippi, atomic testing in, 68

Mitchell, Cameron, 90
Mitchell, Marty, 92
Monticello, Utah, 105
Morgan, Karl, 85
Morton, Rogers C. B., 51, 106
Morton, W. J., 3
Moss, Frank, 103
Mossman, Ted, 93
Motion pictures: public attitude toward atomic warfare reflected in, 89–93, 172 n. 23; science fiction, 91, 92, 153 n. 10, 172 n. 24; promotion of atomic use and safety in, 77, 170 n. 36
Mt. Charleston, Nev., 57
Mt. McKinley (ship), 44
Muller, Herman, xiii, 85, 98

Nagasaki, Japan, atomic bombing of, 20, 21, 51
Nagato (Japanese warship), 37
National Aeronautics and Space Agency, 66
National Association of Atomic Veterans, 111
National Association of Radiation Survivors, 112
National Cancer Institute, 105
National Center for Atmospheric Research, 54
National Committee for a Sane Nuclear Policy, 98
National Defense Research Committee, 6
National Electric Light Association, 2
Nehru, Jawaharlal, 50
Nelson, Barry, 91
Nernot, Walter, 4
Nevada: AEC assurances about atomic test safety to, 58, 80–85, 106; agreement with AEC regarding Workmen's Compensation claims, 125–26; capitalizes on atomic testing to promote tourism, 93–94; newspaper sup-

Nevada: *(cont.)*
    port of nuclear testing in, xiii,
    95–99, 100, 106; officials support
    nuclear testing in, xiii, 97–100;
    suggestions to end testing in, 96–
    97, 99–100; supports Eisenhower
    reelection, 87–88. *See also* Neva-
    da Test Site
Nevada (battleship), 37, 160 n. 4
Nevada Highways and Parks, 94
Nevada Industrial Commission,
    125–26
Nevada Proving Ground, 56–58,
    63. *See also* Nevada Test Site
Nevada Test Site (NTS), xii–xiii,
    11, 70, 92; accidents at, 57, 59,
    64–65, 83–84, 96, 97, 105–6; civil
    defense tests at, 63–64; civilian
    employees at, 68, 84, 88, 106,
    112, 125–26; description of, 56–
    57, 59, 97; first atomic tests at,
    56, 58–59; geology of, 57; jour-
    nalists at, 14, 95; military ma-
    neuvers at, 59–63, 107, 126–36
    passim; non-weapons testing at,
    66–67, 79–80; Plowshare Pro-
    gram at, 79–80; protests at, 99–
    100; site selection of, 55–57, 70,
    97–98
Nevada Test Site Radiation Victims
    Association, 112
New Mexico, atomic testing in,
    68. *See also* Trinity test
Newsweek on Bikini Atoll atomic
    tests, 38, 39
Newton, Isaac, 1
New York (battleship), 43
New York Chamber of Com-
    merce, 30
Nichols, Kenneth D., 27, 30
Nickles, Dan, 138
Nitze, Paul, 30–31
Nuclear Defense Agency: cleanup
    of Eniwetok Atoll radiation and,
    53–54; tests of levels of radiation
    exposure and, 83–84

Nuclear fallout. *See* Radioactive
    fallout
Nuclear power plants, 31, 78, 97;
    AEC control of, 33; accident at
    Three Mile Island, 112–13, 147;
    compensation for claims against,
    134
Nuclear Regulatory Commission,
    34, 110
Nuclear Rocket Development Sta-
    tion, 66
Nuclear waste disposal, 58, 67–68,
    79–80, 100
Nuclear Waste Policy Act, 175 n.
    85
Nunamaker, Richard, 106
Nunamaker v. United States
    ("Baneberry" case), 106, 119,
    121, 122–24, 130
Nye County, Nev., 56, 88

Oak Ridge, Tenn., 7, 18, 89
Operation Castle. *See* Bikini Atoll,
    Marshall Is.; Bravo atomic test
Operations Research Office, Johns
    Hopkins University, 61–62
Oppenheimer, Frank, 153 n. 15
Oppenheimer, Robert, 4, 12, 21,
    24, 26, 90; as AEC advisor, 28,
    30; dismissal of, 75, 85, 151 n.
    27; first atomic test and, 13, 16–
    17; as Los Alamos director, 8–9,
    15; opposes H-bomb, 75
Overton, Nev., 57

Pahute Mesa, Nev., 56, 65
Palmer, Q. O., 15
Panama Canal Company, 115
Parawan, Utah, 105
Pastore, John, 49
Patel, Marilyn, 129–30
Pauling, Linus, xiii, 85, 98; sup-
    ports atomic test ban, 101, 172 n.
    24
Pearson, Drew, 19
Peckarsky, J. C., 107

Pennsylvania (battleship), 37
Pensacola (U.S. naval vessel), 37
Pike, Sumner T., 28, 55
Pioche, Nev., 57
Pleasant Grove, Utah, 105
Power, Thomas, 102
Prescott, Keith, 126
Prescott v. United States, 126, 142
Preston, Ron, 141, 142
Price-Anderson Act, 134
Prinz Eugen (German warship), 37
Purnell, W. R., 7

Quesada, Elwood R., 46

Rabi, I. I., 13
Radiation, 163n. 67; emitted by
first atomic test, 16; exposure
limits to, 14, 62; ground contamination from, 21; ground
venting of, 57, 65, 83, 103, 105–
6, 123–24, 133, 139, 165n. 13,
180n. 48; illness from, 41, 48;
monitoring, 39, 42–43, 57, 62,
80, 132; safety standards and
practices and, xiii, 14, 45, 53, 62,
121; understanding of at first
atomic test, 14–16, 21. *See also*
Radioactive fallout
Radiation Exposure Compensation
Act of 1981, 136–39, 141
Radioactive fallout, 12, 80–81; contamination of Japanese fishery
from, 50; dangers of minimized,
76, 82–85, 87, 91, 96, 104, 132–
33, 137, 155n. 53; effect on
livestock of, 18; medical effects
on humans of, 48, 49, 82, 85,
87, 98, 101, 103–13 *passim,* 121–
22, 124, 132, 136, 137, 146;
monitoring at first atomic test
of, 15, 17; in South Pacific, 39,
40, 46–50, 76. *See also* Sheep
Radioactivity, discovery of, 1–4
Radiogenic Cancer Compensation
Act, 141

Rainier Mesa, Nev., 75
Rallinson, Marvin, 85
Reagan, Ronald W., 154n. 39: ad-
ministration opposition to com-
pensation for atomic test victims,
139, 143–44; "star wars" pro-
gram and, xii, 68
Reed, Stanley F., 116
Reynolds Electrical and Engineer-
ing Co., Inc., 68, 85, 106, 126
Rice, Calif., 11
Roberts, Harley, 106
Roberts v. United States, 119, 124
Rock Flats, Colo., 125
Rogers, Paul, 109
Rongelap, Marshall Is., fallout
from Bravo atomic test at, 47,
48–49
Rongerik, Marshall Is.: Bikini na-
tives moved to, 37, 51; fallout
on, 47
Röntgen, Wilhelm, 2
Rooney, Mickey, 91
Roosevelt, Franklin D., xii, 5–6, 8,
26
Roper, H. McKay, 59
Rosenburg, Ethel, 8, 73
Rosenburg, Julius, 73
Royal, Kenneth C., 23
Rubens, Heinrich, 4
Runit, Marshall Is., 45, 54
Russell, Charles, 94, 97
Russell, James, 76
Rutherford, Ernest, 3, 4

Sachs, Alexander, 5
St. George, Utah, 57; radioactive
fallout from Nevada Test Site in,
64–65, 96, 142
Sakawa (Japanese warship), 37
Salt Lake City, Utah, 105
Sandia National Laboratories, 68
Sands Hotel, Las Vegas, 93
San Luis Valley, Colo., 11
San Nicholas Island, Calif., 11
Santa Fe, N.M., 19

Saratoga (aircraft carrier), 37
Schlesinger, James, 51
Schriever, Bernard, 102
Schweitzer, Albert, 74, 83
Science News Letter, on Bikini Atoll atomic tests, 38
Seaborg, Glenn, 6
Segre, Emilio, 6
Sheahan, Dan, 99
Sheep, effect of radioactive fallout on, 18, 65, 117–18, 122–23, 132–33, 135, 166 n. 42
Sheppard's Furniture Store, Las Vegas, 93
Silver City, N.M., 19
Simon, Paul, 143
Skate (submarine), 41
Smith, Bill (U.S. Marine tank driver), 17
Smith, Billy (REECo engineer), 85
Smith, Margaret Chase, 103
Smith Act, 72
Smith v. Humboldt Dye Works, Inc., 125
Smyth, Henry DeWolf, 8; report on Manhattan Project, 20–21
South Africa, atomic weapons in, 103
South Pacific: atomic testing in, xiii, 36, 46, 55, 65, 69, 70–71; cleanup efforts in, 133. *See also* Bikini Atoll; Eniwetok Atoll
Stalin, Joseph, 15, 30
Stevenson, Adlai, 87–88
Steward, Stanley L., 18
Stimson, Henry L., 8, 19, 20, 24
Storke, H. P., 63
Story, Richard, 51
Strategic Air Command, 102
Strauss, Lewis L., 76, 99; as chairman of AEC, 19, 27–28; on Bravo test accident, 47–48, 49–50, 76; on safety of atomic testing, 80, 82–83, 84; supports development of H-bomb, 30, 74, 76
Stringfellow, Douglas, 96

Styer, W. D., 7
Subversive Activities Control Board, 72
Sutherland, Ross, 64
Suzuki, Kantaro, 20
Swayze, John Cameron, 95
Swing, Joseph, 60
Szilard, Leo, 5

Taft, William, 136
Teague, Archie, 96
Tecolote, N.M., 18
Teller, Edward, 5, 29: on first atomic test, 13; urges atomic weapons testing, 74–75, 102
Tennessee Valley Authority, 29, 115
Texas, 11
Thornburgh, Richard, 113
Thornwell v. United States, 128, 129
Three Mile Island, Harrisburg, Pa., nuclear power plant accident at, 112–13
Thurmond, Strom, 138
Tibbets, Paul, Jr., 20, 90
Time, on first Bikini Atoll atomic test, 39
Tonopah, Nev., 57, 99
Trading with the Enemy Act, 115
Trinity test, 11–17, 57
Truman, Harry S, xii, 8, 21, 29, 151 n. 25, 155 n. 52; atomic energy policy of, 22–24, 25, 26, 43–44, 58, 71, 90, 161 nn. 33, 35; McCarthy and, 72; South Pacific atomic bomb tests and, 36, 38; internal security program of, 73; Potsdam meeting and, 15, 19; supports development of H-bomb, 30–31, 46; urges weapons development, 55, 162 n. 58
Tularosa Basin, N.M., 11
Twining, Nathan, 102
Tyler, Carroll, 62

U.S. News & World Report, 84; on Bikini Atoll atomic tests, 38

Udall, Stewart, 111
Ujae, Marshall Is., 37
Ujelang Atoll, Marshall Is., 44, 52
Union of Soviet Socialist Republics: arms control and, 79, 86; "cold war" and, 31, 43–44, 71, 91–92; first atomic bomb ("Joe One") of, 30, 46, 55, 71, 162n. 55; monitoring of U.S. atomic tests by, 45, 80; nuclear testing treaties with U.S., 65, 100, 101–3; weapons capacity of, 46
United Airlines v. Weiner, 117
United Nations Trusteeship Agreement, 48
United States: arms control and, 79, 86; claims against in tort cases, 114–44 *passim;* "cold war" and, 31, 43–44. 71–74, 87, 91–92; compensation to victims of atomic testing by, xi, 11, 48–53, 110–11, 125, 140, 147; testing liability concerns of, 11, 15, 17, 18, 50, 109; testing treaties with U.S.S.R., 65, 100, 101–3
U.S. Army Corps of Engineers, 7
U.S. Center for Disease Control, 105, 107; studies effects of radiation on humans, 108, 110
U.S. Coast Guard, 99, 116
U.S. Department of Defense: authority at Nevada Test Site of, 68, 97; interest in psychological effects of atomic war on troops of, 60–61; involvement in atomic test maneuvers of, 59–63, 107–8, 127–38 *passim;* suits against, 141–42
U.S. Department of Energy, xiii, 160n. 69; authority at Nevada Test site of, 68; public relations regarding atomic testing and, 53, 70, 75–76, 80–82, 84
U.S. Department of Health and Human Resources, radiation-cancer link study of, 137, 143

U.S. Department of Health, Education, and Welfare, 105, 110, 111
United States Information Agency, 77
United States–Japanese Radiation Effects Research Foundation, 155n. 52
U.S. Marine Corps, at Eniwetok, xiii
U.S. Public Health Service, 104–5
United States v. Kubrick, 120–21
U.S. Veterans Administration, 110, 111, 127, 128; claims against for radiation-induced illnesses, 107–9, 128–29, 131, 135, 136, 137, 138, 143
University of Utah, Salt Lake City, 142
Uranium Miners Association, 112
Utah: AEC assurances to, 81; radiation fallout from Nevada Test Site in, 64–65, 85, 104, 105, 111, 117–18, 132; supports Eisenhower reelection, 88
Utah State Department of Health, 105
Utirik, Marshall Is., fallout from Bravo atomic test at, 47, 48–49

Vandenburg, Arthur H., 25, 26, 28, 156n. 11
Vaughn, N.M., 18
Villard, Paul, 3
Voice of America, 77

Wackenhut Services, Inc., 68
Wald, George, 113
Wallace, Henry, 44
Warner, John, 141–42, 143
Warren, Shields, 62
Warren, Stafford, 14–15, 17, 42, 153n. 15
Washington County, Utah, 88
Watson, Edward M. ("Pa"), 5–6
Weisgall, Jonathan, 52

Weiss, Edward, 104–5
Weizsäcker, Carl Friedrich von, 9
Welles, Orson, 90
Westinghouse Advanced Energy
    Systems Division, 67–68
West Virginia Republican Club of
    Wheeling, W.Va., 72
Weyzen, Walter, 85
Wheeler, John Archibald, 4
White Sands, N.M., 12, 56
Widmark, Richard, 91
Wigner, Eugene, 5
Woodruff, Nathan, 104

Workmen's Compensation, 125–26,
    180 n. 58
World War I, 4
World War II, 4, 5, 20
Worman, Frederick, 57
Wyatt, Ben, 37

X-rays, 2–3

Yucca Flat, Nev., 57, 59, 65
Yucca Mountain, Nev., 68, 175 n.
    85
Yaizu, Japan, 49, 50